Educational Psychology

Studies in the
Postmodern Theory of Education

Joe L. Kincheloe and Shirley R. Steinberg
General Editors

Vol. 329

PETER LANG
New York • Washington, D.C./Baltimore • Bern
Frankfurt am Main • Berlin • Brussels • Vienna • Oxford

Educational Psychology

An Application
of Critical Constructivism

EDITED BY
Greg S. Goodman

PETER LANG
New York • Washington, D.C./Baltimore • Bern
Frankfurt am Main • Berlin • Brussels • Vienna • Oxford

Library of Congress Cataloging-in-Publication Data

Educational psychology: an application
of critical constructivism / [edited by] Greg S. Goodman.
p. cm. — (Counterpoints; vol. 329)
Includes bibliographical references and index.
1. Education psychology. 2. Constructivism (Education).
3. Postmodernism and education. 4. Educational sociology.
LB1051.E36124   370.15—dc22   2007044389
ISBN 978-1-4331-0112-0 (hardcover)
ISBN 978-1-4331-0111-3 (paperback)
ISSN 1058-1634

Bibliographic information published by **Die Deutsche Bibliothek**.
Die Deutsche Bibliothek lists this publication in the "Deutsche
Nationalbibliografie"; detailed bibliographic data is available
on the Internet at http://dnb.ddb.de/.

Cover design by Clear Point Designs

The paper in this book meets the guidelines for permanence and durability
of the Committee on Production Guidelines for Book Longevity
of the Council of Library Resources.

© 2008 Peter Lang Publishing, Inc., New York
29 Broadway, 18th floor, New York, NY 10006
www.peterlang.com

Printed in the United States of America

This book is dedicated to Andrea Lynn Goodman
for her unyielding support.

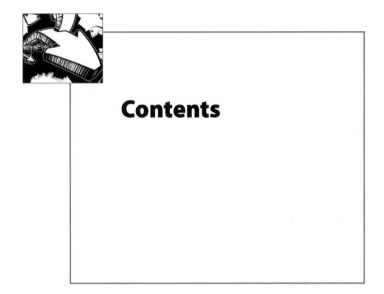

Contents

Foreword

This book takes educational psychology out of the hands of scholarship that examines how people learn as individuals and places it squarely in the palms of lived realities of today's children and adolescents, arguing that learning is social as well as cognitive, and that learning has social consequences. All of the authors in this book ask readers to consider that *what* students learn is as important as *how* they learn it. To this end, the book seeks to engage readers in a dialogue about social justice, and the need to engage in school experiences where students pose critical questions about the curriculum, expose its vested interests and hidden agendas, and ultimately, become agents of change.

Much of the early work in educational psychology viewed learning as something that happens entirely inside the head of learners, which eschews the role of social interaction learners have with the environment and thus avoids dealing with critical issues that impact students. From its beginning, educational psychology focused its attention on social, moral, and cognitive development, with an eye toward the creation of theoretical ideas that could be applied to educational settings, such as schools and classrooms. Teacher education programs, in particular, have relied on the seminal work of Piaget, Bandura, and Bloom, among others, to help students become acquainted with theoretical principles that underlie the strategies, lessons, and classroom management processes they will be expected to learn and use in teaching. While many of the principles created by these educational psychologists continue to inform teacher education programs, this book argues for a stance toward teaching and learning that goes well beyond individual learning, to one that necessarily ties teaching and learning to issues of social justice for children and adolescents who have been historically and are presently underserved and marginalized by school practices and policies.

It is important to consider that early theoretical ideas about teaching and learning were developed either in laboratories or in countries outside the U.S. long ago. Moreover, since social factors and social contexts were considered extraneous for understanding how learning occurs, the theoretical principles resulting from this early work were thought to apply to any and all contexts where students were in a position to learn. After all, if the conditions were right, so it was thought, students would acquire the knowledge inside their heads just as the teacher presented it, following the principles of learning dictated by theory that was discovered in laboratories and other places where conditions were controlled and learning was observed.

This book asks readers to reconsider educational psychology and to place it in real settings, where children and adolescents bring to classroom a wide range of experiences and background knowledge that earlier theoretical pioneers of learning theory

could not have imagined. Remember that when Bloom, Bandura, Piaget, and Skinner (and to some extent, Vygotsky) created their theoretical work, they worked with students from dominant groups. Their work was developed at a time in the U.S. when schools for minority students were drastically unequal, when the lives and experiences of non-White students and other marginalized students were absent from the curriculum. Few of their followers questioned the generalizability of their work to situations where learners of diverse language, gender, social class, and ethnic backgrounds were together in classrooms. None of these early educational psychologists questioned whether their work legitimized the interests of the dominant groups and at the same time suppressed the knowledge and experiences of minority and marginalized groups. The authors in this book do, and they offer ways to counter social injustices that have accumulated from decades of neglect resulting from a concern for individual learning that ignores the social realities of poverty, racism, intolerance, and social stratification.

In today's classrooms, many students are immigrants and children of immigrants who live in poverty and are likely to enter school speaking a language other than English. Many schools in urban settings are likely to be hypersegregated, attended mainly by students of one ethnicity who are bilingual or becoming bilingual. There is a growing trend of schools where the overwhelming majority of students are African American, or Mexican and Mexican American, or Puerto Rican and African American, with few White students as classmates. Likewise, much like in the days of legalized segregation, there are schools where almost all of the students are White and have little or no contact with students of other ethnicities or language groups. As the authors of this book point out, in today's schools, it takes much more than understanding learning theory to address the learning needs of diverse school populations. It takes a critical stance for social justice, where students are led to question what is legitimate knowledge in light of the lived experiences of marginalized and oppressed groups.

This brings us to the central thesis of this book: The need for critical consciousness and change to be firmly embedded in our work in schools. The authors in this book point out the limitations of educational psychology concerned with how children develop socially and cognitively through constructivism, which highlights the role of learners in actively constructing and appropriating what for them are new ideas. The main area of concern is not entirely with the theoretical principles associated with constructivism but rather the absence in the early work of any reference to *what* students learn, especially as it relates to social justice issues and critical consciousness of social stratification based on language, ethnicity, social class, gender and race. Constructivism implies that students are active learners in creating meaning through scaffolded interaction with others. Critical constructivism, using Vygotskian social learning principles and following Paulo Freire's approach to critical pedagogy, goes well beyond the creation and appropriation of new meaning; it asks students to question whose meanings count and who benefits from meanings that exclude, that place the values of the dominant group over others, and that perpetuate myths about the poor and oppressed peoples of the world. These are serious questions that need to be posed and addressed in today's schools as teachers are strapped with standards, testing, and accountability. On top of all these encumbrances, bilingual education is increasingly outlawed as an educational approach. These dictates are a thinly veiled attempt by the dominant group to maintain its power by implementing educational policies that in fact are a means to ensure that the voices and needs of immigrant children, poor children, English language learners, and other stigmatized groups are not heard. This book challenges readers to engage

in dialogue with students about the world around them, to pay attention to social injustice, and to put forth solutions to the problems they pose. Among the many themes and topics that inquire about social justice are the following:

Advocacy	N-word
Bilingual Education	Oppression
Critical Race Theory	Poverty
Discrimination	Queer Theory
English-Only	Racism
Feminism	Spanglish
Genocide	Tracking
Homophobia	Undocumented
Immigration	Varieties of Language
Jingoism	White Privilege
Ku Klux Klan	Xenophobia
Linguicism	Youth Movements
Minutemen	Zealots

Each of these social justice topics is open-ended and requires much scaffolded discussion and dialogue, reading and writing, as well as inquiry and action to critically construct deep understanding of their meanings and implications for a better world for marginalized and oppressed groups. The hope of creating a more socially just world by understanding how students learn coupled with what they learn rests squarely on the shoulders of teachers and students who engage in topics that challenge systems of domination. This book provides students of educational psychology with new hope and a set of tools for reaching that goal.

Christian Faltis
Professor, Arizona State University, Tempe

Artwork by Christian J. Faltis

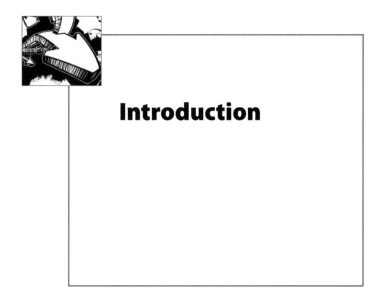

Introduction

The essential question for all preservice teachers and educators is "How do children learn?" This question is so simple, yet the implications for the children, their teachers, and ultimately, the community these new and future citizens will inhabit are profound. Our work to prepare children for a world of dynamic change, characterized by unknown opportunities and obstacles, is inextricably linked to this question: How do children learn? Although many receive the call to come to the classroom to teach, the process of comprehending the meaning of the question of how children learn is complex, and your learning the answer to this question begins as you encounter the writing of the authors of this book and will continue throughout your career.

Your responsibility as a preservice teacher or educator is to develop the knowledge, skills and dispositions necessary for all children to be able to learn and to develop themselves to their full potential. As you strive to live up to your own expectations of what it means to be a teacher, you will progress through a series of stages in your own development of becoming an accomplished and successful professional. What you will discover as you work to fully comprehend how children learn is that you will be the leader in the community of learners known as your classroom. Teaching is a mutually rewarding endeavor.

When I graduated from the University of New Hampshire and began working in the public schools, I remember confronting obstacles for which I felt completely unprepared. Angry and demanding parents, frustrated and disaffected students, disgruntled and burned-out colleagues all made me question my decision to become an educator. I was seeking excitement and stimulation, and I was meeting resistance and refusal to change. Immediately, I felt that my college professors failed to prepare me for the reality of the public school. I needed to blame someone for the collision between my expectations and the reality I discovered.

Forty years later, as I reflect on my experience, I understand that the process of becoming a successful educator is more like becoming a Jedi knight, a 5th degree black-belt, or any other highly accomplished professional. This esteemed position is not given. It is attained through many years of hard work, motivation, reflection, and the strength of purpose within one's self. As I learned at Outward Bound: To serve to strive and not to yield. The answer to that simple question: How do children learn? is continually evolving in my brain and being fostered by my soul.

As you begin your career, remember to always consider this question: how do children learn? This book can guide your inquiry into many of the techniques and theories of learning, but more importantly these authors call to you to consider why it is so important to teach, to lead, and to care for our children. Simply, our future depends upon these

young people. How we treat and teach them and how and what they learn are critical for our survival as a world community and as an ecosystem. As the planet flies through space, slowing one's personal pace to reflect and consider the importance of teaching and learning can create a reinforcing loop to maintain our motivation to continue to strive for the success of all of our students.

Although many deserve credit for their contributions to a book's process and production, this editor owes the greatest debt of gratitude to the authors who have contributed well-researched and carefully considered critical constructivist pedagogy to this text. Tamar Jacobson was the inspiration for this book's beginning. As we traveled across Pennsylvania following her visit to Clarion University, we schemed a proposal for a book and began with the naïve notion that all that lay ahead were sweet chords and chocolate. Also principal in the initiation of the process was the work of Suzanne Gallagher. Having published *Educational Psychology: Disrupting the Dominant Discourse* in 2003 (Peter Lang Publishing), Suzanne laid the groundwork for this text by driving a wedge into the staid and static discipline of educational psychology. Her courageous feminism creates a formidable leadership to guide educators in the pursuit of teaching for social justice.

Also an advocate for social justice in education, Jeff Duncan-Andrade is among the few members of the academy who put their pedagogy and praxis to work in the public schools and on the streets. In addition to a scholarship that is extraordinary for its depth and breadth, Jeff's dedication to the causes of social justice education has benefited many people in his immediate Oakland, CA, community and beyond. Standing with Jeff, Floyd Beachum and Carlos McCray are visionary leaders in the movement to create cultural bridges of understanding between the white and black alienated and segregated communities. Using Hip-Hop as a metaphor for culture, they propose using the appealing opportunities of youth culture to connect black, brown, white, and other youth through one cause: social justice.

Joanne Washington is a Hip-Hop Presidential Scholar, and her communication study aims to bring us all together in one connected community. Using language as a link, we can grow together and gain from furthering our understanding of each other's identifications and human needs. This Freirean concept of shared identifications is also adopted by Chinese scholar Binbin Jiang. In her approach to teaching English as a Second Language, Binbin goes beyond language to the soul of our connection with one another. Seeking an understanding of who is present, Binbin takes the learners on an adventure to find out and to learn through the discovery of one another.

Karen Carey is a psychologist and her love is children. Karen presents prospective teachers with an opportunity to find out how assessment can benefit their classroom practices and enhance their connection with their students. Also coming from a practitioner's perspective, Patty Kolencik knows and can demonstrate the importance of feelings in the process of learning and the creation of school culture. Her contribution of affective education's role in learning is critical to the teacher's success in the student's achievement. With Patty, I also thank my other colleagues in the Education Department at Clarion University of Pennsylvania for their support of my scholarship and teaching.

A special thanks to Christian Faltis for his contribution of this book's preface. Christian's work in multicultural education and his prolific contributions to teacher education have earned him the respect of his colleagues throughout the world. We are deeply honored to have his endorsement.

Other important individuals in this book's creation include our mentor, Peter McLaren. Peter's work is always ahead of the pack, and his leadership in critical constructivism and revolutionary critical pedagogy is visionary. This book is a

direct reflection of Peter's mentorship of all people seeking social justice in education. Sharing this esteemed leadership with Peter stand Joe Kincheloe and Shirley Steinberg. Their selection of this work for publication in the series CounterPoints is a compliment to all of these authors, and we respectfully express our gratitude to them for this recognition.

The book's visual distinction is directly credited to the editorial work of Barbara Morton and Bernadette Shade. Their countless hours of proofreading, layout, and design have resulted in a readable and attractive text.

Grateful acknowledgment is hereby made to copyright holders for permission to use the following copyrighted material:

The two frontispieces, paintings by Christian Faltis, appearing in the front matter section of this book are printed by permission of the artist.

"Developing Social Justice Educators", by Jeffrey M.R. Duncan-Andrade. In the March, 2005 issue of Educational Leadership, 62(6), p 70-73. Used with Permission. The Association for Supervision and Curriculum Development is a worldwide community of educators advocating sound policies and sharing best practices to achieve the success of each learner. To learn more, visit ASCD at www.ascd.org.

Just Kidding cartoons for cartoon #144 which appears on page 72 of this text. Used by permission.

***

The article, "Your best friend or your worst enemy: Youth popular culture, pedagogy, and curriculum in urban classrooms" by Jeffrey Duncan-Andrade, appeared in Taylor & Francis' The Review of Education, Pedagogy, and Cultural Studies 26: 313-337, 2004.

Every attempt has been made to secure proper permissions from copyright holders. Any person or company that feels that there is any issue pertaining to copyright of material contained in this volume is encouraged to contact the publisher.

Artwork by Christian J. Faltis

CHAPTER ONE

Developing Social Justice Educators

How Can the Subject Tell the Truth About Itself?

Jeff Duncan-Andrade

In a teacher inquiry group, educators collectively examine how to teach for social Justice.

Although many teachers in high-poverty urban schools struggle to meet the needs of their students, some gifted educators achieve consistent success. What enables some teachers to effectively reach the same students whom other teachers can't seem to reach? Three highly effective teachers recently articulated their teaching philosophies as they participated in a teacher inquiry group at Power Elementary School in South Central Los Angeles. As these effective teachers shared the philosophies guiding their instructional practices, curriculum designs, and relationships with students, they made it clear that the strength of their teaching came from a focus on student empowering **social justice pedagogy**. The inquiry group shed light on two questions: "How

Social justice pedagogy
A style of teaching that offers hopeful alternatives to the oppression of poverty, racism, and injustice.

can a focus on teaching for social justice energize teaching and learning in an urban school?" and "How can urban schools create a formal space for teachers to investigate and question their philosophies and beliefs and learn from colleagues who provide relevant, socially transformative instruction?"

A Social Justice Philosophy

I proposed the teacher inquiry group at Power Elementary as a three-year program. Its purpose was to support the development of student-empowering social justice themes in teachers' practice. Seven teachers signed up to participate. All were fairly new to teaching when we began; the most senior had six years of experience. At the outset of the program, their students' test scores covered the schools achievement span: Three of their classes consistently scored in the top quartile of the school, two were in the middle, and two were in the bottom quartile.

How Can a Focus on Teaching for Social Justice Energize Teaching and Learning in an Urban School?

Ms. Grant, Ms. Kim, and Mr. Truong, the teachers with the highest student test scores in the group, all subscribe to Paulo Freire's idea that effective education for marginalized groups must employ a **liberatory pedagogy**—that is, one that aims to help students become critical change agents who feel capable of and responsible for addressing social injustices in their communities (Freire, 1970). Ms. Grant, a fourth grade teacher, explains: Racial, cultural, ethnic, and socioeconomic status has no effect on students' abilities to acquire knowledge. Schools should provide students with the fundamental skills and ideas necessary to develop within the system while also preparing them to transform the system.

Mr. Truong, a fifth grade teacher, cites a series of problems with the institutional culture of urban schools.

Liberatory pedagogy

A style of teaching that seeks to end oppressive policies and to free people from injustices.

The first thing I wonder about urban schools is 'Where is the love?' Even a surface-level analysis of our school reveals that students dislike the school; they are unengaged and exhibit resistance. The environment is not child-centered. This is reflected in the scripted or mandated programming . . . a set of decontextualized academic exercises, an overemphasis on basic skills. Students have become machines; they are not allowed to question the relevance of what they are learning. They are forced to perform for the sake of the task at hand. In short, our schools reflect a prison system mentality, a lot like the conditions in urban communities.

Mr. Truong believes that he can best care for his students by giving them the academic and critical skills to act as change agents in their communities. He teaches his students using what he calls the "4Es" of **emancipatory pedagogy**:

Emancipatory pedagogy

A style of teaching that seeks to free people from the limitations of injustices.

- *Engage*—Provide culturally responsive teaching that validates students' funds of knowledge.
- *Experience*—Expose students to various possible realities by presenting narratives that show the perspectives of those often unheard in society.
- *Empower*—Use a critical and transformative pedagogy to give students a sense of agency, both individual and collective, to act on the conditions in their lives.
- *Enact*—Create opportunities for students to act out their growing sense of agency, learning from and reflecting on their successes and struggles.

Ms. Kim also develops traditional academic skills by paying attention to students' cultures, critical thinking, and agency.

My practice begins with the recognition of the students' cultural capital: language, culture, family, interests, and so on. . . . My goal is to offer counter-discourse to the traditional curriculum and to incorporate this in a fluid, meaningful, and empowering way. It is important that my pedagogy identify forms of oppression—and not ambiguously, either, or else students feel like things cannot change.

These three successful teachers are keenly aware of the dire conditions in which many of their students live. They believe that they should not ignore these conditions but instead should talk about them in the classroom. They design their pedagogy to empower students with tools for recognizing, naming, analyzing, and confronting the most acute social conditions facing them: poverty, racism, violence, and inequality.

To these teachers, success means both raising students' test scores and developing students' ability to think critically and act constructively. They insist that one without the other is unlikely to reduce the opportunity gap for urban students. They do not accept urban poverty as an excuse for underachievement by either teachers or students. Instead, they see unequal material conditions as a set of constraints that students can and should transform.

The philosophies of social justice embraced by these educators go beyond the traditional narrative, which sees education as a vehicle to escape financially impoverished communities. These teachers view education as a vehicle to invest in that can improve conditions in urban areas. They want their students to become college graduates who will come back and transform their urban communities. Less successful urban teachers tend to have more modest ambitions, such as wanting their students to study for tests, behave well in class, and persist in school.

Social Justice Teachers in Action

Ms. Grant:

Although Ms. Grant does not approve of the school district's scripted reading program (Open Court), she rejects the arguments of those teachers who claim that they are pedagogically handcuffed by it. She develops social justice-oriented units that incorporate media and critical literacy into the scripted Open Court themes. For example,

as her class worked with the program's "Mysteries of Medicine" unit, she had students view the popular *John Q*, discuss inequities in the health care system, and follow up with writing assignments and poster projects examining how these issues affected their own lives and the lives of other people in their community. In these assignments, students developed individual and collective policy positions on health care issues.

After the class participated in these learning activities, class members significantly raised their scores in three of the reading program's measured areas: applications, strategies, and conventions, but Ms. Grant is especially proud of her students' **transformative thinking** about their own community. A typical student, D.T., not only made notable academic gains but also connected what he learned to local conditions. He wrote:

Transformative thinking
Being able to visualize a different, and life-changing perspective.

> I went to Ralph's and I seen strikers. One striker's son had a broken arm, and they was on strike because they didn't have enough health care. And it made me think about John Q., when his son didn't have enough money to get a new heart. It made me feel bad because a lot of people have more health care than the people who are on strike.

Ms. Kim and Mr. Truong

Ms. Kim is only in her third year as a teacher, but her students have some of the highest math and literacy test scores in the school. She attributes this success to three things: her social justice pedagogy, her collaboration with colleagues, and the fact that she was able to stay with the same students through second and third grades.

Mr. Truong's fifth grade students also show exceptional growth on standards based testing—an amazing achievement considering the inexcusable working conditions he has experienced. Because of Mr. Truong's reputation for being effective with students other teachers could not reach, the school administration shuffled several "challenging" students into his class and collapsed an undersized fifth grade class into his room, leaving him with 38 students and no additional support. At the beginning of the year, fewer than 50 percent of the students in this class were scoring at or above proficiency in spelling, vocabulary, and proofreading. By February, however, class proficiency in these skills had risen to 83, 88, and 92 percent, respectively. In the same time frame, the class average in reading fluency jumped by 20 words, exceeding the district fluency benchmark, and the percentage of students at benchmark in reading comprehension tripled. Mr. Truong's students showed similar gains in math.

Both Ms. Kim and Mr. Truong contend that their students' success is a result of instructional strategies that enable students to apply what they learn in the classroom to real issues in their lives. An example is their collaborative response when the school disciplined several students for having toy guns on campus—guns that the students had purchased from an ice cream truck in front of the school.

As part of their learner-writing unit, Ms. Kim's students wrote to the ice cream truck vendor, telling him that toy guns were creating a negative environment in their school and asking that he stop selling them. Mr. Truong's class wrote to toy manufacturing companies expressing similar concerns during their persuasive writing unit. When neither party responded, students from the two classes got together to organize an official protest. Under the supervision of teachers, parents, and the principal, students boycotted the ice cream truck.

They held signs that read "No More Toy Guns" and "Don't Sell Guns Here" while chanting, "What do we want? No more toy guns at Power Elementary. When do we want it? Now!"

The ice cream truck left after several minutes of the protest, and it did not return. Although a rethinking of the school policy of letting a vendor sell toy guns near school property would have represented a greater victory, Ms. Kim and Mr. Truong emphasize the importance of letting stu-

dents come to conclusions about their effectiveness on their own. They believe the real victory here is that students felt empowered to apply the lessons they learned in school to challenge the immediate conditions of their lives.

Teachers Teaching Teachers

It is not news that exceptional urban teachers like Ms. Grant, Ms. Kim and Mr. Truong exist. To help the majority of teachers attain such success, however, urban schools must rethink their approach to teacher development. A promising approach is to create opportunities for successful teachers to reflect on their practice and share with less successful colleagues.

At Power Elementary, this strategy has proven effective and mutually beneficial for all the participants. The seven teachers in the inquiry group meet once a week for two hours in a four-week cycle of activities guided by the following themes.

Intellectual Development

During the first week of each cycle, the teachers discuss their written reflections on a reading chosen by one of the participants. Each reflection includes a classroom action plan for addressing issues raised by the reading. Group members who are already effectively addressing the issue use this time to share their practice with the other teachers. Those who are having less success can prepare an action plan informed by their colleagues' successes.

For example, Ms. Kim used her reflections on Henry Giroux's introductory chapter in *Literacy: Reading the Word and the World* (Freire & Macedo, 1987) to share with the group; an activity she finds effective for implementing Giroux's emphasis on "naming and transforming" negative ideological and social conditions (p. 5). In her class, she explained, she uses periods of open dialogue to encourage students to identify and critique non-democratic structures in their lives. She used the 2004 presidential elections, for instance, to develop dialogue about democracy. As students expressed their strong opinions about the candidates, Ms. Kim observed, they were empowered to "be dynamic, intellectual, and critical of what is going on."

Ms. Kim detailed how she charts student discussions on a Concept/Question Board in the classroom, which is used to continue previous dialogue and to display the students' various opinions. These discussions also enable her to assess students' functional and critical literacy skills. She uses these assessments to develop additional support structures in basic phonics for struggling readers and more advanced literacy techniques for those students who are ready.

Other teachers in the inquiry group were able to use Ms. Kim's ideas to address challenges in their own classrooms. Mr. Ballesteros, for example, began using similar student discussions to identify individual student needs and provide skill development appropriate to those needs in his math instruction. He started to decrease his use of whole class instruction, adding more individual and small-group instruction tailored to his students' performance levels. As a result, he reported, "I'm now seeing progress in the student work; they are showing greater understanding and they are getting it."

Professional Development

During the second week of the cycle, teachers pair up and observe their partner's classroom practice, debriefing afterward one-on-one to learn from their partner's reflections and feedback. When the entire group meets later in the week, each teacher reports on what he or she saw and learned from the observation. At these meetings, teachers use dialogue, questions, and suggestions to build a culture of teaching and learning.

Participants use the second hour of this meeting to discuss student work. Each teacher brings work samples from specific students (one high, one middle, and one low performer) whose progress they are following over the year. They draw from

the samples to highlight challenges and successes and to get critical feedback from their colleagues. This activity allows for concrete support. It also develops accountability among colleagues because of the expectation that all the students will show academic progress.

Ms. O'Leary, for example, brought to the group her concerns about keeping her lowest performing students on task. She was welcomed to observe in Ms. Grant's class to generate more effective strategies. After the visit, Ms. O'Leary reported to the group:

> I recently tried something I never wanted to do because it seemed time wasteful, but it worked well when I saw it in Ms. Grant's room. She had kids line up to check work with her, rather than stay seated and do something else when finished. My kids got one another distracted when I let them stay at their seats when finished with writing as I saw kids one at a time. So I tried Ms. Grant's method and it seems to work well. The kids worked harder and made more significant changes when I did the writing conferences this way.

Community Development

During the third week of each cycle, the teachers collaboratively develop out-of classroom projects, such as after-school sports and game clubs, academic support systems, and parent and community partnership plans that the teachers want to implement or improve. With each new cycle, teachers evaluate the progress of their projects and discuss issues with the group to keep the projects moving forward.

Holistic Growth

During the final meeting, teachers review their reflections from the first week. They prepare new reflections detailing their progress on the issues they addressed in week one, discuss their growth, and ask for additional support in areas in which they would like better results.

The opportunity for teachers to articulate new-found feelings of motivation, professionalism, and commitment is central to the development of a positive professional climate. As Ms. O'Leary, one of the improving teachers, explains:

> This group makes me feel like things are gonna change. I'm gonna need to change because it makes me always want to get better, and I want to offer what I have. As long as this group is available, I'll feel professional. In fact, this is the first time I've felt like a professional. I no longer feel replaceable or like the goal of professional development is to make all teachers the same. This community of professionals is going to help everyone get better and keep people [in teaching] longer.

The holistic growth meeting also enables highly effective teachers, such as Mr. Truong, to improve their practice and model an enduring commitment to professional growth:

> Thinking back to my goals and previous reflections, I am reminded that I am not where I want to be with my goals . . . I am not satisfied that I have fully taken advantage of potential literacy moments in science . . . By the next reflection, or sooner, I will come back to this and see if I have ironed out the wrinkles.

The opportunity to be reflective ensures that all inquiry group participants, not just the struggling teachers, have the opportunity to identity themselves as achievers and learners.

Toward Better Teaching in Urban Schools

Urban schools face sizeable challenges. Two components that can help urban school leaders meet these challenges are: 1) developing a better understanding of effective urban teachers' philosophies and practices, and 2) putting a system in place to support the professional growth of all teachers. School leaders can develop these supportive systems of professional development if they use successful practitioners as resources.

Power Elementary School's inquiry group enables highly effective teachers who espouse a

pedagogy of social transformation to share their philosophy and practice with colleagues. The structure of the group balances high expectations with teacher autonomy, support, and collaboration. Such professional development communities hold great promise for helping urban schools improve professional practice and student achievement.

(School and teacher names are pseudonyms.)

References

Freire, P. (1970). *Pedagogy of the oppressed.* New York: Continuum.
Freire, P., & Macedo, D. (1987). *Literacy: Reading the word and the world.* South Hadley, MA: Bergin and Garvey.

CHAPTER TWO

Coming to a Critical Constructivism

Roots and Branches

Greg S. Goodman

How do children learn? How can my teaching positively affect the future lives of these young people? What can I do in my classroom to make a contribution to our environmental quality? What are the components of the democratic classroom? As you consider becoming a teacher, you may have already asked yourself some of these questions. If you have, you are not alone. Most pre-service teachers are filled with questions as they consider their future in education.

One of the most important questions to ask concerns the style of teaching you will adopt: what type of pedagogy should I practice? **Pedagogy**, the philosophic and theoretical foundation for teaching, has been one of the fundamental foci of teachers since Socrates, the ancient Greek philosopher, first questioned Meno about how we obtain knowledge (Sesonske & Fleming, 1965). During the past

Pedagogy
The art and science of teaching based upon a philosophy or set of beliefs.

Constructivism

A pedagogy that features the learner's discovery and creation of knowledge.

Praxis

The application of critical pedagogy featuring reflection and action.

fifty years, educators have been presented with a wide array of pedagogical possibilities: objectivism, behaviorism, social learning theory, cognitive learning theory, **constructivism**, and critical constructivism. Today, the pedagogical positions or perspectives recommended by postmodern learning theorists reflect the growth of educators' knowledge of what makes for both better teaching and improvements in student outcomes or learning. The continuing conversation on teaching and learning is supported by thousands of volumes of scientific research (Wheldall, 2006). As you begin your career in education, you will be well informed by reading some of the literature of educational research and considering questions you may like to investigate on your own.

There is much to consider in the development of your own pedagogy for professional practice (**praxis**). Arguments for pedagogical positions are enlivened by political, humanistic, sociological, philosophic, and artistic appeal. A good example of this can be taken from the recent film, *Freedom Writers* (2007). As the film begins, the protagonist, Mrs. Gruwell, is confronted with her own naiveté, or innocence, concerning how to run a classroom within an urban high school. As she considers the students' needs to understand historic events like the Holocaust, she begins to help them understand the implications of their own racist and prejudicial behaviors. In a perfect world, perhaps Mrs. Gruwell would have been better prepared for her first teaching assignment. If she had come to her first teaching assignment prepared for critical constructivist praxis, she would have been ready to present relevant challenges to her students. However, in that scenario there would have been no story, because there would not have been the essential conflict that captivates us as viewers.

Despite its distorted, Hollywood depiction of a middle-class woman saving the hood/ghetto, *Freedom Writers* can give you good insights into the

application of the pedagogy identified as critical constructivism. Critical constructivism is an engaging process of enriching students' learning experiences by challenging the known world with intellectually and spiritually invigorating experiences (Kincheloe, 2005). Mrs. Gruwell wanted to attack the racism and sexism in her classroom by using dynamic, experiential processes. She learned, as did her students, that the best way to teach is through authentic engagement with relevant issues.

To assist you, the pre-service teacher, in developing a pedagogical position to inform your future teaching, some of educational psychology's most recent research, philosophic thought, and pedagogical theory will be discussed. I will briefly cover some of the traditional constructivist concepts and theory from the Swiss psychologist Jean Piaget and his Russian counterpart Lev Vygotsky before branching out into an approach more congruent with today's research and the youth you will serve. Although the eclectic, critical constructivist position will be strongly suggested to you, you are encouraged to create your own unique and personal pedagogy. The major purpose of this chapter is to inform you of some of constructivism's foundational thought and then to aid you in the development of your own, unique pedagogical stance. The knowledge of constructivism past and the critical constructivism of the present can be an essential tool for enhancing your teaching practice in the classroom and the larger community.

A secondary purpose of this chapter is to help to prepare you to pass the section of the Praxis Two examination titled "The Principles of Teaching and Learning." In most states, beginning teachers must pass this examination before they can acquire a teaching credential. The authors of this text do not support the use of single, high stakes tests for any selective sorting. However, over 800 occupations in America currently require a competency examination (Drummond, 2006), and education is aligned with mainstream policy considerations in this regard. Since the passing of No Child Left Behind (NCLB, 2001), the Praxis exam has been required of all prospective teachers in an attempt to insure their basic literacy (Praxis One tests reading, math, and writing skills) and to evaluate subject specific competency (Praxis Two: mathematics, English, sciences, etc.). Although this author takes exception with both the content and predictive validity of Praxis One and Praxis Two, these evaluations must be passed if one desires to teach in most American public schools (Goodman & Carey, 2004). To deny this reality is to do you, the pre-service teacher, a major disservice. However, you can transcend the banality of the Praxis by understanding the foundational theories and moving beyond their limited perspective (Watson-Gegeo & Gegeo, 2004). Through understanding some of the dominant discourse, you will then be able to grow beyond primary comprehension to improve your professional practice and reach the broad audience of today's multicultural classroom.

Jean Piaget: The Developmental Psychologist

To better understand and appreciate the significance of Piaget's contribution to our understanding of development, it is helpful to briefly review previous conceptualizations of childhood. Before Piaget's systematic observations and scientific evaluation of children, young people were viewed as either small versions of their adult counterparts or insignificant and bothersome burdens on society (for example: the satire *A Modest Proposal*). Although this was not a universal position, children were often considered cognate with adult roles and activities. In the world of art, they were depicted in adult clothing and formally represented. These artistic images of children portrayed them as iconic prizes of the aristocracy. Yet in real life, young people worked beside adults, or substituted for adults, in factories and in fields. Much of the motivation for these activities was economic. Mouths were difficult to feed. In colonial New England, families would send young

boys to wealthier neighbors to live and work during the long, difficult winter months (Kennedy, 2006). When Pilgrim children were released from work to attend school, they read and studied the Bible. Prior to the twentieth century there was no conception of developmentally appropriate reading material or children's literature. Children were treated as little adults in almost every aspect except, of course, in rights and freedoms. There were little to no protections for children or their rights.

To understand the significance of Piaget's scientific inquiry into children's development, some historical facts may help you to understand how children were mistreated. In the late 1800s, one third of Britain's boys and one half of the girls between the ages of five and nine were working 12 to 15 hour shifts in shops and factories (Colón & Colón, 2001). During these Victorian times (circa 1830 through 1900), approximately 100,000 children were employed in factories within the immediate vicinity of New York City (Calvert, 1893). This practice of exploiting children was ubiquitous in industrial and in agrarian cultures around the globe, and it continues today throughout much of what is referred to as the third world; i.e., the undeveloped nations of the world, especially in Asia and Africa (historyplace.com/uniterstates/childlabor/about.htm). Exploitation of children as "sex workers" continues in the United States as thousands of children are smuggled into America to be sold as prisoners of this ethically repugnant and criminal enterprise. Campagna and Poffenberger estimate that 1.2 million children are sexually exploited within the United States every year (Campagna & Poffenberger, 1998).

The sad reality of the history of children in both Europe and America is that children were so widely mistreated and abused (Colón & Colón, 2001). Although child labor laws were first enacted in the 1830s, most children of poor families were manipulated as insignificant pawns in a labor market supported by unconscionable greed. A famous poem penned from the period by Sarah Cleghorn (1917) entitled "Golf Links" laconically laments:

> *The golf links lie so near the mill*
> *That almost every day,*
> *The laboring children can look out,*
> *And see the men at play.*
> (In Metcalf & Burnhart, 1997, p. 3)

To combat the continuing subjugation of children as wage slaves to cruel corporations, photographer Lewis Hine (1874–1940) used his camera to chronicle the exploitation of children for the National Child Labor Committee. "From 1908 to 1912, Hine took his camera across America to photograph children as young as three years old working for long hours, often under dangerous conditions, in factories, mines, and fields. In 1909, he published the first of many photo essays depicting children at risk. In these photographs, the essence of wasted youth is apparent in the sorrowful and even angry faces of his subjects. Some of his

images, such as the young girl in the mill glimpsing out the window, are among the most famous photographs ever taken" (historyplace. com/unitedstates/childlabor/about. htm).

The stories of the abuses of children and the ignorance with which they were mistreated are a large part of the reason Piaget's scientific study of children has been so influential. Piaget helped to change the way in which society viewed children by adding a scientifically based inquiry into their cognitive development. Consequently, Piaget's work is foundational to modern educational psychology, and his observations of children have been important in our understanding of developmental changes throughout childhood and into adolescence (Piaget, 1969).

Piaget is still considered the most influential developmental psychologist in the history of the Western world (Diessner & Simmons, 2000). Piaget brought us out of the dark age of thinking that children were either naïve urchins or small people with lives largely undifferentiated from adults.

Although the world of education, and, more specifically, America's classrooms are fundamentally different than the 100% Caucasian Swiss audience of Piaget's study, Piaget's contributions bring two things to our attention: (1) children's developmental processes change over time, and (2) we can improve as teachers if we make careful observations of how young people construct meaning or knowledge within normal developmental sequences (Piaget, 1964). Piaget applied scientific methods to the study of children, and he paid close attention to the cognitive or thinking processes. Piaget's genius is all the more important when we consider that he was one of the first psychologists to reveal these gradations within a developmental sequence (Vidal, 2000).

The foundation of developmental psychology posits that children progress through stages of growth beginning at the most fundamental and progressing toward the most advanced or "adult" stage. David Jardine (2006) has contributed a "commonsense legacy of Jean Piaget's work" to simplify our understanding:

> An astonishing number of near commonsensical beliefs in educational theory and practice owe their origins directly or indirectly to Jean Piaget's legacy, including the beliefs that:

- Children go through stages of development, and one must be sensitive to "where the child is at";
- A student should be presented with materials and curricular expectations appropriate to the stage of development he or she is at;
- The development of intelligence occurs not only in stages but in a traceable sequence of stages;
- Developmentally appropriate curriculum materials must therefore also be sequenced to fit the stages of development in the child;

- In any real classroom, individual children will be at different levels of development;
- "Ages" and "stages" and "grade levels" are not equivalent except as very broad generalizations that are, more often than not, overgeneralizations;
- In order to learn, young children especially (but not exclusively) are greatly helped by active manipulation of objects (an early thread of hands-on learning);
- Children sometimes need to use concrete materials (objects, images, examples, visual or auditory aids, etc.) not only to learn, but also to show, demonstrate or articulate what they have learned;
- Experiencing and knowing the world in deeply embodied, sensory, playful and image-filled ways are ways of being intelligent (a thread of what has come to be known as "multiple intelligences" (Gardner, 1993);
- Children's play is a central feature of the development of intelligence;
- The healthy establishment of a previous stage is necessary to the healthy achievement of the next stage, and finally,
- In knowing the world, we don't just take in the world passively—rather, we actively construct our experiences and understandings of the world according to our own concepts, categories, levels of development and previous experiences. (pp. 2–3)

Jardine notes that the stages of development are not set or fixed, but these changes do occur in a systematic, observable order in the lives of healthy, fully-functioning children. Piaget (1969) made thousands of observations of children, and he specifically delineates four distinct periods of cognitive growth that occur in a chronological order. The first period is identified as the sensori-motor stage of development. The sensori-motor stage begins at birth and continues until approximately two years

of age. As the stage's name suggests, during this period of development, children explore the world through their senses: smelling, seeing, hearing, tasting, and touching. Through sensory exploration, children come to understand their immediate world and eventually learn to coordinate multiple sensory inputs, for example, hearing mother and seeing mother. This awareness of mother extends over time to knowing mother is near by even though the child can't see her because he or she can hear her. Piaget called this phenomenon "object permanence." Before this is developed, if the mother is out of sight, she does not exist.

The sensori-motor stage of development is a very exciting time for parents. Parents anxiously await the arrival of developmental milestones such as focusing, grasping, standing, walking, and saying the first word. The key concept in all of the activities was the "operation" of the child. As the child would develop, more and more "operations" were being conducted by the child. Piaget used this term to define all of the later stages of child development to build a case for expanding capacities of the child.

At roughly two years of age, children begin to transition from the sensori-motor stage into the pre-operational period of development. From two years of age until approximately age seven, children use various forms of play to develop language and other life skills. This is another period of tremendous growth in children. The two-year-old enters this period as a dependent infant and begins to develop some basic independence from mother/caregiver. The primary job of the young child is to develop language and communication skills to represent and interpret the world. This is a time of play and of exploration. As meaning is developed, reality is only of marginal importance. Psychologists often call these the magic years. Many children believe in Santa, and talking animals are within the scope of conceivable occurrences. The fanciful, magic years of children play an importance part in their construction of meaning as they travel through worlds of make believe and experience the loss of innocence.

Many child psychologists believe that healthy and positive experiences are of utmost importance during this period for later school and life success (Jacobson, 2002). There is a strong body of research-based evidence claiming a valid link between the quality of play in the preoperational period and readiness for school instruction (Bowman, Donovan, & Burns, 2000). In his facetious essay, *All I Really Need to Know About Life, I Learned in Kindergarten*, Robert Fulgram reviews for adults the life lessons of the pre-schooler/kindergartener. The lessons of "take turns," "the golden rule," "don't hit or hurt" help the young child move from a life of self-focus (narcissism) to a world of successful intrapersonal and interpersonal relations. In the article, "The Importance of Being Playful" (Bodrova and Leong, 2006) conclude, "in classrooms where play was on the back burner, teachers struggled with a variety of problems, including classroom management and children's lack of interest in reading and writing. These results confirm that thoughtfully supported play is essential for young children's learning and development" (p. 29).

As children progress through school years, they enter into Piaget's third stage: the concrete operational stage of development (Piaget, 1969). Beginning at approximately seven years of age (roughly first grade) and continuing until about eleven years of age (roughly fifth grade), children begin to learn addition and subtraction, spelling, and other mental tasks. Before this time, children could manipulate objects physically, but in this new stage, their mind begins to comprehend how people and events can be organized or structured. For example, when preoperational thinkers would see a woman, and they might immediately identify her as a mother or 'mommy.' Concrete operational thinkers can see a woman and simultaneously identify her as a mother, wife, and sister. The ability to

classify sets or subsets is the key component of this stage of development.

During the concrete operational stage, students like to actively participate in their learning through group work and using manipulative objects. Making books, building dioramas, and acting out roles in simple plays are all good examples of ways in which students between the ages of 7 and 11 can construct knowledge using their logical and imaginative qualities. Making learning fun, social, and meaningful goes a long way toward creating an effective learning environment for these rapidly growing youngsters. Many educational psychologists credit Piaget with the development of the notion that children create meaning (knowledge) on their own. This phenomenon is known as constructivism, and it holds as one of its basic precepts that children create (constructs) their own reality. Therefore, the child's own actions and interactions with the environment are a reflection of unique interests and desires (Langer & Killen, 1998).

The last period of a child's development is the formal operational stage. This stage emerges at roughly 12–15 years of age. The logical thinking ability that developed during the concrete operational stage is enhanced by thought processes that can include abstract and hypothetical ideas. For example, a formal operational thinker can be given hypotheses to test or imaginary scenarios to consider. How much water will a boat's hull displace if the boat weighs a ton, or how would our government be structured today if the British had won the Revolutionary War? Piaget called the adolescent's ability to solve problems and devise solutions hypothetical-deductive reasoning. "What if" questions make good formal operational thinking exercises for the curious adolescent learner.

Adolescents have many unique developmental characteristics. One of their most interesting attributes is their self-centeredness or egocentricity. Adolescent egocentrism (Elkind, 1978) is a term to describe the teenager's belief that the rest of the world is as interested in them as they are. Another term for this phenomenon is "imaginary audience." Problems associated with adolescent egocentrism include a sense of being invincible or invulnerable. This sense that "it will never happen to me" can lead to reckless driving, drug taking, and/or unprotected sexual experimentation. "Egocentrism is a constant companion of cognitive development" (Wadsworth, 2003, p. 130). Knowing about this powerful personal motivator can be the teacher's best aid in gaining the attention of this narcissistic population.

Although Piaget has obtained iconic status among traditional educational psychologists, critical constructivists do not take such a positive view of his work. The main critique of Piaget stems from the reductive division of development into four fixed stages. Although this conceptualization may have been valid in the rigid, strict Swiss monoculture, this perspective fails to account for the diversity of children's experiences within the larger, global context. As Watson-Gegeo and Gegeo (2004) state: "Research has seriously challenged the notion that the 'stages' of human development are universal in the Piagetian sense, because what is expected of children from an early age and the kinds of socio-historical processes in which they are undergoing development vary across cross-culturally in substantial ways . . ." (p. 244). Piaget is important to know, but it is also essential to situate his study within the 100% white, 1950's Swiss culture. How Piaget's theory applies to twenty-first century American inner-city students (who represent Puerto Rico, Cuba, Mexico, Cambodia, Ethiopia, Somalia, etc.) is certainly up for question and requires critical re-examination.

Lev Vygotsky and the Socio-cultural Theory of Development

All children grow up in a context of a family, a community, and a culture. Lev Vygotsky (1896–1934) theorized that the influences upon our lives by these significant others contributed the most to the individual's cognitive development. Vygotsky (1987) took objection to Piaget, and he wrote, " . . . our research confirms . . . and allows us to put the question about using psychological research data on children's concepts applicable to teaching and training problems in a completely different way from Piaget" (p. 235).

Vygotsky contributes several very valuable concepts to the process of teaching and learning, and many of these constructivist notions are still valid. One of the first is the concept of **scaffolding**. Vygotsky believed that children's growth occurred incrementally within a space he called the Zone of Proximal Development. Vygotsky (1987) stated, "It is the distance between the actual developmental level as determined by independent problem-solving and the level of potential development as determined through problem-solving under adult guidance or in collaboration with more capable peers" (p. 86). A learner needs to be in a position from which they can make the next incremental step in learning. For example, a non-swimmer is not in the Zone of Proximal Development for learning to water ski or to skin-dive. Although this concept is easy to grasp in our minds, it can be very difficult to apply in a classroom of 30 or so students, each on a different learning level.

Scaffolding

Building a support system for learners to better achieve.

I like to teach the concept of scaffolding through the example of a term paper. At the beginning of each semester, I assign a 2,000–2,500-word term paper on a research topic of the student's choice. To mitigate the effects of resistance to writing and the inevitable sad consequences of late papers, I give the students four different assignments in one: choosing the topic, writing an outline of the paper, completing the first 1,000 words, and the final draft. By having three assignments to turn in before the final draft is due, most students attend to the paper and complete their work on time. This assignment works to demonstrate the process of scaffolding and its benefit to both the student and the teacher. Necessary corrections and other editing can be completed well in advance of paper deadlines and, most importantly, student outcomes improve.

Vygotsky's work on the Zone of Proximal Development spurred the creation of the notion of cognitive apprenticeship (Collins, Brown, & Newman, 1987). Applying the axiom "Two heads are better than one," you can understand the benefit of using social motivation to improve learning. Vygotsky's thinking that social relations, and the culture from which social interaction is defined, helped to shape the child's cognitive functioning is most useful for teachers to consider. "He believed that the development of memory, attention, and reasoning involves learning to use inventions of society, such as language, mathematical systems, and memory strategies. In one culture, this could consist of learning to count with the help of a computer; in another it could consist of counting on one's fingers or using beads" (Santrock, 2006, p. 51).

Using socially motivated techniques to improve learning provides multiple benefits for the student. Once the teacher has trained or mentored the student in a learning process, the students are able to actively engage the curriculum in an effective manner. For example, I use the teaching of methods to create critical questions to help my students direct their thinking to the daily lesson. Each class, students are required to read the assigned text and to create a critical question using an allusion from the reading. When the student comes to class, they are given time to meet with 2–4 other students and to ask their questions of one another. I call this process CALT, Constructivist Action Learning Teams. When I break from my lecture and students begin CALT, the entire class becomes actively engaged. Sometimes called **cooperative learning**, student's natural peer to peer motivation is enhanced by the discovery process. Because I am trying to train college age students to think and act like teachers, peer-to-peer teaching through cognitive apprenticeship can be

Cooperative learning

Using groups to reinforce learning.

an effective scaffolding tool for developing critical questioning skills.

Both Piaget and Vygotsky have made great contributions to the development of the educational theory known as constructivism. Although these men differed in their perspectives, many teachers combine elements of both theorists to create their own, eclectic pedagogical practices. Whether you choose to use Piaget's more individual discovery-based learning or Vygotsky's socially motivated cognitive apprenticeship techniques, or a combination of the two approaches, students will appreciate the fact that you trust in their ability to learn.

Criticisms of Piaget and Vygotsky have reflected changes in educational psychology during the last 50 years. Specifically, Vygotsky and Piaget began their scientific investigations before the advent of the civil rights movement, preceding the woman's movement, and ahead of the development of critical pedagogy. Although it may not be fair to critique their contribution's lack of attention to such a key component as **social justice** education, it may be more appropriate to suggest that their work opened the way to a refinement of their constructivist contributions to what is now referred to as critical constructivism.

Social justice
Practices that work to provide fairness and equality.

Critical Pedagogy

Critical pedagogy
This is the liberatory teaching method created by Paulo Freire.

Critical pedagogy is the contribution of the mentor Paulo Freire (1970). Paulo Friere was a Brazilian schooling and social visionary. Among his most impressive accomplishments, Freire developed a process of using social motivation to improve learning. He called these groups literacy circles. As described by biographer Peter McLaren (2000), "In 1962, the town of Angicos, in Rio grande do Norte, was witness to a remarkable event: Freire's literacy program helped 300 rural farm workers learn to read and write in forty-five days. By living communally with groups of peasants and workers, the literacy worker was able to help campesinos identify generative words according to their phonetic value, syllabic length, and social meaning and relevance to the workers" (p. 143). Freire's project was the development of literacy and the liberation of all poor and oppressed people.

Paulo Freire appealed to the world's educators to consider the provision of social justice as the preeminent mission for all teachers. Social justice in Freire's eyes meant giving citizens the ability to read and, therefore, the key to learning how to break away from the oppressive domination of poverty and social inequality (McLaren, 2000). Throughout all of his life, Freire championed concern for the poor, illiterate, and under-represented citizens by developing literacy circles and calling for the education of all, not just an elite few. Out of his love of the people and a desire to provide education for the empowerment of all, Freire has inspired educators interested in social justice to adopt critical pedagogy as essential to the development of meaningful educational practice (McLaren, 2000).

For all students, especially for those attending urban schools, critical pedagogy has wide applicability in our educational community. As our national educational system continues to confront crises of relevance and is challenged in all areas for improvements, the need for educational reform is most critical in urban settings where unemployment and under-employment are pervasive and alienation from successful role models predominates. For most urban youth, large-scale efforts to provide equal opportunity appear to be economically and socially unsupported. In response to the need to bring excitement and relevance back to the schools, educators for social justice link to Freire's critical pedagogy to support and teach underrepresented individuals and groups.

In today's confusing culture, it may be fair to add that almost all youth require authentic activities to build connection to real world meaning for the value of one another and the need to protect our environment. Often lost in a make-believe world of video games and a mass-marketed culture of vio-

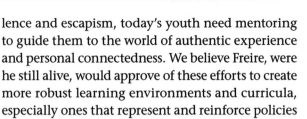

lence and escapism, today's youth need mentoring to guide them to the world of authentic experience and personal connectedness. We believe Freire, were he still alive, would approve of these efforts to create more robust learning environments and curricula, especially ones that represent and reinforce policies of social justice and environmental education.

Critical Constructivism

Critical constructivism has evolved from a combination of the philosophic foundation provided by constructivist theory (we create our own unique reality and knowledge) and the contribution of myriad critical pedagogy scholars led by the mentor, Paulo Freire. Despite years of scientific inquiry into the nature of the child and how best to teach them, much of the **technical rationality** of initiatives such as No Child Left Behind have betrayed educators. Chased by standardized test scores and running away from the fear of the discrediting failure to achieve Adequate Yearly Progress (AYP), today's teachers need support for the good work they do in their classrooms not threatening mis-applications of evaluation. In support of the social justice needs our students require, the authors of this book advocate critical constructivism's democratic and emancipatory perspective. Critical constructivism offers a view of the child and his or her multidimensional and wonderfully unique characteristics that defy any technical or scientific explanations (Jardine, 2006).

Technical rationality

A belief that science can control classroom outcomes.

Critical constructivists believe that their students can acquire the knowledge necessary to lead productive and satisfying lives. This belief is supported by the conviction that individual students can create meaningful experiences and that these students are capable of not only analyzing the world around them, they can affect change in their world.

The authors of this book believe that the acts of learning which are most important are the ones that directly affect the lives of students and both the immediate and international world they inhabit. To demonstrate the relevant interconnection of children and their real identifications, these authors have linked urban culture, hip-hop culture, and the multiple cultural possibilities of youth with a critical constructivist approach. Through the reading, you will see how you can integrate socially just practices within your classroom to make the learning relevant, authentic, and exciting. Because the issues you will address are relevant, the topics will enliven discussions and create discomfort. Your classroom will be a process-driven ecosystem as students construct meaningful discussions and provoke democratic action.

Our schools have a long way to go to help our students to fulfill the failed promise of the signers of the Declaration of Independence. All wo/men have not been created equally, and their opportunities to frequently mirror the inequities brought on by a lack of education, health care, and other "savage inequalities" (Kozol, 1992) are what our poorest 25% of children experience. Critical constructivists are sensitive to the needs of all children, especially the needs of marginalized and abandoned youth. Critical constructivists understand that there is a real need to help these youth create a viable and sustaining life, free from the threat of violence, disease, and poverty. But rather than defining what critical constructivism is, these authors wish to show you applications of this theory so you can get to work and change the world of your future students. As Joe Kincheloe observes, "To assume a position which refuses to seek the structural sources of human suffering and exploitation is to support oppression and the power relations which support it (Freire, 1970; Perry, 2001)" (p. 13). The authors of this book hope you will grow to see our critical constructivist applications of educational psychology as a dynamic and relevant method of changing the lives of your students in positive ways.

References

Bodrova, E. & Leong, D.J. (2006). The importance of being playful. In K. Cauley, J. Mcmillan, & G. Pannozzo (Eds.) *Educational psychology: Annual edition.* Dubuque, IA: McGraw-Hill (pp. 27–30).

Bowman, B., Donovan, M.S., & Burns, M.S. (2000). *Eager to learn: Educating our preschoolers.* Washington, D.C.: National Academies Press.

Calvert, K. (1893). "The little laborers of New York City." In *Harpers New Monthly Magazine,* Vol. xlvii, no. cclxxix, pp. 325–332 (August 1893).

Campagne, D.S. & Poffenberger, D.L. (1988). The sexual trafficking in children. Dover, MA: Auburn House Publishing Company.

Collins, A., Brown, J.S., & Newman, S.E. (1987). Cognitive apprenticeship: Teaching the craft of reading, writing, and mathematics (Technical Report No. 403) BBN Laboratories, Cambridge, MA. Centre for the Study of Reading, University of Illinois, January 1987.

Colón, A.R. & Colón, P.A. (2001). *A history of children: A socio-cultural survey across millennia.* Westport, CT: Greenwood Press.

Diessner, R. & Simmons, S. (2000). Sources: Notable selections in educational psychology. New York: McGraw-Hill/Dushkin.

Drummond, R. & Jones, K.D. (2006). *Assessment procedures for counselors and helping professionals.* Englewood Cliffs, N.J.: Prentice Hall.

Elkind, D. (1978). Understanding the young adolescent. *Adolescence, 13,* 127–134.

Freire, P. (1970). *Pedagogy of the oppressed.* New York: Herder and Herder.

Fulgram, R. (2004). *All I really need to know, I learned in kindergarten.* New York: Balentine Books.

Gardner, H. (1993). Multiple intelligences: The theory in practivce. New York: Basic Books.

Goodman, G. & Carey, K. (2004). Ubiquitous assessment: Evaluation techniques for the new millennium. New York: Peter Lang Publishing.

The History Place: Child Labor in America 1908–1912. Photographs of Lewis W. Hine. (retrieved 5/13/2007) http: www.historyplace. com/uniterstates/childlabor/about.htm Para 3 & 4.

Jacobson, T. (2002). Confronting our discomfort: Clearing the way for anti-bias in early childhood. Portsmouth, NH: Heinemann.

Jardine, D. (2006). *Piaget and education.* New York: Peter Lang Publishing.

Kennedy, D. (2006). Changing conceptions of the child from the Renaissance to post-modernity: A philosophy of childhood. Lewiston, NY: Edmin Mellon Press.

Kincheloe, J. (2005). *Critical constructivism.* New York: Peter Lang.

Kozol, J. (1992). *Savage inequalities: Children in America's schools.* New York: Harper Perennial.

Langer, J. & Killen, M. (1998). *Piaget, evolution, and development.* Mahwah, N.J.: Erlbaum.

McLaren, P. (2000). *Che Guevara, Paulo Freire, and the pedagogy of the revolution.* Lanham, MD: Rowman & Littlefield.

Metcalf, A. & Burnhart, D. (1997). *America in so many words: Words that have shaped America.* Boston, MA: Houghton Mifflin.

No Child Left Behind Act (2002). Public Law 107–110, 1st session (January 8).

Perry, P. (2001). *A composition of consciousness: Roads of reflection from Freire to Elbow.* New York: Peter Lang.

Piaget, J. (1969). *The child's conception of the world.* Totowa, New Jersey: Littlefield, Adams, & Company.

———. (1964). *The moral judgment of the child.* New York: Free Press.

Santrock, J. (2006). *Educational psychology: Second edition.* New York: McGraw-Hill.

Sesonske, A. & Fleming, N. (1965). *Plato's* Meno*: Text and criticism.* Belmont, CA: Wadsworth Publishing.

Vidal, F. (2000). Piaget, Jean. In A. Kazdin (Ed.), *Encyclopedia of psychology.* Washington, D.C. & New York: American Psychological Association and Oxford University Press.

Vygotsky, L. S. (1987). Thinking and speech. In R.W. Weber & A. S. Carton (Eds.), The collective works of L. S. Vygotsky (translated by N. Minick). New York: Plenum Press.

Wadsworth, B. (2003). Piaget's theory of cognitive and affective development: Foundations of constructivism. New York: Allyn & Bacon.

Watson-Gegeo, K. & Gegeo, D.W. (2004). *Pushing the epistemological boundaries of multicultural education.* In G. Goodman & K. T. Carey, Eds., Critical multicultural conversations. Cresskill, N.J.: Hampton Press.

Wheldall, K. (2006). *Developments in educational psychology: How far have we come in twenty-five years?* New York: Routledge.

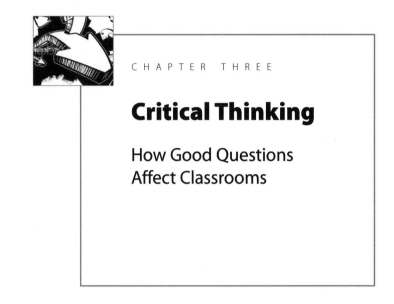

CHAPTER THREE

Critical Thinking

How Good Questions Affect Classrooms

Greg S. Goodman

Critical thinking
Thought that is more analytical and avoids simple solutions.

This chapter presents the notion that **critical thinking** is one of the keys to your success as a person: be that as a citizen or as a teacher. Developing ways to use your mind to explore concepts, theories, events, or assumptions is a good place to start. To begin this discussion, let us ask ourselves some questions: How is critical thinking different than thinking in general? Is it always necessary to think critically? What values or benefits exist in asking critical questions? How do we begin to create critically meaningful questions?

Many professors of education consider John Dewey (1944) to be one of the foremost philosophers in American's history. Philosophers are valued for their critical thinking and intellectual contributions to society. As an educational philosopher, Dewey gave us many ideas to ponder. One of the best of Dewey's contributions was the notion that learning is the process of thinking about experience. In Dewey's (1944) words, "No experience having meaning is possible without some element of thought" (p. 143). This contribution is immediately simple to understand, yet it is profound in its implications for us as teachers, and it is worthy of a deeper investigation. To assist in displaying how Dewey's words affected me as a teacher, I will share this example from my favorite teaching lesson: rappelling.

As a young college student, fresh out of 13 very boring years of public and private schooling, I was eager to learn of exciting and new ways to use my mind. Encouraged by my mentor Peter Ordway to attend a school called Outward Bound, I discovered how to rappel (how to descend mountains using a rope). Having had this experience of scaring myself half to death and realizing that I could do very bold things and not be limited in my experience by fear, the thing that I wanted to do most was to share this natural high with others. To teach outdoor education became my goal, and teaching rappelling would become my best lesson.

The days of climbing and rappelling always held excitement, and they were never boring. This is not to say that teaching on the edge of the cliff

was sufficient for me as a teacher. I took inspiration from some instruction by Jed Williamson, president of Sterling College. Jed once shared with me that my rappelling lesson had a high "C.T." factor. When I asked what "C.T." meant, Jed smiled and said, "Cheap Thrills." For those unable to get beyond the immediate experience of rappelling, this is true. Jed inspired me to seek something more from the experience. My challenge as a teacher was to help my students see this experience as a metaphor for other challenges in their lives. Rappelling was my best teaching aid for overcoming fear and personal obstacles. The real learning for climbers is not the obvious technique business of knots, slings, and belays, but it is in the internal examination of one's fear, courage, ingenuity, integrity, and identity.

I would instruct my students that for some of them, the courage to attend this class on the cliff required more character than it does for the ones who blithely hop down the rock face, high on adrenaline. In my introductory safety, outdoor "bathroom" rules, etcetera lecture, I would allude to Dewey's words, learning is the process of thinking about experience, to communicate the message that this day and lesson were not about learning to rappel. Today's lesson was about reflecting upon your own courage and ability to overcome personal limitations. To give this meaning to sixth graders, I would add, "There are no chickens on the rock today. For several of you, it took more courage to get up and get on the bus to come out here than it will take for others to descend this cliff."

Rappelling can be a pathway to personal discovery; however, the real learning comes from reflecting on the experience and using that knowledge for your life's benefit. Learning that you can overcome obstacles and that you do have the courage that you will need to endure: these are the big lessons. Teaching something as important as this was the reason I so enjoyed my lesson on rappelling. I was really trying to teach students to think critically about themselves. What does it mean to have courage? What is a moral equivalent for your bravery today? In what ways did you confront your own perceptions of self by doing this rappel? How did today's experience change the way you see someone else in your class?

As a climbing teacher, it is relatively easy to make learning exciting. It is all in the rock. What about math, English, or social studies teachers? How will you make your subject have personal meaning for your students? Some would argue that the subject matter is not relevant. What is important is teaching learning processes: logical thinking, creative and divergent thinking, critical thinking, and using the mind's multiple capacities or intelligences (Gardner, 1983). For all teachers, assisting in the development of the knowledge, dispositions, and skills of critical thinking may be the most valuable of the contributions they can imbue upon their students regardless of the specific subject matter at hand. In fact, educators may argue that some of the most important work ahead within in this century is in engaging students through meaningful and relevant discourse to consider their potential role and become critical citizens (Giroux, 1998). Critical citizens are individuals who take seriously their ethical, moral, and philosophic responsibilities to create communities that care about the environment, the culture, and the people they include.

> More than ever, the sheer magnitude of human knowledge renders its coverage by education an impossibility; rather, the goal of education is better conceived as helping students develop the intellectual tools and learning strategies needed to acquire the knowledge that allows people to think productively about history, science and technology, social phenomena, mathematics, and the arts. Fundamental understanding about subjects, including how to frame and ask meaningful questions about various subject areas, contributes to individuals' more basic understanding of principles of learning that can assist them in becoming self-sustaining, lifelong learners.

From "How People Learn: Brain, Mind, Experience and School" (p. 5) http://newton.nap. edu/html/howpeople1/ch1.html

The Bellevue Community College "Critical Thinking and Information Literacy Across the Curriculum" faculty have developed a solid rubric for defining critical thinking.

Critical Thinking recognizes:

- Patterns and provides a way to use those patterns to solve a problem or answer a question
- Errors in logic, reasoning, or the thought process
- What is relevant or extraneous information
- Preconceptions, bias, values and the way that these affect our thinking
- That those preconceptions and values mean that any interferences are within a certain context
- Ambiguity—that there may be more than one solution or more than one way to solve a problem

Critical Thinking implies:

- That there is a reason or purpose to the thinking, some problem to be solved or question to be answered
- Analysis, synthesis and evaluation of information

Critical Thinkers:

- Can approach something new and in a logical manner
- Look at how others have approached the same question or problem but know when they need more information
- Use creative and diverse ways to generate a hypothesis, approach a problem, or answer a question
- Can take their critical thinking skills and apply them to everyday life
- Can clarify assumptions and recognize that they have causes and consequences

- Support their opinions with evidence, data, logical reasoning, and statistical measures
- Can look at a problem from multiple angles
- Can not only fit the problem within a larger context but decide if and where it fits in the larger context
- Are comfortable with ambiguity (www.bcc.ctc. edu/lmc/ilac/critdef.htm)

The Role of Critical Thinking in the Promotion of Social Justice

One of the most important functions of a relevant educational pedagogy (philosophy of teaching) is to confront social injustice and environmental destruction with some meaningful and relevant questions. Some philosophers have suggested that the notions of what is right or wrong are already within us. We begin as children questioning simple fairness. In adulthood, we look at right and wrong as more complex questions, with answers other than simply yes or no.

As David Jardine (2000) has shared in his book *Ecopedagogy,* the word "educate" derives from the Latin root *educatus:* to bring out or to rear (raise). We take this meaning literally to state that we, as educators, are helping to develop, or to bring forth, the whole collective of body, knowledge, mind, soul, and character within our students. The important questions are within us and stem from the life experiences we have lived with our families, our friends, and our foes. What burns inside our students, future teachers, are the questions of meaning-making and the discovery of truth. When we present real questions to our students, relevance and meaning–making enhance our perspectives and help us to feel worthwhile.

Conversely, our disaffected (at risk or turned-off) students are overloaded with frustrations, and they often display a refusal to learn or even look inward. In the book, "I Won't Learn from You," Herb Kohl (1994) called this phenomenon (refusing to learn) "creative maladjustment." Could a

student's refusal to learn also stem from her inability to create questions of real personal and social relevance? That often our students are frustrated by a lack of personal power and disconnected from the real issues of their time may be the logical consequences of an educational system that has been imposed upon them by distant leaders and policy makers. Educational and social change begins with the questioning of the ideas that have maintained a broken system in which many of our students fail. In our culture, we need individuals who dare to come forward to question the big problems such as: "Why do we continue to wage wars outside our borders?"; "How can we judiciously resolve the issue of 12.5 million illegal aliens living in our country?"; "How can we allow such large numbers of our students to fail or drop out of high school?"; and "Why are we failing to correct the achievement gap between minority and poor students and their white and affluent classmates?" These are just some of the critical questions.

From John Lennon (*Give Peace a Chance*) to Emenim (*Feel the Love*) to John Mayer (*Waiting for the World to Change*), the call is for real pedagogical changes: to question the boredom and the alienation brought on by teachers and schools that perpetuate policies of social reproduction. We cannot continue to operate schools that foster failure through poor educational practices. The new psychological and educational knowledge required to facilitate human growth and learning should be a primary focus of today's te   low we can enliven a passion for d learning processes of the keys to c requirements of

Technology advancements hav ways (Peters, 2006). tion emerge from ac   private organizations with suc   volume that the total amount of info-d knowledge available far exceeds anyone's capacity for comprehension. Even the processes we are using for the creation of this book may become obsolete within a short period.

As you read this book, assuming you are holding a hard copy, the 5,000,000 books in print are being electronically copied to supplant and possibly to replace actual hard-copy manuscripts. This act symbolizes the dynamic growth of information and communication technologies (ICTs). As our world continues to "shrink," a factoid's value will diminish, too. What this implies for educators is that learning as a process of thinking and evaluating new information is much more important than rote memorization. Of course, the need to learn facts will continue to be of value; however, its importance is of diminished significance in comparison to one's ability to assimilate new information and to accommodate that information in relation to this rapidly changing world. This process-driven quest for learning is inspired and enlivened by critical questioning

How to Create Critical Questions

Changes in technology call for a re-examination of old paradigms of critical thinking and beg the development of new behaviors to execute pathways for understanding our role within these new ICT defined cultures (Peters, 2006). Thinking critically will be key to one's ability to negotiate life's chaotic and confusing constellation of choices. Because of the importance of this skill, thinking, it is important for students to begin to build understanding of the ways one develops critical questioning skills and dispositions. For purposes of applying educational psychology, you, as a student/teacher can implement the processes of critical thinking for every developmental level from emergent critical thinkers (pre-school) to fully matured critically thinking citizens (college graduates?).

One of the many markers of the educated person is the ability to think critically. This activ-

ity, critical thinking, is associated with informed query (questioning) and concomitant intellectual attributes including linguistic facility and research-based knowledge foundations. When these attributes are linked with an attitude or disposition of inquisitiveness characterized by honest curiosity (versus a haughty snobbishness defined as hubris), the quality of interaction is markedly higher. Critical thinkers are lively discussants at political events, participants in positions of community leadership, or situated within academic communities as professors or students. Supporting traditions of discursive activity has been a primary function of the academy, the name given to all members of institutions of higher learning. Interactions between academy members (for example, dialogues and published papers) are opportunities for publicly displaying and testing research and newly developed ideas. In fact, the tradition of dialogue is older than the academy. As an example, the *Meno,* Plato's dialogue of virtue, pre-dates the inception of academic institutions such as the university.

Historically, the activity of critical thinking is foundational to the western tradition of intellectual endeavor. Most scholars would concur that Socrates (father to the Socratic method) taught us all to further our investigations into truth and knowledge until we answered the questions fundamental to our being such as "What is virtue?" "Can virtue be taught?" In the ancient Greek dialogue *Meno,* Socrates seeks to find the answer to how virtue connects to humans (Phillips, 2006). His explorations in search of an answer lead him to question Meno as to the nature of education and knowing. How do we come to know virtue?

SOCRATES: And thus we arrive at the conclusion that virtue is either wholly or partly wisdom?

MENO: I think that what you are saying, Socrates, is very true.

SOCRATES: But if this is true, then the good are not by nature good?

MENO: I think not.

SOCRATES: If they had been, there would assuredly have been discerners of characters among us who would have known our future great men; and on their showing we should have adopted them, and when we had got them, we should have kept them in the citadel out of the way of harm, and set a stamp upon them far rather than upon a piece of gold, in order that no one might tamper with them; and when they grew up they would have been useful to the state?

MENO: Yes, Socrates, that would have been the right way.

SOCRATES: But if the good are not by nature good, are they made good by instruction?

MENO: There appears to be no other alternative, Socrates. On the supposition that virtue is knowledge, there can be no doubt that virtue is taught.

This is not the end of the discussion. (Does it ever end for Socrates?) To conclude Plato's *Meno*. . . .

SOC: If virtue was wisdom [or knowledge], then, as we thought, it was taught?

MENO: Yes.

SOCRATES: And if it was taught it was wisdom?

MENO: Certainly.

SOCRATES: And if there were teachers, it might be taught; and if there were no teachers, not?

MENO: True.

SOC: But surely we acknowledged that there were no teachers of virtue?

MENO: Yes.

SOCRATES: Then we acknowledged that it was not taught, and was not wisdom?

MENO: Certainly.

Socrates may well have believed that teaching was truly the way in which virtue was acquired, but his method of teaching was to push others to deeply investigate each question. As we seek to apply this process of developing critical questions in our classes today, we are fortunate to have had a series of mentors following these lines of query and refining the applicability to meet the changing needs of our students and the world they inhabit. Socrates, though important in the tradition of western thought, is of note historically. Bringing the concepts forward 2,000 years, perhaps Bob Dylan, Mary Oliver, 50Cent, Tupac, or other members of Hip-Hop or other cultures would frame it better for the youth of today (White, 1997)?

As an example, let us critically look at questions of virtue from some of these more current challenges of mainstream thinking: Mary Oliver and Tupac Shakur. Mary Oliver is a widely anthologized American poet who lives in Provincetown, Massachusetts. She grew up in eastern Ohio, and as a young woman, she summered in the woods of Western Pennsylvania in a place called Cook Forest. Living in an old army tent, she would imagine herself a poet, and she spent her time as a *flâneur:* an idler. She would roam the forest in search of herself, and she used the time to observe nature's beauty and man's destruction. Years later, she would write *The Wild Geese:* the poem that won national attention and admiration.

> *You do not have to be good.*
> *You do not have to crawl through the desert for a hundred*
> *   miles repenting.*
> *You just have to let that soft animal in yourself love what*
> *   it loves.*

This poem frees; it liberates. Reading this brings back our childhood and the time of our freedom from oppression of schedules, responsibilities, and obligations. It relates to our work as educators, but how does it connect? What rules do you need to adhere to and what callings do you answer?

Tupac Shakur grew up in the shadows of America's 1960s. His mother, Afeni Shakur, was a Black Panther, and Tupac's life was just starting as the civil rights movement had achieved national attention. The hope and the frustration of civil rights failed promises left Tupac as a ten-year-old proclaiming: "I want to be a revolutionary!" (White, 1997). Tupac took this calling and transformed himself into an icon of Hip-Hop. His lyrics were both a rant and raging against a world of racism and discrimination of the Black man. The words of his songs were also an appeal to bring the changes necessary to free oneself of the oppression of the hood:

> *We gotta make a change. . . .*
> *It's time for us as a people to start makin' some changes.*
> *2PAC Lyrics "Changes"*

Tupac challenges us to look at the injustices of the inner city and to feel the pain of ghetto traps: pimps, drugs, violence, and alienation. Tupac calls to his brothers and sisters to examine the situation they find themselves in and to adjust their lives before the violence changes them. Unfortunately, Tupac was a victim of his own prophesies. On September 13, 1996 in Las Vegas, Nevada, Tupac Shakur died from gunshots inflicted upon him six days earlier (White, 1997). However, his lyrics live on as a reminder of the continuing need to "make a change." As future teachers, you are in a unique position to ask questions of your own. What role will you play in the production of social change? As a teacher, what aspects of social change do you want to incorporate within your classroom? Do the women's movement, civil rights, democratic processes, students with disabilities, and care for the environment have a place within your curriculum or classroom culture?

For the authors of this book, the dynamic and pressing issues of social change and the problems associated with our modern civilization's ecological

mismanagement are drivers of our motivation to increase the critical thinking capacity of our students. We take inspiration from the mentor to many subscribers of critical thinking: a man named Paulo Freire (1970). Freire's work has ignited a new political revolution in American educational dialogue (Goodman, 1999; Kincheloe & Steinberg, 1997; McLaren, 1997). Informed by Freire's thought and word, educators for social justice are inspired to have hope for the future through Freire's critical pedagogy: the pedagogy of love. Love in Freire's eyes was a love for humanity. This love is not a romantic love, but a mindful compassion and connectedness with all people to create successful communities. Successful communities, in Freire's eyes, were ones in which all citizens could read, develop personal **agency**, and safely co-exist in an atmosphere of collective harmony and social justice.

Agency

A person's ability to determine their own destiny.

Following the loving legacy of Paulo Freire, we feel a responsibility to prepare our students for the world of diversity and the demands of proper earthly stewardship. Helping to prepare future teachers of yet unborn generations of citizens makes the issues of critical thinking and its application into a real and relevant problematic not a solitary, esoteric, or academic exercise. Critical thinking and questioning will make your classroom come alive!

Paulo Freire's critical pedagogy is deeply imbedded into the practice of the teaching. His teaching has given us a sense of personal responsibility that motivates and guides us to help our students to work toward issues of social justice and to confront problems of our environment. These important activities require thinking that is critical and well informed. Freire's goal was to bring literacy to an illiterate and exploited mass of millions of Brazilians. By forming literacy circles, he applied social learning theory to support individual learning. The result was the creation of literacy for thousands of Brazilians (McLaren, 2000).

Constructivist Action Learning Teams

From Freire, I have taken the notions of critical pedagogy and literacy circles and created a process called Constructivist Action Learning Teams (CALT). Constructivist theory comes from the work of developmentalists Jean Piaget and his contemporary, Lev Vygotsky. These men affirmed our ability to create and construct our own lives through the multifaceted and experientially based existence that we continuously evolve and participate in. We are the agents of our own destiny. This agentic process posits people as the essential creators of their own life experience. Students' experiences contain relationship choices, activity decisions, and learning opportunities. Constructivists believe that individuals re-structure the chaos of life to create meaning and order within their own worlds. In this model, teachers provide stimulation, guidance and extrinsic motivation in order to maximize the intrinsic motivation of our students and to help them to further their understandings and knowledge.

In the CALT process, I begin by teaching my students about framing critical questions. This teaching includes a rationale for using critical query. Critical query reflects the knowledge of the conversationalist, and it furthers the discussion beyond simple reductive yes and no questions. Questions and their quality do reflect upon the individual, and there are, contrary to popular wisdom, "stupid" questions. Questions like, "Is our children learning?" (Begala, 2000) reflect extraordinarily dim light upon the interrogator. I want my students to get beyond the reductive "Yes" and "No" conversant critique and to move the conversation deeper into an intellectual and informed discussion.

How to achieve this higher learning is no mystery. The information and grist for the student's mental mill are located within the research of the topic at hand. Using the common research forms contained within the literature review process, the students will find information and fact to bring meaning to their questioning. Within the books,

journal articles, and myriad other sources of information, students will find facts (or untruths) upon which they can build questions and arguments for discussion.

Adolescents are known for their developmentally linked, reductive, either/or thinking. As adolescents mature in their ability to define their world, they begin to eschew perceptions of either/or. As college students, it is incumbent upon you, as emerging adults, to see that over-generalizations are invalid and that the answers to important questions are not "Yes" or "No," but are complexities of response belonging rightfully upon a continuum ranging widely across a spectrum of culturally driven and diverse possibilities. Questions like, "As a nation, what policies should we develop to reverse global warming?" are not answered with simple solutions.

The writers of this book want you to share in the knowledge contained in the readings we have selected for your edification. Some of these readings are deep, and some of them are easy to comprehend. However, all of these readings are made meaningful by your thinking about the reading's content and by developing critical questions to make their investigations more enlivened and experiential.

Related to each chapter assignment in the classes I teach, I ask my students to create a critical question and to bring it to class with them. At the end of my lecture, I ask the students to query their peers with their question and to spend some time in discussion. What I get from this process is an enthusiasm and a participation that is lively. The students enjoy each other's company, and they like having the ability to share their opinions and to challenge their learning. Topics such as racism, discrimination, poverty, No Child Left Behind, Hip Hop culture, and other relevant issues spark a dialectical discourse that makes the traditional, teacher-directed questioning pale in comparison. In my classroom during CALT, the noise level picks up and the interaction is healthy and enlivened. I believe that higher levels of learning are accomplished through the CALT process and the use of critical pedagogical practices.

College is a time of great intellectual and emotional growth. However, the greatest purpose of college may be in the social learning that can occur within the classroom and throughout the campus community. Learning how to work with diverse student groups and to develop dispositions that foster successful team working skills can be among the most beneficial tools one can acquire during the college years. Using the CALT process helps students stretch themselves and ask the tough questions. Students like to challenge each other's thinking and to investigate multiple pathways for solving problems. Hopefully, by building positive cultures of learning and fostering values of respect for diversity (of opinion, personality, style, etc.) within our classrooms, we can help our larger university community and extend these pro-social behaviors for everyone's benefit.

The Real Questions

Carlos Santana demands, "Give me your heart, make it real, or else forget about it." It is time to "make it real" in the classrooms. Our students have been mesmerized into boredom with the traditional curricula of sterilized textual representations of cultural reproduction. The frontier of education and the point of adventure and excitement are within working through problems of the present moment to meet the challenge of preparing our students for the future. Valid questions for today's students confront inequalities and alienation from hope of ever changing our culture. John Mayer sings, "We're waiting… waiting for the world to change." But if all we are going to do is wait, the world is never going to change in a direction other than the direction corporate and political leaders choose for their profit. Building more fences around our Nation's borders and producing gated communities to surround our suburban estates changes nothing of the inequality or alienation most Americans experience. Instead,

we need our future citizen/leadership to ask, what can I do to stop the violence in my communities? What are the real reasons for drug use of epidemic proportion in this country? What is wrong in our communities that gangs are viable social units? How can I work to stop the spread of sexually transmitted diseases? When will our schools stop focusing on standardized assessments of the past with no plans to prepare students for a future? When will we experience a real and meaningful connection with our earth instead of viewing it as an object to be trashed and exploited? These are examples of the types of questions students of a critical constructivist educational psychology need to ask themselves in preparation for teaching today's youth.

Questions of social justice and personal relevance are the critical problems to examine if we want to make a difference in the lives of those we teach. Until we engage our students in the types of real questions that need confrontation, the process of education will work to reproduce the same alienated, disconnected, mind-numbed citizens who are unprepared to find solutions to the vexing social and political questions of our time. It will not be their fault that they cannot see the solutions, because they were tacitly taught to deny their complicity and to blame or ignore the victims of social malaise. Just like the miscreants at school, society shoves misfits aside and attempts to coerce them back to work (Goodman, 1999). Meanwhile, in other locations, the shootings continue; the drug cartels have a lucrative market for their goods; and the criminal justice system finds work for the unemployed. These are the real, present issues that need questioning, and the indignation of young people is the fuel for possibility and change.

The leadership in the teaching of educational psychology must ask: what are our social and professional responsibilities as educators? The root of the word psychology . . . psyc . . . comes from the Greek word psyche. Psyche means soul, and it also, in psychiatry, means "mind." The mind is "an organic system reaching all parts of the body and serving to adjust the total organism to the needs or demands of the environment" (Friend & Guralnik, 1953, p. 1175). If our soul is our essence, then we need to consider questions of essential importance to the education of our future citizens. As the children of Birmingham, Alabama seized the day and left the schoolhouse for the jailhouse to force the end of segregation, we need to bring the spirit of the civil rights movement back to our classrooms and communities needing equally important transformations. Teaching our youth how to develop critical questioning may allow their minds to develop the congruence and courage to empower greater social changes.

References

Begala, Paul. (2000) *"Is our children learning?" The case against George W. Bush.* New York: Simon & Schuster.

Bransford, J.D., Brown, A.L., & Cooking, R.R., Editors. (1999). *How people learn: Brain, mind, experience, and school.* Washington, D.C., National Academy Press. http://newton.nap.edu/html/howpeople1/ch1.html

Dewey, John. (1944). *Democracy and education.* New York: The Macmillan Company.

Freire, Paulo. (1970). *Pedagogy of the oppressed.* New York: Continuum Press.

Friend, J.H. & Guralnik, D.B. (1953). *Webster's new world dictionary.* Cleveland, OH: The World Publishing Company.

Gardner, Howard. (1983). *Frames of mind: The theory of multiple intelligences.* New York: Basic Books.

Giroux, H. (1998). *Channel surfing: racism, the media, and the destruction of today's youth.* New York: St. Martin's Press.

Goodman, G. S. (1999). *Alternatives in education. Critical pedagogy for disaffected youth.* New York: Peter Lang Publishing.

Jardine, David. (2000). *Under the tough old stars: Ecopedagogical essays.* Brandon, VT: The Foundation for Educational Renewal.

Kincheloe, Joseph & Steinberg, Shirley. (1997). *Changing multiculturalism.* Buckingham, England: Open University Press.

Kohl, Herb. (1994). *"I won't learn from you" and other thoughts on creative maladjustment.* New York: The New Press.

Lennon, J. (1970). *Give peace a chance.*

Mayer, J. (2006). *Waiting on the world to change.*

McLaren, Peter. (2000). *Che Guevera, Paulo Freire, and the pedagogy of revolution.* Lanham, MD: Rowman & Littlefield.

———. (1997). *Revolutionary multiculturalism: Pedagogies for dissent for the new millennium.* Boulder, CO: Westview.

Peters, Michael. (2006). *Building knowledge cultures: Education and development in the age of knowledge capitalism.* Lanham, Maryland: Rowman & Littlefield.

Phillips, J. "Memo." (Lecture, Clarion University. Clarion, PA, April 10, 2006).

White, Armond. (1997). *Rebel for the hell of it: The life of Tupac Shakur.* New York: Thunder's Mouth Press.

CHAPTER FOUR

Dealing with Cultural Collision in Urban Schools

What Pre-Service Educators Should Know

Floyd Beachum & Carlos McCray

I think your ears have lied to you
And your eyes have implied to you
That Urban means undeserving and absent of purpose
So give me back!!
Give me back my identity!!
Give me the opportunity
To break free of influential essentials that my community
*   seeks*
And have been lead to believe
Either from Hip Hop vultures disguised as moguls
Or mass media outlets that televise and overemphasize
What is deemed a destructive culture
Broadcast and typecast misguided black youth
That lives below the reality of broken homes, economic
*   oppression, and a multitude of Half-truths*
And finding no salvation in my inner city school
Because educators aren't there to educate
But instead baby-sit and dictate
Further reinforcing and filtrating the messages that dis-
*   tort who I am*
And who I could grow to be

So I ask why haven't you extended your hand
To enhance my ability, expand my ideals and possibilities
Versus leaving me to discover my identity through manipulated mediums
And an environment that welcomes my bemused condition
I mean more to this society
My articles of clothing, vernacular, or demographic
Do not define me.
Contrary to popular belief I am also aspiring, inspiring, and operating as a prodigy born out of art
So it is evident that I have the ability to play more than just this part
But I am also a product of my surrounding . . . and my underdeveloped mind often has no protection . . .
Then difficult to discover my identity and direction
This is a burden that I cannot overcome alone
Give me something additional to relate to before I become prone
To embracing what is put into the universe to be adopted as my own
Way of thinking, living, feeling . . . I am a king on my way to being dethroned
Understand me rather than abandon me and pierce me with labels
This is when you find distrust, despair, and anger
I need positive influence to rival the issuance of negative imagery so common in my world
I am young, black, impressionable, but imperiled
Look at me!!
—"Look at Me" a poem by Krystal Roberts
(of Atlanta, GA)

The goal of educational psychology is to effectively solve problems. In many urban schools, many educational problems remain unsolved. As it stands, we can clearly identify the epidemic of failures for ethnic minorities . . . Urban practitioners must become problem-solvers and functional decision-makers. As problem-solvers, they must value ethnic, linguistic, and racial differences to effectively teach in urban schools (Smith & Sapp, 2005, p. 109).

The dispositions and beliefs of pre-service educational professionals are of extreme importance. The fate of urban school children largely rests in the hands of educational professionals who may not share the same cultural backgrounds as their students or clients (Kunjufu, 2002; Landsman & Lewis, 2006). Therefore, it is critically important for these individuals to understand social context, appreciate differences, and champion change for a more multicultural organization (Cox, 1994; Cox, 2001; Irvine, 2003). Sometimes the problem is cultural, where the culture of educators' clashes with that of their students, thereby creating a phenomenon called **cultural collision** (see Beachum & McCray, 2004). By critically examining and understanding youth culture, educators can gain educational insight (i.e., how to tailor teaching strategies and arrange classroom management policies) and make significant connections with their students, which would help reduce many of the problems African Americans face in schools. The above poem gives an acute voice to the legions of voiceless young people who are trapped in neglected neighborhoods, segregated schools, and cultures of chaos.

Cultural collision

A clash of values or beliefs.

African American (the term Black will also be used synonymously) youth identity is unique and multi-faceted. It can be affected by a multitude of factors including parents, peers, music, school, television, religious influences, and life experiences (Harro, 2000). For many inner-city youth in particular, self-identity is a combination of various complexities. These youth may face several critical issues such as socioeconomic despair, pressure from gangs, a lack of faith in institutions, and society's concentration on materialism and individualism (Berman & Berreth, 1997). These issues also have an effect on youth identity. Of the numerous influences and factors that shape youth identity, two, sometimes conflicting factors, Black youth popular culture (hip-hop culture and television) and school culture are of particular importance.

This chapter will concentrate on the development of secondary school-aged urban youth (i.e., those in grades 7–12). Urban Black youth popular culture will be examined by means of hip-hop culture and the media. Both of these variables have the awesome potential to shape youth identity. The American phenomenon known as hip-hop can affect youth in both positive and negative ways (Kunjufu, 1993). In a like manner, television too, can exert a powerful influence over youth. The media have the power to alter the habits, feelings, and minds of young people, especially Black youth (Kunjufu, 1990). This chapter is written to assist in the understanding of psychological and cultural/ social forces on urban youth, with special emphasis on Black youth culture. For you, the emerging teacher, this information is critically important in your work with these impressionable young people.

Notions of Contemporary America and Schools

If you work hard can you really be "successful" in America? How much of your success is due to individual merit (your own efforts)? To what extent do structural barriers inhibit the life chances of certain groups in America? Are schools agents of change or do they perpetuate the inequalities found in American society? These are difficult questions, especially if you have never really considered them. Though difficult, these are important questions for educators and professionals dealing with diverse populations. Why can't we readily identify oppression, inequity, and injustices? The answer might very well be that we are socialized into believing and acting out various roles as related to race, class, gender, ability, status, age, and social class (Harro, 2000). Tatum (1997) states that this socialization process is similar to smog in the air that we all breathe and are inevitably impacted by. This smog is found in notions of **meritocracy**, individualism, and old-fashion hard work. The cultural ethos of the United States is full of idealistic concepts such as the Protestant work ethic, and the Horatio Alger myth (belief in the idea of going from rags to riches as applied to everyone equally). Such ideas are ingrained into the psyches of nearly all Americans.

Meritocracy

Belief that hard work and accomplishments are rewarded.

Writing of pre-service educators, Villegas and Lucas (2002) asserted:

> They are insensitive to the fact that power is differentially distributed in society, with those who are affluent, white, and male having an advantage over those who are poor, of racial/ethnic minority groups, and female. They lack an understanding of institutional discrimination, including how routine practices in schools benefit young people from dominant groups while disadvantaging those from oppressed groups; and they have an unshakable faith that American society operates according to meritocratic principles and that existing inequalities in social outcomes are thereby justified. (p. 32).

Thus, you must be willing to question deeply held beliefs and be willing to challenge foundational assumptions. Of course, you might be thinking to yourself, "I made it, why can't anyone else?" Villegas and Lucas responded, "Because the educational system has worked for them (pre-service teachers), they are not apt to question school practices, nor are they likely to doubt the criteria of merit applied in schools" (p. 31). The next factor in understanding how cultural collision operates is to realize how people are affected by the geographic isolation of many urban areas.

The Urban Context and Popular Culture

For the purposes of this discussion it is important to also understand the significance of the urban context. Many urban areas across the nation are plagued with all types of social and community problems. Urban schools in these areas face challenges such as inadequate funding and teacher apathy. Resentment from external powers fuels the fire for the marginalizing and criticism of these schools (Ayers, 1994).

As it appears, the urban context creates an environment that affects urban schools and the youth within them. "The situation in far too many schools is one of despair, poverty, isolation, and distress" (Obiakor & Beachum, 2005, p. 13). Noguera (2004) wrote, "In poor communities, the old, persistent problems of overcrowded classrooms, deteriorating facilities, and an insufficient supply of qualified teachers and administrators remain largely unaddressed" (p. 176). These are but some of the many problems that these schools and sometimes districts encounter. The attitudes and behaviors of urban youth of color begin to reflect the structural inequities that create their environments. Kozol (2006) traces the segregation, poverty, and inequity found in such schools in his book, *The Shame of the Nation*. At the same time, this situation has resulted in the increasing pseudo-police state found in many urban areas and schools (Wacquant, 2001) as well as feelings of alienation (Rothstein, 1996; Yeo & Kanpol, 1999).

Black popular culture, many times, tends to originate from this urban context. According to Damen (1987), "Culture is learned and shared human patterns or models for living; day-to-day living patterns; those models and patterns pervade all aspects of human social interaction; and culture is mankind's primary adaptive mechanism" (p. 367). Black popular culture was born amidst "social, cultural, political, and economic segregation—initially as a vibrant expression of black political and cultural strivings" (Guy, 2004, p. 48).

Gause (2005) stated that "popular culture is the background noise of our very existence" (p. 336). When we consider the origin, expansion, and influence of "Urban America" we realize that its inhabitants are molded and shaped by history, experience, and social context. The global phenomenon known as hip-hop culture can be viewed as an expression of Black popular culture with its roots found in the plight and promise of the urban context.

Hip-Hop Culture

Hip-hop culture has a great influence on American youth. White and Cones (1999) write, "Hip hop is a catch-all term for a contemporary, urban-centered youth lifestyle associated with popular music, break dancing, certain dress and hair styles, graffiti, and

street language" (p. 96). Hip hop culture has gone from primarily rapping, break dancing, dj-ing, and graffiti to including dialects, attitude, expression, mannerisms, and fashion (Dyson, 2001; Kitwana, 2002). In reference to its wider appeal, Kitwana (2002) asserts, "Rappers access to global media and their use of popular culture to articulate many aspects of this national identity renders rap music central to any discussion of the new Black youth culture" (p.11). This emphasis on media opens up rap artists to audio and visual media. McCall (1997) writes:

> Dr. William Byrd, a black clinical psychologist, pointed out that for young, impressionable people the mere fact that explicit gangsta lyrics are aired on the radio lends credence to their messages as truth. "When you bombard someone with those messages, it causes conflict, even with those young people who may have been taught other values. With these rap messages, not only are they being bombarded with radio, they also get video." So it's what you hear and what you see. It confirms that these are acceptable values in a subculture (p. 60).

Therefore, this "message bombardment" can be influential to impressionable youth. Kitwana (2002) agrees, "Today, more and more Black youth are turning to rap music, music videos, designer clothing, popular Black films, and television programs for values and identity" (p. 9).

Hip-hop culture has become an integral part of the lives of many urban youth. Through its influence they develop various ideas about sex, relationships, success, and life (Kunjufu, 1993). In addition, these influences can have positive or negative effects on youth identity. "The ages between 13–17 are when they [youth] are particularly vulnerable to outside influence and before their values and ideas have fully developed" (Kunjufu, 1993, p. 81). Hip-hop culture is expressed through songs on the radio, glamorized by video, and reinforced by peers. The result is a particularly powerful form of infiltration and indoctrination. However, this influence can be good or bad. Most of the controversy surrounding hip-hop culture has to do with its emphasis on male chauvinism, open gunplay, and illegal drug usage.

Much of the criticism revolves around a certain mode of hip-hop expression called gangsta rap. Gangsta rap usually refers to a style of rap that references/overemphasizes drug selling, hyper-macho posturing, disrespect for authority, the use of violence to settle disputes and to gain respect, and negative attitudes towards women (Guy, 2004; Kunjufu, 1993; White & Cones, 1999). In reference to this form of rap, Dyson (1997) wrote:

> The gangsta rap genre of hip-hop emerged in the late 1980s on the West Coast as crack and gangs ruled the urban centers of Los Angeles, Long Beach, Compton, and Oakland. Since hip-hop has long turned to the black ghetto and the Latino barrio for lyrical inspiration, it was inevitable that a form of music that mimicked the violence on the streets would rise (p. 113).

In recent years, the label gangsta rap has seemed to apply less to the contemporary forms of hip-hop displayed in popular culture. Today, much of the music incorporates strands of this theme along with others making it into an eclectic combination of macho-posturing, **misogyny**, violence, and materialism. Thus, gangsta rap is less identified as a societal pariah of previous years but now a common part of "normalized" hip-hop culture. Hip-hop culture has the ability to affect the values of Black youth through various media. Another important medium is television.

Misogynistic
Woman hating.

Television Media

The American media are a source of news, entertainment, and information. They include radio, newspapers, the Internet, and television. For our purposes, the authors will concentrate on the media as represented by television. The media have the ability to spread truthful and positive knowledge or misrepresent people, events, and data. Unfortunately, many times the latter is the case. Moreover, televi-

sion is responsible for imagery that negatively influences youth (Bush, 1999). Consequently, this imagery has the ability to affect youth identity.

Television is an important part of life to many Americans. Black youth, in particular, watch seven to eight hours of television a day, as compared to four and a half hours for white youth (Browder, 1989). Bush (1999) notes, "negative images presented in all of the media conspire with many hours of television viewing to produce a negative effect on Black children's self-image" (p. 36). In reference to Black youth and television, Browder (1989) observes the following:

- Black children tend to use TV as a source of role models. They imitate other people's behavior, dress, appearance, and speech.
- TV provides examples of relationships with members of the opposite sex.
- TV is used as a primary source of learning and perfecting aggressive behavior.
- Black children closely identify with television characters—particularly the Black characters. (p. 47)

Given the amount of television watched by Black youth and its influence on their development, the images portrayed by the television medium become extremely important.

Television many times promotes gender stereotypes and negative images of Blacks. A study conducted by Mamay and Simpson (as cited in Bush, 1999) concluded that "women in commercials were typecast according to three stereotypical roles: mother, housekeeper, and sexual objects" (pp. 35–36). This research indicates that television has the ability to affect the way people view gender roles. Katz (1995) writes:

> Stressing gender differences in this context means defining masculinity in the opposition to femininity. This requires constantly reasserting what is masculine and what is feminine. One of the ways that is accomplished, in the image system, is to

equate masculinity with violence (and femininity with passivity) (p. 135).

In addition to gender, the television medium also influences many youth towards violence. For instance, a 14-year-old Black male was sentenced to life in prison for the murder of a six-year-old girl. He was imitating pro wrestling moves he watched on television (Ripley, 2001). Today's Black youth are many times criticized and labeled as violent or rebellious (Dyson, 1997; Kitwana, 2002). Wilson (1990) asserts, "Deeds of violence in our society are performed largely by those trying to establish their self-esteem, to defend their self-image, or to demonstrate that they too are significant" (p. 54). This is not to excuse individuals for violent behavior, but it provides insight into other influences impacting behavior. Moreover, the television medium promotes a value system based on materialism and immediate gratification (Kunjufu, 1990). In accordance with these values, too many youths resort to violence. Thus television exposure to negative imagery could possibly encourage an inner-adversarial conflict of self-identity.

Identity Theory and Black Youth

Black youth who are matriculating through middle and high school deal with a considerable amount of transition. The transitions here are related to grade levels, geographic location of schools, maturation, and identity development (to name a few). Considering the latter, young adults share a certain amount of curiosity, exploration, and discovery with regard to the development of identity (Tatum, 1997). However, Black youth in particular, begin to examine their own ethnic/racial identities even more than their white counterparts (Negy, Shreve, Jensen, & Uddin, 2003). Tatum (1997) posits that "given the impact of dominant and subordinate status, it is not surprising that researchers have found that adolescents of color are more likely to be actively engaged in an exploration of their racial or ethnic identity than are White adolescents" (p. 53). In this

state of heightened identity awareness is where salient and unconscious messages and imagery can influence ideas and values. Black youth are more sensitized to society's view of them with regard to race. "Our self-perceptions are shaped by the messages that we receive from those around us, and when young Black men and women enter adolescence, the racial content of those messages intensifies" (Tatum, 1997, p. 54). Hence, identity development for Black youth is complicated by notions of race/ethnicity more than for their white peers, making this a time of complexity and vulnerability. This situation creates the need for direction and guidance from influential individuals and institutions, one of which is the school.

School Culture

The school itself can have a major impact on the development of students. During school, students are afforded opportunities for academic, emotional, and social growth. Students also interact with teachers and administrators within this educational environment that is founded upon certain values. Academics, opportunities for growth, different types of interaction, and value systems all play a role in a school's culture. The school's culture also has the ability to shape student identity.

A school is commonly defined as a place of teaching and learning. The culture of an organization is the set of values and beliefs of the organization, and these values and beliefs are normally shared with the majority of people in the organization (Cunningham & Cordeiro, 2006; Fullan, 2004; Karpicke & Murphy, 1996). Thus, school culture is the shared value system of a given school. Specifically, school culture involves certain components. According to Pawlas (1997), "The key components of a strong effective school culture include shared values, humor, storytelling, empowerment, a communication system for spreading information, rituals and ceremonies, and collegiality" (p. 119).

School culture is important to all who are involved with the school.

The school culture can affect student identity. Banks (2001) notes "the school culture communicates to students the school's attitudes toward a range of issues and problems, including how the school views them as human beings and its attitudes toward males, females, exceptional students, and students from various religious, cultural, racial, and ethnic groups" (p. 24). When the school's culture is characterized by value disagreement, lack of communication, and little collegiality (among teachers and students), many students see themselves as incapable, incompetent, and worthless. However, when an environment promotes a schoolwide value system, good communication, collegiality, and the utilization of ceremonies, students' attitudes are much more positive. Karpicke and Murphy (1996) agree that a healthy (school) culture has a great impact on the success of students.

Taking all of this into account we find that those teachers who are interested in changing a culture must first try to understand the existing culture. In doing this, those teachers would have to begin by understanding the various cultures that come to the schoolhouse on a daily basis, before imposing another culture.

Intersection of School Culture and Black Popular Culture

The values as dictated by negative hip-hop culture and the media many times conflict with the values of the school. Kunjufu (1990) notes that gangs and negative media promote immediate gratification and materialism, while many parents and teachers promote long-term gratification and qualities such as moral integrity and honesty. Kunjufu (1993) also states that there is a concern about some hip-hop artists' misogynistic and violent messages. In effect, students obtain certain values from this segment of hip-hop culture and television and then bring those values to the school. Therefore, there is a conflict of value systems, which sometimes results in disci-

pline problems and lack of communication between students and educators. In addition, peers can have a great influence on each other, even more than the influence of adults (Kunjufu, 1990). Thus, the values are shared and become pervasive because of the influence of peer communication and pressure. Furthermore, Black youth spend much more time with peers, listening to music, and watching television than they do having meaningful conversations with teachers and parents (Bush, 1999; Kitwana, 2002; Kunjufu, 1994). The task for educators is to familiarize themselves with youth culture/value systems and realize the subsequent effect on youth identity.

Hip-hop culture has undergone tremendous growth as an artistic form of expression, fashion, as well a money-making venture. Many have advocated censorship in order to curtail much of the negative influence of rap music. However, censorship may not be an appropriate or realistic response. It sends the message that artistic expression can be stifled by those who simply disagree. But what are we to make of the violent themes readily found in hip-hop culture? In response to this over-emphasis on violence in hip-hop, Dyson (2005) explained:

> . . . hip-hop has been nailed for casting glamour on thuggish behavior and for heartlessly painting violent portraits of urban life. It's all true, but still, the whole truth of hip-hop as art form and, because of generational lag, as agitator of adults, must not be overlooked . . . At its best, hip-hop summons the richest response in the younger generation to questions of identity and suffering (p. 115).

Dyson (1996) wrote, "While these young black males become whipping boys for sexism and misogyny, the places in our culture where these ancient traditions are nurtured and rationalized—including religious and educational institutions and the nuclear family—remain immune to forceful and just criticism" (p. 186). Therefore, a certain amount of responsibility must be placed on parents, guardians, and school officials. In effect, parents and educators should take a greater role in involving themselves in the lives of these youth. One must remember that hip-hop culture has a business aspect and the supply will meet the demand. What would happen if the consumers demanded more positive conscious images?

The media also have to be held accountable for negative imagery. If not, then youth identity could be at stake. Chideya (1995) writes, "In the final analysis, it's up to the reader and viewers to keep the media honest . . . pointing out times that the media has misrepresented the African-American community can only make the community better. The media belongs to all of us. If we want it to work, we have to work" (p. 11).

Implications for Educators

In summary, there are many factors that influence the identities of urban Black youth. Hip-hop culture, television media, and school culture do have a serious impact on this particular group. At the heart of this analysis is the creation of a healthy positive value system. Consequently, those students who develop this strong value system have less of a chance to be affected by negative aspects of hip-hop culture and misrepresentation in television media and more of a chance to be influenced by the "positivity" exemplified in a healthy school culture.

Educators have a critical role to play in students' academic and social development. First, you must recognize the inherent inequities within our society and how they impact people, especially in urban areas. Secondly, realize how cultural collision plays out in our schools. By acknowledging the background experiences of urban students, which includes their cultural expressions, educators can gain insight into addressing student behavior, communication, and values. Lastly, Milner (2006) proposed some questions for educators as they begin to self-examine; he referred to it as *relational reflection.* The questions are as follows: 1) Why do I believe what I believe?; 2) How do my thoughts and beliefs influence my curriculum and teaching [managing

and disciplining] of students of color?; and 3) What do I need to change in order to better meet the needs of all my students? (p. 84). Educators engage students in a mutual process of liberation for completeness. "Completeness for the oppressed begins with liberation. Until liberation is achieved, individuals are fragmented in search of clarity, understanding, and emancipation. This liberation is not outside of us or created or accomplished through some external force. Rather, it begins with a change in thinking" (p. 85). The essence of this "education for liberation" is a change in thinking for educators, making them realize their own power with students and potential in society.

Due to the increasing amount of cultural and social diversity found in society and in our schools, educators must find the right balance which promotes a healthy school climate while also embracing some degree of **cultural pluralism** (Villegas & Lucas, 2002). There should be a willingness and effort among educators to structure the school culture to ensure that individuals of diverse backgrounds are well positioned to achieve regardless of their predispositions in life. A school culture structured in a pluralistic manner can lead to the self-efficacy and self-determination of students who may bring conflicting values from their environment (Banks, 1995). Banks (2001) insists "The culture and organization of the school must be examined by all members of the school staff . . . in order to create a school culture that empowers students from diverse racial and ethnic groups" (p. 22). This is extremely important because it helps to ensure that students are not being labeled incorrectly and are not subjugated because of inadequate cultural capital. Therefore, it is important for educators to help such students develop the kinds of value systems that encourage positive self-identities and give them the legitimate opportunity to become successful in school as well as in life.

Cultural pluralism

A mix of different identities.

References

Ayers, W. (1994). Can city schools be saved? *Educational Leadership, 51*(8), 60–63.

Banks, J. A. (2001). Multicultural education: Characteristics and goals. In J. A. Banks & C. A. McGee Banks (Eds.), *Multicultural education: Issues and perspectives* (4th ed.), (pp. 3–30). New York: John Wiley & Sons, Inc.

———. (1995). Multicultural education: development, dimensions, and challenges. In J. Joll, (Ed.), *Taking sides: Clashing views on controversial education issues* (pp. 84–93). New York: The Dushkin Publishing Group, Inc.

Beachum, F. D., & McCray, C. R. (2004). Cultural collision in urban schools. *Current Issues in Education, 7*(5). Available: *http://cie.asu.edu/volume7/number5/*

Berman, S., & Berreth, D. (1997). The moral dimensions of schools. *Educational Leadership, 54*(8), 24–27.

Browder, A. (1989). *From the Browder file: 22 essays of the African American experience.* Washington, DC: The Institute of Karmic Guidance.

Bush, L. V. (1999). *Can black mothers raise our sons?* Chicago: African American Images.

Chideya, F. (1995). *Don't believe the hype: Fighting cultural misinformation about African-Americans.* New York: Penguin Books.

Cox, T., Jr. (2001). *Creating the multicultural organization: A strategy for capturing the power of diversity.* San Francisco: Jossey-Bass.

———. (1994). *Cultural diversity in organizations: Theory, research, and practice.* San Francisco: Berrett-Koehler Publishers.

Cunningham, W. G., & Cordeiro, P. A. (2006). *Educational leadership: A problem-based approach* (3rd ed.). Boston: Allyn and Bacon.

Damen, L. (1987). *Culture learning: The fifth dimension on the language classroom.* Reading, MA: Addison-Wesley.

Dyson, M. E. (2005). *Is Bill Cosby right? Or has the Black middle class lost its mind?* New York: Basic Civitas Books.

———. (2001). *Holler if you hear me: Searching for Tupac Shakur.* New York: Basic Civitas Books.

———. (1997). *Race rules: Navigating the color line.* New York: Vintage Books.

———. (1996). *Between God and gangsta rap.* New York: Oxford University Press.

Fullan, M. (2004). *Leading in a culture of change: Personal action guide and workbook.* San Francisco: Jossey-Bass.

Gause, C. P. (2005). Navigating the stormy seas: Critical perspectives on the intersection of popular culture and educational leadership. *Journal of School Leadership, 15*(3), 333–345.

Guy, T. C. (2004). Gangsta rap and adult education. *New directions for adult and continuing education, 101,* 43–57.

Harro, B. (2000). The cycle of socialization. In M. Adams, W. J. Blumenfield, R. Castaneda, H. W. Hackman, M. L. Peters, X. Zuniga (Eds.), *Reading for diversity and social justice: An anthology on racism, anti-Semitism, sexism, heterosexism, ableism, and classism* (pp. 79–82). New York: Routledge.

Irvine, J. J. (2003*). Educating teachers for diversity: Seeing with a cultural eye.* New York: Teachers College Press.

Karpicke, H. & Murphy, M. E. (1996). Productive school culture: Principals working from the inside. *National Association of Secondary School Principals, 80,* 26–32.

Katz, J. (1995). Advertisement and the construction of violent white masculinity. In G. Dines and J. Humez (Eds.). *Gender, race and class in the media: A text reader.* Thousand Oaks, CA: Sage Publications.

Kitwana, B. (2002). *The Hip Hop generation: Young Blacks and the crisis in African American culture.* New York: Basic Books.

Kozol, J. (2006). *The shame of the nation: The restoration of apartheid schooling in America.* New York: Crown Publishing Group.

Kunjufu, J. (2002). *Black students—Middle class teachers.* Chicago: African American Images.

———. (1994). *Countering the conspiracy to destroy black boys* (vol. IV). Chicago: African American Images.

———. (1993). *Hip-hop vs. MAAT: a psycho/social analysis of values.* Chicago: African American Images.

———. (1990). *Countering the conspiracy to destroy black boys* (vol. III). Chicago: African American Images.

Landsman, J., & Lewis, C. W. (Eds.) (2006). *White teachers/diverse classrooms: A guide to building inclusive schools, promoting high expectations, and eliminating racism.* Sterling, VA: Stylus.

McCall, N. (1997). *What's going on.* New York: Random House.

Milner, H. R. (2006). But good intentions are not enough: Theoretical and philosophical relevance in teaching students of color. In J. Landsman & C. W. Lewis (Eds.), *White teachers/diverse classrooms: A guide to building inclusive schools, promoting high expectations, and eliminating racism* (pp. 79–90). Sterling, VA: Stylus.

Negy, C., Shreve, Jensen, B. J., & Uddin, N. (2003). Ethnic identity, self-esteem, and ethnocentrism: A study of social identity versus multicultural theory of development. *Cultural Diversity and Mental Health, 9*(4), 333–334.

Noguera, P. (2004). Going beyond the slogans and rhetoric. In C. Glickman (Ed.), *Letters to the next president: What we can do about the real crisis in public education* (pp. 174–183). New York: Teachers College Press.

Obiakor, F. E., & Beachum, F. D. (2005). Urban education: The quest for democracy, equity, and excellence. In F. E. Obiakor & F. D. Beachum (Eds.), *Urban education for the 21st century: Research, issues, and perspectives* (pp. 3–19). Springfield, IL: Charles C. Thomas.

Pawlas, G. E. (1997). Vision and school culture. *National Association of Secondary School Principals, 81,* 118–120.

Ripley, A. (2001, March). Throwing the book at kids. *Time, 157* (11), 34.

Rothstein, S. W. (1996). *Schools and society: New perspectives in American education.* Englewood Cliffs, NJ: Prentice Hall.

Smith, R., & Sapp, M. (2005). Insights into educational psychology: What urban school practitioners must know. In F. E. Obiakor & F. D. Beachum (Eds.), *Urban education for the 21st century: Research, issues, and perspectives* (pp. 100–113). Springfield, IL: Charles C. Thomas.

Tatum, B. D. (1997). *Why are all the Black kids sitting together in the cafeteria?: And other conversations about race.* New York: Basic Books.

Villegas, A. M., & Lucas, T. (2002). *Educating culturally responsive teachers: A coherent approach.* Albany, NY: State University of New York Press.

Wacquant, L. (2001). Deadly symbiosis: When ghetto and prison meet and mesh. *Punishment and Society, 3*(1), 95–134.

White, J. L. & Cones III, J. H. (1999). *Black man emerging: Facing the past and seizing a future in America.* New York: W. H. Freeman and Company.

Wilson, A. (1990). *Black on black violence.* New York: African World Info Systems.

Yeo, F., & Kanpol, B. (1999). Introduction: Our own "Peculiar Institution": Urban education in 20th-century America. In F. Yeo & B. Kanpol (Eds.), *From nihilism to possibility: Democratic transformations for the inner city* (pp. 1–14). Cresskill, NJ: Hampton Press, Inc.

CHAPTER FIVE

Communication, Culture, and Media Influence in the Classroom

Joanne Washington

Advances during the past twenty years have sparked a revolution in technology and communication systems. Today, communication is instantaneous as it travels in digital form via a wide variety of media. Communication has shifted from passive to active. No longer does the student sit passively in the classroom, eyes fixed on the teacher—center stage—the focus of attention.

Think about the changes in communication that have occurred: Twenty years ago telephones were only used for spoken communication and television and film were our primary entertainment outlets. Advances in communication technology have changed the way we use technology and how we depend on it for most of our communication. We expect instant connections and expect that our interactions will garner immediate responses (think instant messaging). What this means for teachers is that we enter the classroom with the expectation that when we communicate with our students, we will be understood and they will give us the responses that we desire. To that end, most schools of education require prospective teachers to take courses on how to use communication technology in the classroom. The most recent trend is the use of cell phones to teach (Mickey, 2005). Yet, will the ability to download textbook readings to students' cell phones, use a blazing PowerPoint presentation, design an interactive wiki or post a blog comparing the writings of Emily Dickinson and Willa Cather actually improve the way you, as a teacher, effectively interact and communicate with your students? Perhaps it will. I believe media technology, when used effectively in the classroom, can enhance instruction. Several years of research conducted on the usefulness of media technology as a tool for instruction concludes that media, while useful for storing and delivering instruction, have little effect on learning outcome. Noted educational technology researcher Richard Clark, summarized the findings of this research writing:

JUST KIDDING

> The best current evidence is that media are mere vehicles that deliver instruction but do not influence student achievement any more than the truck that delivers our groceries causes changes in nutrition (Clark, 1983, p 445).

Meta-analysis
Research that analyzes the findings of similar studies.

Some believe that Clark's findings are outdated. This is understandable given that his **meta-analysis** was conducted more than twenty years ago. Yet, recent work in this area has not yielded any differ-

ent results. Although students enthusiastically use media technology at home, little technology is used in the classroom experience (Clark, 1998; Molenda and Sullivan, 2001; Peck et al., 2002a)

In interviews with high school students in San Francisco (close to Silicon Valley and the world headquarters of high-tech industries), it was found that these students used computers but not in the way educational experts expected.

> . . . most students surveyed at each school reported home access and serious rates of usage . . . Some used computers mostly for schoolwork; others used their home access mostly for social pursuits. Students also expressed much enthusiasm about computers and other technologies. Yet despite experience with home computers, enthusiasm for technology, and abundant access to technology in school, technology had but little impact on students' school experiences (Peck et al, 2002b, 477).

Hopefully, no one believes that the use of media technology alone has the power to effectively connect the student and teacher in meaningful ways that communicate interest and care about the relationship between the two. Nor, can technology alone create a classroom environment that impacts the students' learning experience. The teacher creates the culture of learning and effectively communicates the instructional message using the various channels at his or her disposal. This can only be accomplished through the establishment of a communication relationship between the student and teacher. The next section will examine exactly how this communication link is formed.

What Is Communication?

There's a famous old comedy routine from the radio days of the 1940s by Bud Abbott and Lou Costello called "Who's on First." A simple synopsis of the routine follows:

ABBOTT: Costello, I'm going to be the new manager of the New York Yankees.

COSTELLO: Good deal. Since you're the manager, will you introduce me to all of the players?

ABBOTT: I certainly will, my friend

COSTELLO: Do you know all the players names?

ABBOTT: Why, yes I do.

COSTELLO: Well, who are the main players?

ABBOTT: Let's see . . . we have Who's on first . . .

COSTELLO: (interrupting) Wait a minute. You're the manager and you don't know who's on first?

ABBOTT: Why aren't you listening? I just told you Who's on first.

COSTELLO: I'm gonna give you one more chance. Who's on first?

ABBOTT: Yes, that's what I just said![1]

Most people find the exchange humorous because of the obvious wordplay and confusion about the baseball player's name. The player on first base is actually named "Who." The second is named "What" and the third base player is named, "I don't know." Abbott believes he is providing Costello with the baseball player's name and Costello is trying to communicate his frustration with Abbott's explanation.

The routine was originally heard on radio and had quite an effect on the listening audience as Abbott and Costello delivered their lines using a rapid fire technique. More than 60 years later, this routine may seem somewhat outdated to us, yet the lesson of distinguishing the difference between simply providing information and engaging in effective communication is worth learning.

---

1.   If you would like to read the radio script or hear the original broadcast, go to http://www.abbottandcostello.net/or one of several hundred websites on Abbott and Costello.

Information is the giving of facts and data about a particular subject while communication requires a much deeper level of understanding.

Communication is defined as *a shared experience between a sender and receiver that contains a message that is understood by both the sender and receiver.* The message may hold thoughts, feelings, information, ideas, and a range of activities that can be intended for communication. For example: How many examples of communication can you find in the following passage?

Thandie, a first-year middle school teacher, checks her reflection in the mirror a few minutes before the bell rings. "Wow," she exclaims out loud, "I shouldn't have stayed up watching that movie last night. My eyes are blood red!" "Oh well," she reflects, "they'll all be here in a few minutes—nothing I can do about it now." (Thandie moves to the front door of her classroom to greet her students). Thandie pats a few students on the shoulder, says good morning to most and returns a hug from an enthusiastic girl who always seems to smile even on the grayish days. Last, but not least, comes Tish. (Tish is big for her age and stands at Thandie's height). "Hey Tish," Thandie begins, giving Tish her most engaging smile. However, before Thandie can ask Tish about her weekend, Tish exclaims in a loud voice "Ms. Mills, what was you doin' last night? *You gotta lay off the bottle–you just gotta.*" Tish breaks into raucous laughter and the whole class joins in. Thandie feels her face tighten and her body tense as she thinks about what to say next . . .

Intra-personal communication

Communication within yourself.

First, let's look at how Thandie used **intrapersonal communication**. Thandie begins her day by speaking audibly about her bloodshot eyes although no one is present to answer her. Sometimes when we *self-talk*, we speak out loud even though there is no one present to answer. The most common type of intrapersonal communication is the self-talk that occurs in our thoughts. We reflect on past events and ponder our future. We think about what we're going to say and do when a situation arrives. Sometimes we rehearse scenes and play out the potential consequences of our actions. Intrapersonal communication is the most basic level of communication. It functions by allowing us to examine our innermost feelings, process events in our lives as they are happening, and prepare us for future potential communication situations. Intrapersonal communication takes on an important function in the communication process by helping prepare a person to communicate. Our self-talk can make us very relaxed in communication situations or create anxiety which, in turn, can negatively impact our communication. Many times, the receiver of our communication attempts can sense our comfort or

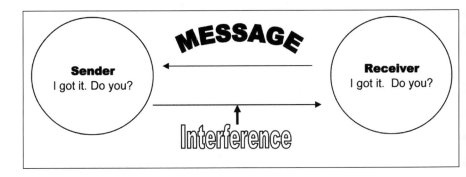

anxiousness in a situation based on the verbal and non-verbal signals that we send out. Let's look at a basic communication model.

The *sender* is the person who initiates the communication. The *receiver* is the intended target of the communication. The arrows go both ways because a communicated message must be recognized as such. A message that goes out without a means to determine if it has been received as intended is no longer a message but is simply an *informational give and take.*

There are occasions in which our communication efforts fall short of the desired effect. The communication attempt fails and both the sender and receiver are left pondering why they were misunderstood. Because our verbal and non-verbal communication is prone to **message interference**, our messages become distorted or are misinterpreted. To better understand the dynamics of both of these modes of communication; the following section examines the characteristics of verbal and non-verbal communication.

Message Interference

Anything that changes the original intent and purpose of a communicated message.

Verbal and Non-Verbal Communication

Verbal communication is the messages we send audibly through language. Our words can be abstract or concrete. Abstract words are open to many interpretations while concrete words have fewer interpretations. Abstract words need not be complex. They simply must have several meanings. Concrete words, on the other hand, have limited meanings and are therefore less likely to be misinterpreted. Here are a few examples of *abstract* and *concrete* words we commonly use in communication.

In communication, our tendency is to use several abstract words to explain concepts that are already very complex. For example, most textbooks on the high school and college level use abstract words to explain complex ideas and principles. I have many students who open their communication theory books and are literally horrified by the thought that their whole school term will be spent reading a 300-page book that contains no illustrations or pictures. Conversely, books on the elementary and middle school levels use many illustrations, charts, graphs, maps, pictures and cartoons. Edgar Dale, noted educationist, was the first to promote the importance of auditory and visual communication in education through the *Cone of Learning Experience Model*. This model advanced the theoretical notion that the most effective way to communicate concepts is through direct experiences. The least effective way is through abstract **symbols**—or words (Dale, 1969). Overall, Dale suggested that

Symbol

an arbitrary sign used as a referent to something of significance.

Abstract Word	Many Ways to Interpret Meaning
Dog	What is the dog's color, type or size?; She was dog tired; or The sawyer placed a dog on the oak log to keep it from moving on the sawmill's carriage.
Home	What is the home's color, type or size? Is the home (meaning home life) happy or sad?
Music	What is the music style or genre? What can be considered music? Is rap or metalcore considered music?

Concrete Word	Limited Ways to Interpret Meaning
Tricycle	A small peddled cycle with three wheels
Sun	A star that is the source of light and heat for a planet
Doctor	Distinguished by area of specialty.

learning will be enhanced if the relationship between direct experiences and abstract symbols is effectively communicated (Seels, 2004). In general, we only tend to remember twenty percent of what we hear (abstract symbols). Yet, that percentage is more than tripled if we also use communication as an active process of both reception and participation to obtain our learning goals (Catt et al., 2007; Dale, 1969). *Communication is an active process that engages both the sender and receiver in direct meaningful experiences that will ultimately translate into a richer and more rewarding learning environment.*

Non-verbal communication involves the messages we send without the use of language. Sometimes non-verbal communication is used alone, and other times its purpose is to emphasize key points given in a verbal message. Even silence is a form of non-verbal communication in a specific **communication context**. How much then, can you really communicate without the use of words? Probably more than you think.

Communication Context

Circumstances that surround a communication situation that provide clues to a message's meaning.

Look back at Thandie's story. When Thandie is standing at the door of the classroom greeting her students, does she talk to everyone? Some students are greeted with hugs, others with a pat on the shoulder. One student even greets Thandie with a smile. A pat on the shoulder is a type of non-verbal communication called a haptic. Oftentimes, non-verbal communication is used to accompany verbal communication and is used to emphasize the verbal symbols (words). There are several types of non-verbal **signals** in communication. Following are a few that are more widely used.

Signal
A sign or gesture used to send a non-verbal message.

If Thandie greets 30 students in the morning, she has potentially 30 different communication

Type of Non-Verbal Communication	Common Use in Communication
Haptics	The use of touch to communicate. A soft touch generally communicates gentleness while a hard or rough touch (for example, a hit, slap or punch) can communicate anger depending on the communication context.
Proxemics	The use of space to communicate. The closer a person is to us when communicating, the closer the intimacy. Therefore, we generally only allow close relationship within our personal space while communicating.
Kinesics	The use of body movements to convey messages. It could be facial movements like a smile, raised eyebrow, frown, or the lowering or raising of our eyes. Shrugging your shoulders or kicking at something also conveys a message without words.
Appearance	A person's visual aspect that is not altered cosmetically. This may include a person's body type and size, ethnic and racial characteristics that communicate an image, idea or belief about an individual.
Vocalics	The use of voice inflection, tone, or accent to add a particular emphasis to the verbal communication.
Affects	Personal mannerisms that give insights about an individual's comfort level in communication situations. Also serves as a calming mechanism. Examples are twisting hair, nail biting, lip biting, finger tapping, wringing hands, clinched fists, thumb sucking, folding arms, hands in pocket, etc.

situations—all within the same relative context. Things appear to go smoothly until Thandie greets Tish. One way to analyze the exchange between Thandie and Tish is through the cultural influences that affect their communication.

Cultural Communication Influences

One of the most difficult tasks for communication mediators is to diffuse a verbal conflict before it accelerates into a non-verbal confrontation or altercation. As you can imagine, non-verbal conflicts are more difficult to assess because the parties are not talking. You can only get a barometric reading through *sensing* the changes in the communication participants. Some people when reassessing a volatile conflict will make comments such as "You could feel the chill in the air" or "I could sense something wasn't going right." Actually, those individuals don't have a sixth sense nor are they clairvoyant. They are simply highly skilled at reading non-verbal signals and the cultural influences that are impacting the communication context.

Recently, a student told me of a late night incident in which several African-American college-aged girls were walking past a dormitory that housed elementary girls who were on campus for a summer sports camp. Some of the elementary girls leaned out the window and called out to the college students, "Hey b———————, you think you're d——— cute don't you?" Well, needless to say, the college girls yelled back for them to stop and a verbal confrontation occurred between the two groups. The African-American girls went to the dorm to look for the camp girls' counselor but found no one. They then returned to their dorms and a few minutes later, the campus police arrived with the girls' counselor. The counselor told the college-aged girls that she had been around Black girls before and knew that the only reason they came up to the camp floor was to fight the elementary girls. Unfortunately, this communication situation accelerated so rapidly

that both the counselor and the college girls filed harassment complaints against each other.

So, what can we learn from this situation? And, how would understanding Tish's cultural communication help Thandie respond appropriately to Tish's comments? First, let's look at the definition of culture as defined by Samovar and Porter:

> Culture—the deposit of knowledge, experience, beliefs, values, attitudes, meanings, hierarchies, religion, notions of time, roles, spatial relations, concepts of the universe, and material objects and possessions acquired by a group of people in the course of generations through individual and group striving (Samovar and Porter, 1994, pg. 11).

I use this definition to illustrate the importance and impact of an individual's culture on the communication process. If we look at our original model of communication and add the cultural influences, we do indeed see a greater sphere of factors that impact the flow of effective communication.

Having specific knowledge of the subject matter is a key influencer in the communication process. If, for example, the sender has more knowledge of a topic than the receiver, how might that person communicate that fact nonverbally? Will he or she show it in their facial expression or tone of voice? How then will the receiver interpret the message? Will he or she resent the sender if the message is sent with a hint of sarcasm or frustration? What if the message is sent with an open expression communicating respect and willingness to accept any response? The same holds true for our attitudes, values, and beliefs.

Attitudes, Beliefs and Values

Bias
An unfair attitude that adversely influences one's ability to be objective.

I know individuals who, after having a bad night's sleep, wake up in a bad mood. If I speak to them (especially in a cheerful voice) before they have time to adjust to their day, I will inevitably receive a wince and a growl in response to my greeting. Yet, their attitude or mood is temporary and does not reflect their attitude or belief about me. We all have **biases**

Stereotype

A belief held about the character or characteristics of an individual based on broad generalizations about a specific class or group. Not treating the individual as a distinct person.

and hold **stereotypes** of individuals and groups that can influence our communication. While these biases and stereotypical attitudes don't generally affect our choice of words, the manner in which we deliver the words can be greatly affected. As we communicate, the non-verbal signals that accompany our verbal messages are delivered as part of the normal reactions to a communication context. If we are not aware of the personal values we bring into a situation, we can unduly influence the outcome of our communication attempts.

Much of what we hold as personal values is learned early in life and is a direct result of our religious and spiritual upbringing as well as our family values and traditions. Think about conversations you may have had with your family members and what might be discussed if the topic were about an individual in any of the following circumstances:

- Someone living in a trailer park
- A person living in a high-rise apartment in Manhattan
- A person living (insert your hometown)
- A person of color living in a (rich, poor) section of town

Our biases are very much a part of life experiences as are the positive events that have occurred during our lifetimes. In Thandie's encounter with Tish, we witness a whole range of communicative reactions, mostly non-verbal which may give us clues to our hidden biases:

- Tish's size can be perceived non-verbally as being on the same level as her teacher. While not directly communicated, Tish may feel free to communicate with her teacher as if she were her peer or equal.
- Thandie makes a friendly gesture by smiling at Tish. While this gesture has been met with a positive response from the other students, Tish does not respond to Thandie as expected, thereby creating a bit of **dissonance** in Thandie's mind resulting in her self-talk: "Have I somehow

Dissonance

An uncomfortable mental state caused by conflicting messages.

offended Tish? Why is Tish trying to embarrass me?"

■ Tish uses a non-verbal—*vocalics*—to question Thandie's previous night's behavior. Tish also makes a stereotypical and biased remark suggesting that Thandie's red eyes are a result of a night of drinking. Tish then ends her communication with laughter—another vocalic.

■ The class joins in the laughter—generally a cultural non-verbal shared by many groups of people who see it as a sign of happiness. However, laughter can also be interpreted as offensive in certain contexts and can sometimes reveal our biases towards certain groups of people.

■ Thandie's face tightens and her body tenses. Her body is non-verbally communicating her discomfort.

How much of the communication that is occurring between Tish, Thandie and her class is culturally influenced? We have little information regarding the cultural, social, economic or racial backgrounds of the parties involved. Yet, we do know that the cultural backgrounds of both Thandie and Tish are going to influence the next communicative event that will occur. What can Thandie do to lessen her tenseness in the communication exchange? How can she improve the interpersonal communication *first* between Tish and herself?

Interpersonal Communication

Communication between an individual sender and one or two receivers.

Impersonal and Personal Interpersonal Communication

Interpersonal communication is the most frequent used level of communication. Most of our everyday exchanges occur on the interpersonal level. Interpersonal communication can be face-to-face but is also commonly transacted through **media** technology (cell phones, Internet, etc.). Interpersonal communication allows both parties in the communication exchange to respond immediately to the communication situation. Therefore, if there is miscommunication, it can be handled right there on the spot. Each individual in the communication

Media

Plural of *medium*, a means of storing and sending communication.

exchange can adjust his or her message to better reach the intended outcome.

Interpersonal communication can be either impersonal or personal. Most of our everyday exchanges are conducted using impersonal communication. We use this type of interpersonal communication when exchanging messages with individuals we interact with based on the person's role. We see no further than that person's function within our need to accomplish a short-term goal. If you're purchasing an item at a local convenience store where you, let's say, purchase gas frequently—chances are that you've seen the clerk many times. Yet, the communication most likely never goes beyond exchanging a few pleasantries. Your goal is to make a purchase. Sometimes we ask questions of individuals and never go beyond receiving the answer we desire. The information exchanged is superficial and we primarily regard the person in his or her role. We are more apt to interact with that person from our perspectives of their cultural or stereotypical role. Even though you may communicate with that person a number of times and over a long period of time, the nature of the communication never goes deeper. It remains on the superficial level.

In contrast, while personal communication may begin similarly to impersonal communication, rea-

Impersonal Interpersonal	Personal Interpersonal
Persons interact by role and/or stereotype.	Persons interact as distinct individuals with distinguishing characteristics.
Accomplishes short-term communication goals without sharing personal information.	Accomplishes long-term communication goals over time through the sharing of personal information.
Relationships remain superficial even though there may be several contacts over time. Individuals are rarely perceived as anything more than an assigned role or stereotype.	Relationships grow deeper over time and develop into an understanding of each individual's personhood as a result of shared communication.

Thandie's Short-Term Communication Goals	Actions	Anticipated Effect
Immediately stop students from laughing	Tell students to stop laughing or "else"	Depends on Thandie's relationship and/or her authoritative position. Will not improve personal or impersonal communication
Stop Tish from laughing	Tell her to stop or "else"	Thandie continues to regard Tish stereotypically and accelerates the potential for conflict by adding a veiled threat.
Take control by letting Tish know that Thandie, as the teacher is in control and that Tish, as student is being disrespectful.	Immediately confront Tish in a voice and tone loud enough for the other students to hear	Accelerates potential for conflict and sets up more communication hurdles
Let Tish know that Thandie has been embarrassed by her.	Immediately confront Tish in a low, stern tone but maintain non-verbal signs (affects) of embarrassment	Tish may be confused by Thandie's mixed communication. Thandie's sternness is an attempt to control the communication situation but her non-verbal communicates discomfortability. The situation maintains its awkwardness.

sons for developing a deeper communication evolve. You find that you have commonalities that grow into both parties sharing more *personal* information. You communicate with the person as a distinct individual. And, as you continue the relationship over time, a deeper understanding of the person's communicative needs develop.

Both impersonal and personal interpersonal communications are needed to navigate through daily interactions. It would be impractical to engage in personal interpersonal communication with each person you greet. As well, our lives would not be enriched without the personal communications we have with significant individuals within our social spheres. Look at a comparison between impersonal and personal interpersonal communication.

So then, how can Thandie manage her communication interaction with Tish? What are Thandie's communication goals? Here are a few short-term goals with action steps and anticipated effects. What other goals can you think of?

All of these goals are understandable if Thandie primarily uses impersonal communication with Tish and does not want to develop a communication relationship based on respect and individual character. However, for unknown reasons, Tish felt that she could make a personal comment about Thandie's personal appearance—her red eyes. This comment presumes that Tish is in a personal relationship with Thandie or that she assumed she could be.

There are several levels of personal relationships from our most intimate (family, spouse, close friends, etc.) to personal relationships that evolve from daily and lengthy interaction. If Thandie has been teaching over a period of time and is still treating the communication with her students as impersonal (i.e., seeing each student in their cultural and stereotypical roles), then a smooth resolution of this communication situation is doubtful.

Let's examine a few options with the assumption that Thandie does use personal communication with Tish on a level appropriate between teacher and student.

It is important to determine a person's motivation before crafting a response in order to resolve a potential communication conflict. If Thandie can understand Tish's motive for making the comment that she...*"gotta lay off the bottle"* she will be in a better position to *improve* the genuine personal communication that is desirable between a teacher and student. Most miscommunication occurs because individuals interact superficially based on stereotypical perceptions. Regarding the personhood of an individual with the goal of improved communication will gain rewards that will continuously pay off. Knowing the "why" of a person's actions and remarks helps to reach the individual's mind, desires, and heart of expression. In this way, the teacher becomes more than a giver of informa-

Thandie's Communication Goals	Actions	Anticipated Effect
Deepen the understanding of Tish's communication motives: Is Tish attempting to divert everyone's attention away from her and onto Thandie? Does Tish really want to know something about Thandie's personal life? Does Tish understand what appropriate comments between children and adults are?	Use light tone that acknowledges Tish's remark. *or* Redirect Tish's attention: "Never mind what I did last night. What about . . ." *or* Tell Tish and the class that you stayed up late watching television. Talk to Tish privately about her comments.	Furthers personal communication by recognizing the individual and by sharing the appropriate level of personal communication. Helps Tish improve her personal communication skills.

To refocus class attention.	Quiet class and give them a task.	This accomplishes an appropriate short-term goal and is communicated on an *impersonal* level. Thandie communicates using her role as 'teacher.' A communication context (such as a classroom) in which you engage the same people over a long period of time appropriately uses both impersonal and personal communication.
To learn not to tense up when in uncomfortable situations.	Immediately engage in calming non-verbal communication. Relax face muscles and engage in self-talk using soothing phrases learned beforehand to cope with stressful situations.	

tion and a repository of facts and data. The teacher becomes a medium of grand expression on several levels as she or he peels back layers of meaning to reveal the true essence of the individual within each student. Reaching this overarching goal will

ultimately make the teacher an effective communicator in and out of the classroom.

Media Influences in the Classroom

A study by the Kaiser Family Foundation reports that children ages 2–18 spend approximately 5.3 hours using media each day. While sixty-five percent of kids aged 8–18 have a television in their room, the average child spends about 20 hours a week at a minimum in front of the television (Roberts et al., 1997). The point of these statistics is not to point to an overuse of media but to underscore the fact that a teacher's communication is only one of many media messages and influences that impact student lives on a daily basis.

In the beginning of this chapter, I wrote about communication technology in the classroom—specifically the prevalence and use of cell phones (not to mention Ipods and other communication devices) in the classroom. This propagation of media influence presents a significant challenge to the teacher who wishes to encourage thoughtful and provocative communication between students and between student and teacher. How much of what your students see and hear is based on stereotypical and market-driven images? What are the commercial messages that are sent along with text messages, instant messages, ringtones and the like meant to communicate? How much of these messages seep into our everyday communications? As a teacher, how much have *you* been influenced by the same messages and images that influence your students?

The fact of the matter is that you, as teacher, are the primary medium in the classroom. For six hours a day, you are in control of the communication flow. Your continual presence, method for managing the classroom environment and respect shown for each student as an individual will set the communicative tone from the first class meeting until the last day of school.

First Class Meeting Preparation

One of the most unnerving tasks for a beginning teacher is to walk into a new school building and stand in front of a classroom of 30 sets of eyes. This is not student teaching but the real thing. You can't leave your class after eight weeks; you have these same people for a whole year—for better or worse. It is like a marriage of sorts. And like any long-term relationship, you don't walk into it unprepared.

Literature related to factors that contribute to effective classroom instruction generally list the following as critical teacher attributes: credibility, delivery, fairness, knowledge, organization and rapport (Catt et al., 2007; McCroskey et al., 2006). Credibility, delivery and rapport are all communicative elements. While delivery and rapport are elements that are implemented while in the classroom, credibility is developed before you teach your first class.

Credibility asks the question whether or not a speaker is believable and confident. While credibility is related to knowledge of the subject matter, it also gets at whether or not you, as teacher, are able to project an air of confidence, responsiveness and assertiveness.

> Responsiveness indicates the teachers' positive reactions to students' needs and a willingness to listen to their students. Assertiveness suggests that the teacher approach students as a leader and maintain appropriate control in the classroom (McCroskey et al., 2006, 404).

Responsiveness is also not learned in a classroom but is practiced each day in the interactions you have–especially with people who are close to you. How well do you listen? How perceptive are you about others' needs? Effective communicators do not focus on themselves; they are attuned to the communicative needs of their receivers and adjust their communication styles accordingly.

Assertiveness deals with your personal comfort levels. How at ease are you in new situations? What methods do you use when resolving conflicts with friends and loved ones? When you walk into a room and others are present, do you speak first or do you wait until someone acknowledges your presence? Hopefully, in asking yourself these questions, you will begin a plan of developing those areas in which you do not assert yourself. Remember, assertiveness is not being "pushy" or belligerent. Someone who is assertive knows when and how to make her point and how to inform individuals (without becom-

Scenario	Confidence-Building Practice Exercises
Meeting your new supervisor.	First look in a mirror and practice your greeting, saying the supervisor's name. Use direct eye contact and a smile. Then, practice with a friend, adding a firm handshake while you make your greeting. Do this as many times as necessary until it becomes natural. Also, try to get a friend to introduce you to an adult that you don't know. Then practice your greeting.
Going to a club or organization meeting alone where you don't know anyone.	Use the same exercise as above. However, many people do not shake hands when they first meet in casual situations. Instead, practice saying your name and then following up with a question such as, "I didn't know there would be ——— many people here." Eye contact is important and remember, being natural is the key.
Making a presentation or a speech in front of a class.	The best preparation is to take a public speaking course sometime during college. Also, learn to speak up and express your opinions in group and classroom situations whenever you have the opportunity. Of course, preparation is the key. Knowing what you're talking about is paramount.　Again, practicing in front of a mirror is useful. Also, having someone videotape you (even using a cell phone is helpful) will provide you with the best assessment of your communication style. Finally, when the big day comes and you're standing in front of your class, just relax. Find a friendly face and look directly at him or her. Smile and move your eyes across the group as you speak. Move around and you will gain confidence with every step. Use your hands as gestures and if you need to hold on to something, place something (pen, pencil, eyeglasses) in one hand. Remember, at this point, you're the pro–not perfect—but willing to try and to make it work.

ing overly anxious or angry) when a boundary has been crossed.

Confidence is learned through experiencing missteps and mistakes but not allowing those life situations to hinder personal growth. "If at first you don't succeed—try, try again" may seem to be a trite cliché; however, not giving up can be a big confidence enhancer. Confidence is gained through practice and experience. If you want to gain confidence in a particular area, you must be able to first visualize your success and then put yourself in situations where you can put your skills to the test. Here are some scenarios that may test your confidence and practice exercises to boost your confidence quotient.

Handling the Unexpected

Loss of control, fear, and dealing with personal prejudices and biases are probably some of the most challenging barriers to overcome in teaching. Even the most seasoned teacher experiences a temporary loss for words or must deal with unexpected conflicts and confrontations. One important indicator of how a teacher will respond to the unexpected is to determine the type of rapport or communication relationship between the teacher and his or her students. Earlier in the chapter we discussed Thandie and Tish's conflict and determined that the outcome would be predicated on Thandie's communication goals and her relationship (personal or impersonal) with Tish. While education books abound on the topic of handling discipline or managing student behavior in the classroom, it is the communication education literature that focuses on the impact of teacher–student rapport and the importance of teacher non-verbal behavior that we now address.

Face-to-face communication is considered to be the most powerful and effective means of insuring a message is delivered correctly (Witt and Schrodt, 2006). Like the difference between a movie and live theatre, the teacher performing his or her craft in a classroom setting is an authentic, vibrant, and convincing medium. Therefore, the things the teacher says or does will be watched very closely—similar to the way people focus on a television screen. The gestures and words spoken cannot be erased and taped over. So, every word and gesture must be weighed and evaluated before delivery, especially because of the closeness of the teacher as medium to his or her audience (students).

A teacher's immediacy behavior is "conceptualized as both the message of closeness and the behaviors that enhance that sense of closeness. . . . The immediacy principle [is described as] one's tendency to be drawn towards persons and things they like" (Rester and Edwards, 2007, p. 35). One mistake some new teachers make is to attempt to become their students' friend. As discussed earlier, teaching requires both impersonal and personal communication. The teacher will always occupy the role of "teacher" but it does not have to be a stereotypical role. Your communication style, non-verbal mannerisms that convey trust and respect will draw you to your students and them to you. Cautions must however be given against inappropriate touching and the sharing of comments about your personal life and those of your students that are too intimate. Too often boundaries are crossed that prove difficult to rebuild. Many times the teacher then only has the use of fear and other threatening consequences as a means of exacting student compliance. While the use of fear appeal alone has been shown to have some effect on student behavior, it does not positively influence student outcome nor the student-teacher relationship for long-term instructional impact (Sprinkle et al., 2006).

In conclusion, each person seeks to be known by his or her individual make-up—as created by a distinctive pattern. There will never be another person as uniquely formed as you–or the students that you will teach over the coming years. Communicate your confidence as you believe in who you are and the importance of what you express to others. That is the best we have to offer and the ultimate hope of all communicators.

References

Abbott and Costello (retrieved August 1, 2007). The official abbott and costello website. http://www.abbottandcostello.net/.

Catt, S., Miller, D. & Schallenkamp, K. (2007). You are the key: Communication for learning effectiveness. *Education, 127*(3), 369–377.

Clark, R. (1983). Reconsidering research on learning from media. *Review of Educational Research, 53,* 445–59.

Clark, R. (1998). Motivating performance: Part I—diagnosing and solving motivational problems. *Performance Improvement, 37*(8), 39–46.

Dale, E. (1969). *Audio-visual methods in teaching,* 3rd Edition. New York: Holt, Rinehart and Winston.

Heinich, R., Molenda, M. & Russell, J. (1998). *Instructional media and the new technologies of instruction.* New York: Macmillan Publishing Company.

Knapp, M. (1980). *Essentials of non-verbal communication.* New York: Holt, Rinehart and Winston.

McCroskey, J., Richmond, V., & Bennett, V. (2006). The relationships of student end-of-class motivation with teacher communication behaviors and instructional outcomes. *Communication Education, 55*(4), 403–414.

Mickey, K. (2005). Companies look at educational potential of cell phones, but questions linger. *Electronic Education Report, 12*(6), 1–4.

Molenda, M. & Sullivan, M. (2001). A watershed year for technology in education. *Techno, 10,* 14–19.

Peck, C., Cuban, L., & Kirkpatrick, H. (2002a). High-tech's high hopes meet student realities. *Education Digest, 67*(8), 47–54.

———. (2002b). Techno-promoters dreams, student realities. *Phi Delta Kappan, 83*(6), 472–480.

Rester, C. & Edwards, R. (2007). Effects of sex and setting on students' interpretation of teachers' excessive use of immediacy. *Communication Education, 56*(1), 34–53.

Roberts, D., Foehr, U., Rideout, V., & Brodie, M. (1997). *Kids and media @ the new millennium.* Menlo Park: Kaiser Family Foundation Report.

Samovar, L. & Porter, R. (1994). *Intercultural communication: A reader,* 7th Edition. Belmont: Wadsworth Publishing Company.

Seels, B. (1997). *The relationship of media and ISD theory: The unrealized promise of Dale's Cone of Experience.* Albuquerque, NM: Proceedings of Selected Research and Development Presentations at the 1997 National Convention of the Association for Educational

Communications and Technology. (ERIC Document Reproduction Service No. ED 409869).

Sprinkle, R., Hunt, S., Simonds, C. & Comadena, M. (2006). Fear in the classroom: An examination of teachers' use of fear appeals and students' learning outcomes. *Communication Education, 55*(4), 389–402.

Witt, P. & Schrodt, P. (2006). The influence of instructional technology use and teacher immediacy on student affect for teacher and course. *Communication Reports, 19*(1), 1–15.

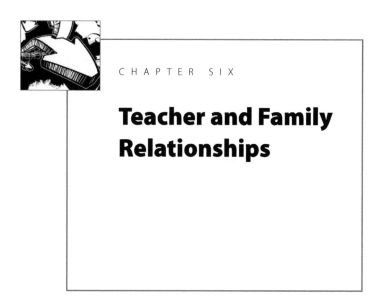

CHAPTER SIX

Teacher and Family Relationships

Tamar Jacobson

Unless you have already experienced parenthood, it may be difficult for you to appreciate fully the enormity of the emotions and roles that parents experience and that affect their ability to function as parents. Even if you are a parent, the diverse cultures, communities and circumstances that influence families in modern America make individual lives unique; one parenting experience and one family will be quite unlike another (Gestwicki, 2007. pg. 1).

Children and Families

Children come with families. When they arrive at our classroom doors, children are already in the process of developing the deepest and most influential relationships of their formative years. Earliest emotional memories will affect them forever, and are being learned and developed with and by the most significant adults in their lives: family members. In order to understand children, the ways they communicate, interact, behave and learn we will need to get to know their families. Knowing the family helps us to understand the child better. Parents have primary responsibility for their children. Teachers and families are partners in helping children learn.

Teachers expect children to be alert and attentive the moment they set foot in the school building, and especially when they enter our classrooms. The reality is children were most likely affected by different family scenarios and situations even just one hour before arriving at school. Their experiences of diverse and complex situations will influence how they feel when they walk through our classroom doors. For example, they may have witnessed a violent argument, experienced harsh scolding or punishment for taking too much time to get dressed, the car not starting, buses too full, trains late, or laundry undone leaving them nothing appropriate to wear. Some children may not have received breakfast and others were yelled at or called names as they were walking out the door. Some children might be feeling ill or did not sleep well the night before. Others woke up with warmth and security, a healthy breakfast and hugs and kisses of support to send them on their way. As we look around at the faces of children in our classrooms, we realize that each and every one has had a unique experience even a very short while before as they set out to meet us in school that morning.

Getting to know families, building those important relationships with parents, and learning how to communicate with family members is perhaps one of the most challenging aspects of the teaching profession and our work with educating children. There are a number of reasons that developing relationships with the families of children in our classrooms is complex. There are numerous and different ways of parenting, and they are affected

and influenced by culture, family style, or socio-economic status. Every unique way of parenting is developed from generations of different life experiences, ways of interacting, solving problems, and, even, expressing feelings. No one way is right or wrong. Just different. As educators we are expected to respect that. This is not easy and causes us discomfort or anxiety.

> Our survival depended upon learning about the cultural mores of our family and community: How to sit and eat at the table, what to say when, how to say it, when to be silent, how to behave with strangers or different family members, what attitudes to have about school, who we could like and dislike, and so on. When we meet people from cultures with different worldviews from us, we immediately feel unsafe. It is as if we have to give up what we learned to survive in order to open ourselves to different cultural mores. We are not sure of how other people will behave or interpret what we say. A lot of the time we do not understand them at all. That makes us uneasy and anxious (Jacobson, 2003, pages 44 & 45).

Reflective practice
Being a thoughtful, pensive practitioner.

Although it is challenging and uncomfortable, it is our responsibility as educators to overcome our discomfort through **reflective practice** where, as professionals, we come to understand why we do what we do, or how we feel the way we do. We learn to make the necessary connections with personal emotions and our own family cultures and understand and monitor how that influences our professional behavior with children and their families.

Parents care about their children. Children are precious to them. However, at the same time they experience many complex feelings about their children including love, anger, guilt, fear, anxiety about doing the right thing, and many more. As teachers, it is our responsibility to learn to understand and respect the challenge of parenting while we attempt to develop relationships with families of children in our classrooms. For example, parents are often frightened of teachers and school. Parents might have had bad experiences while they were in school themselves and are not fond of the institution. They have their own memories about schools from when they were children. Some of these memories are unpleasant. School was not always a fun place for many parents of the children in our classrooms.

In addition, they might feel inferior to the teacher, who they believe knows more than they do, and so they will find it difficult to approach the school with ease and openness. Even more frightening for parents is the fact that teachers are able to know their family secrets through how their children behave and what they say. For example if a child wets her pants or behaves aggressively, the parents fear that we will think it is their fault and that they look bad. When a child is sent out into the world the family is exposed. Until a child leaves her or his home to interact with the community at large, all the family secrets are intact. Once the child goes to school the truth will come out, and parents fear being judged for what kind of parent they are through the behaviors of their children. Types of secrets include behaviors like bathroom accidents, not paying attention at group time, learning how to share or socialize, or manners at the lunch or snack table. However, they could also include larger, more serious secrets like family fights, alcoholism, sex abuse, beatings or abuse and neglect. These fears or complex emotions will affect ways that parents interact with teachers. At times they might seem defensive or confronting, or perhaps they will withdraw and keep away from the school even when invited. It is our responsibility as teachers to reach out to parents in all these different situations and find a way to help them feel emotionally safe with us.

Being judgmental, having inappropriate expectations, and not understanding our biases with regards to the diversity of families are all obstacles as we work to develop relationships with families of children in our classrooms. In this chapter, we think about how to develop the types of relationships with families that will enhance and support children's well-being and academic success. Children

thrive emotionally, socially and academically when teachers and parents or guardians cooperate and collaborate. We will need to develop skills of communication, reflect on our own biases and emotions in order to break down the barriers, and address the obstacles that prevent us from developing healthy and productive relationships with families.

Teachers as Parents

As I write this chapter, the day after Mother's Day, I think about how my son forgot to call me until very late that night. I smile to myself because now that I am older, I have decided that Mother's Day is not about my son remembering me or acknowledgment from others about how good a mother I am. It is not even about how much love I put into my time as a mother. It is about how I loved giving birth to my son. It was a privilege and honor to have him enter my life and accompany me on my turbulent and interesting journeys. I learned so much from him about myself, especially regarding unconditional love and commitment. It is I who should be remembering him on Mother's Day, and thanking him for sharing his joys and sorrows, musical talent, truthful opinions, humor and love, and, especially, for being a child of my womb, who changed my life in so many ways, forever.

Nowadays, I see a tall, lean young man standing before me. My son is thirty-four, a talented jazz pianist, and a credentialed family therapist. I hear his deep voice as he speaks. He was not always like this, for even as I see and hear him now, at the same time I can clearly recall many years ago, as if they were today, his chubby toddler cheeks and sweet little voice. He sat straight and tall in his car seat at the back, when we drove around the neighborhood, pointing at trucks or trains and calling out, *"Look! Twucks"* or *"Look! Twains, Mommy."* As a young mother I learned very early on that no one would fight for my son but me. As a result, I would always come to his school to talk with his teachers from pre-school right up until he graduated from high school. I would speak to his teachers about his progress, share with them our changing family situations, discuss ways to treat him better, and talk about concerns regarding appropriate education practices. I was also involved with the community life of his various schools whether they were in Israel (where we lived until he was fourteen), or in America after we immigrated to the States when he was fifteen. I would volunteer to cook, bake, make craft-type things for fundraisers, help out in his classrooms, or attend meetings and parent-teacher conferences. I knew that parent involvement was very important for his well-being and academic success.

You see, I am a teacher myself and learned from the beginning of my career that all children come with families. When a child enters my class, she is like an emissary from her family. Not only did I learn this in teacher education classes or staff development trainings, but I knew it because I was a child once. I have memories of my own parents' participation in my educational life. Indeed, I can recount each time my mother celebrated my accomplishments when I was growing up. I also remember the times she did not show up and how much I missed her, or felt excluded when my friends' parents were present and mine were not. It affected my general sense of well-being one way or the other.

What do you remember about your own family's involvement in your education? Did they show up for all your scholarly events to which they were invited? How did they participate in your school life? How did that make you feel? What would you have liked them to do more of, or less? What kind of a parent will you be or are you now? Will you be defensive or confronting, or will you withdraw and keep away from school? How do you think about involvement in your children's education?

Teachers Are Not Parenting Experts

We are teachers of children. Our work is not to know the best way to parent. Either we will parent our children the way we were parented because it worked

Subjective
Being affected by personal views, experience or background.

for us, or, we might try something completely different because it was not pleasant for us as children. Ways of parenting are **subjective**, handed down from generation to generation, and as teachers we can only know the best way to parent our own children based on our life experiences. Even though teachers are not parenting experts, we care deeply about the well-being and education of children in our classes. This influences how we perceive parenting styles, and causes us to be judgmental of family systems and dynamics that are different from our own. We are not here to educate parents how to parent. We are here to educate their children. Teachers do not realize that parenting is not a profession. Therefore, we have expectations of families that are inappropriate or not relevant to who they are and what they

Objectivity
Being able to distance oneself from the situation and think it through.

do with their children. In other words, we expect parents to be **objective**, or at the very least, knowledgeable about child development, treating them as if they had studied and learned about the right way to be a parent—as if it were a profession.

Parenting Is Not a Profession

It is difficult for teachers to comprehend that parenting is not a profession. When we say, parents are children's first teachers, we must be careful not to confuse that with the education profession, which we have chosen as a career. Parenting is part of life, nature's way of perpetuating and nurturing our species. Teaching is a profession with a code of ethics, policies, knowledge base, which includes pedagogy and curriculum, and licensure. Anybody can be a parent. Teachers must be specialized in education and credentialed. Oftentimes we have expectations of parents that are inappropriate. We want them to understand child development or the best educational practices without having to explain that to them. We send home complicated homework assignments for them to work on with their children. In his book, *The Homework Myth: Why Our Kids Get Too Much of a Bad Thing*, Alfie Kohn describes the way homework affects family relationships (Kohn, 2006):

> Beyond its effects on parents and children, homework's negative impact—and specifically the nagging, whining, and yelling that are employed to make sure assignments are completed on time—affects families as a whole. As one writer remarked, "The parent-child relationship . . . is fraught with enough difficulty without giving the parent a new role as teacher" or enforcer. Ironically, the sorts of relaxed, constructive family activities that could repair the damage are among the casualties of homework's voracious consumption of time (page 12).

We mistakenly call this *parent involvement.* We invite family members in for parent-teacher conferences and scold them for how their child behaves, demanding that they fix it at home, expecting them to follow through with what we have decided are the best remedies for improving their child's behavior or learning abilities. We are surprised and frustrated when they do not comply. We even judge them as not caring about their children because they do not follow our instructions. We mistakenly call this *empowering families.*

Some more appropriate ways that teachers can support families are by encouraging them to love their children unconditionally, and to be as subjective as possible. It is natural for parents to be attached emotionally, and, hopefully, unconditionally with their children. We can and should encourage parents that their child is their one and only—the very best—and that we understand that no one will fight for their child but them. On the other hand, as an objective and unbiased professional, we have been taught to be engaged with the whole class and be present for all children. In other words, we have learned not to have favorites and to be fair to everyone. As teachers, we are able to do this because we are the professionals. We have learned to be objective, see the bigger picture, and know what is best for the whole group as well as individual children. We understand that parents

must be subjective for the good of their one child. We understand that family support and encouragement is the foundation for a child's self-worth, security and confidence. We have learned about it in child development classes, through keeping up with the current research in our professional field, and by reflecting on our own early childhood experiences within our families of origin. We know that children are more precious to families than anything else in their life.

Children Are Precious to Parents

For many years, I was the director of a large university child care center, which included five preschool and eight infant-toddler classrooms. From time to time I would receive letters from student or faculty parents expressing gratitude for the care and education their children received at the campus center. I was always reminded how precious their children were to them. Following, are examples of two letters I received from different parents when they were preparing to leave the Center. While the letters expressed gratitude, they also described how much these parents cared about their children, how sensitive they were to their children's well-being, the importance of their role as parents, and especially how precious their children were to them:

> Our daughter will be leaving your center at the end of this month. We just wanted to take the time to thank you, the teachers and staff for all your hard work and dedication. In May of 1996 we brought our daughter to your center, a scared and shy toddler, who preferred the company of teachers to children. I can remember how I would sneak in at the end of the day hoping to find her playing happily with some of the children. But a lump would grow in my throat when I would instead find her riding safely in the pack on the back of "friend teacher" (that's what my daughter called her). Looking back, I am extremely grateful for the patience and understanding afforded her during her first months at the center. Now my daughter leaves the center a young girl full of curiosity and eager to make new friends. We as parents leave

equally anxious and excited about her future at "big school." (It is difficult to leave the security of the family-like atmosphere.) Yet we are certain that the strong foundation provided by wonderfully giving and loving teachers has instilled our daughter with the confidence that will support her throughout her elementary years. You are nurturing the future of the world and that is not an easy task. Keep up the good work! Thanks for taking such great care of our precious one. (Parent one)

As I prepare to celebrate my graduation from school, I am very aware of my struggles to get this far and how so many people have helped along the way. Graduating is certainly an accomplishment—but I am most "proud of" and fulfilled by my role as mother to my children. They are more important to me than anything else in this world. In order to go to school, I had to entrust their care to others—something I found very had to do in light of my beliefs about my duties as a mother. So as I prepare to graduate, I realize just how thankful I am and how blessed I have been to have met all of you and to have your help in caring for and teaching my children. If I did not have your help to care for my children, a duty I feel is so very important I can't imagine anything more so, I would not be graduating now. Thank you, all, so much for all your giving to my kids and me, for all you have taught me about child development, and for all the love you have shown my children. (Parent two)

Negotiating the Relationship: Teacher and Parent Cooperation

Teacher-parent cooperation is beneficial for children's socio-emotional development and academic achievement. In May 2007 a report was published by *PolicyBridge,* a non-partisan public policy think tank founded in 2005 to monitor urban policy issues affecting the quality of life for minorities in Northeast Ohio (McShepard, Goler, & Batson, 2007: www.policy-bridge.org). In a proposed "*Policy of Personal Responsibility,*" the authors base their recommendation for more involvement from parents on recent research published by the *Southwest Educational Department Laboratory* indicating:

... that students with involved parents, no matter their income or background, are more likely to earn higher grades, have better test scores, enroll in higher level programs, pass their classes, attend school regularly, have better social skills, adapt well to school, graduate high school, and go on to postsecondary education (Page 15).

While we all know that parent involvement is beneficial, at the same time it often seems difficult for teachers and parents to cooperate. A partnership between adults who care for and educate children is complicated. For, while teachers are professional and objective educators, families are the subjective and emotional caregivers for the children. Indeed, parent-teacher cooperation is very much like a negotiation between those two very different perceptions and attitudes: one subjective and emotional and the other objective and professional.

What Does It Take to Become a Parent?

Think about the following questions as you consider what your own choices or decisions might be as you contemplate becoming a parent. Does having an education influence what kind of parent you will become? Why? What kind of a relationship would you need to develop with your partner in the raising of your children? Who would you choose as a partner in life to share in the raising of your children? Would that person be a lover or a friend? What do you think about your partner's beliefs and values? What do you think about your partner's religion or culture? Would these things matter to you in raising your children? Why? Would you be willing to give up time, money, career, or whatever it takes, to become a parent? How would you negotiate that with a partner of choice? How would your financial situation play a part in parenting your children? What do you think about your physical and mental health affecting your ability to parent? What type of support systems would you need to be a competent and capable parent? What do you feel about the child's gender? Would this play a part in your parenting styles? After you discovered you were pregnant or had decided to adopt a child, how would you prepare for the future? What are any other questions you might want to explore as you consider becoming a parent? If you are already a parent, what advice could you give to future parents?

Write these answers down and discuss them with friends, peers, teachers, your own parents or counselors. What were some of the surprises (if any) that you experienced as you thought and talked about this subject? Write a summary titled: *Becoming a parent: What does it mean for me?*

Creating a Safe Emotional Environment

Now that we are reading, talking and thinking about creating a family, becoming a parent or guardian, and are beginning to understand how fearful parents are of being judged and how they all want the very best for their child, let us look at ways to negotiate an effective and productive parent-teacher relationship. But first, some reminders about how parents feel and what some of their anxieties are.

Parents are guilty from the day their child is born. They are expected to raise their children in the correct manner (whatever that means) by family members, society and the popular media. Advice is abundant and diverse, through books, television talk shows, extended family members, religious leaders, neighbors, pediatricians, professors, teachers, and counselors. It is amazing that people feel capable of parenting at all with all the different advice they are given. Teachers must learn that parents have their own life experiences and different ways of dealing with things. Their ways of interacting, expressing feelings or solving problems could almost be considered a different language from our own. In order to understand parents without judgment, we must learn to listen to their stories. If a parent asks my advice, I usually say something like, "Well, I don't know what would work in your family, but for me, and considering the kind of family I came from, this or that works for me." In fact,

my advice might not work for someone else. Our parenting styles are just too different. For example, some families physically express love with hugs and kisses, stroking and close eye contact. Others are a little more distant and not as physical.

One of the ways to make parents feel comfortable is by letting them know that we are human. Let parents get to know who you are. It is important to let parents know that you are human, fallible, flexible, and respectful of their way of parenting. Make yourselves available and approachable to parents. When I was a teacher of young children I always gave the parents my home phone number. At the first parent meeting of the year, I would tell them all about me. I shared with them stories about my marriage, my experiences as a mother, and informed them that I did not have all the answers. I have always told parents that no one will fight for their child but them, and I want them to feel safe to come and tell me anything that would help me in understanding their child better.

Practice an open door policy, where parents can feel free to drop by any time they want. Invite their concerns. If you know that parents are subjective and naturally emotionally attached to their children, you will expect them to be indignant or afraid if their child gets hurt. When a parent confronts you or is upset, the best thing is to acknowledge their pain and listen to what they have to say. Usually I say something like, "I am so sorry that happened." And then I write down all their complaints and concerns and listen carefully to what they are feeling. After that I explain what I can do to see that it does not happen again, and I warn them that it might because when children play together things happen. However, I list all the actions I can take to improve the situation and promise to apprise them of my progress. I make sure to follow through with my promise. It is important that parents feel safe and trusting with their child's teacher in order for effective communication and cooperation. As professionals we must learn to see the whole picture, the bigger picture of the classroom and the best practices for all the children. Respect parents' feelings, including anger and hurt for their child. Give them steps on how you will help, be professional, listen to all the wants and needs of parents even if you cannot meet all of them. Always write down conversation points with a parent. Take them seriously. Remember just how precious their children are to them.

Involving Families and Facilitating Cooperation

Welcome parents and children into your classroom every day. Mostly, children travel to school on buses, but if they are dropped off by parents, there is nothing as powerful as a warm and welcoming greeting each and every day. Families and teachers will need to communicate about many different issues relating to the care and education of children: things to bring to school; children's clothes, needs, naps, food, behaviors; the child's progress; various and sundry concerns; curriculum; fund raising; participation; meetings; holidays; religion; ideology; philosophy; and beliefs, just to name a few. Almost all of those items listed require discussion, listening, negotiation, explanation and understanding. Some will become complex and challenging conversations and others will be easier to resolve or work through together. The difficulties or ease with which problems are solved and each party is understood will depend on the family's mode of communication and the teacher's biases. It is first and foremost the teacher's responsibility to make it work. It is especially difficult for beginning teachers who feel as judged or as insecure as the parents. If you are unsure about how to react in the beginning, try and listen to the parents and get to know their way of communicating. Before you react or become defensive, try and remember: "Ah, they are being *subjective* and emotionally attached to their child. This is good. This is how it should be. I am the professional, the *objective* person and must work out what to do

that will be best for *all* of the children in my class as well as each individual child."

It is important to arrange conferences twice a year where parents and teachers can discuss the child's progress and share information back and forth respectfully. If you remember the parents' subjectivity and fear of being judged, you will make an effort so that by the end of the conversation, parents leave proud and feel empowered and loving of their children. Parent-teacher conferences are not a time for scolding or warnings. Concerns should be shared and discussed all year long in a respectful and caring manner.

There are many different ways to organize whole group activities for parents: Open house before school starts; meetings with an expert guest speaker on curriculum, behavior management, children's literature, or some other topic of interest to parents; holiday parties; and general informational meetings. Inviting parents to participate and become involved in their child's education can also take many forms. For example, as a classroom teacher, I always organized a parent advisory committee where once a month parents, who acted as representatives of all the parents in the class, would meet with me to discuss any issue of concern, including curriculum, facility, teacher interactions, food, equipment, fund raising, playground or anything of specific interest to them. We would notify all the parents about participation and they were encouraged to contact the committee members with concerns that their representatives could bring up for discussion at our monthly meetings.

Parents might want to come into their child's class to share a talent, their expertise or to read a story. When I was director of the campus child care center, parents were invited to celebrate a "special day" of their choosing with their child's class. It could be related to a holiday they liked to celebrate, birthday, or anything at all. Field trips are another excellent opportunity to invite parents to participate. Teachers always need many adult, helping hands when organizing a trip with a class full of young children.

If you invite parents into your class to participate with the class in general, be aware that their child might be sensitive to sharing their parent with others. It is natural for a child and parent to want to spend time together. When parents were invited to participate in my classroom, I gave them one simple task—*be with your child*. I did not turn them into a helper or a teacher of the other children. If they wanted to do that and their child was willing for that to happen, I was supportive and encouraging. However, I did not expect them to take on that role.

A bulletin board is a good way to let parents know what is going on in the classroom. Articles or suggested parenting books can be posted there too, or other kinds of information that can suggest parenting support of one kind or another. Newsletters or daily news bulletins are a good way for parents to be kept up to date with what their children are learning day by day. In child care settings, where children spend many long hours away from their parents, a notebook is a good way to communicate with parents with an intense and busy work schedule who are unable to spend time in the center. Teachers write information and parents can reply if they do not find the time to speak in person with the teacher.

Home visits are an excellent way to get to know children in their own natural environment, away from the institutional setting and the teacher's *turf* that everyone is accustomed to. When the teacher comes to the child's home she opens herself up to the parent's domain and levels the playing field.

> Home visiting has been a central part of working with families and their young children in many programs all around the country, all through the century. . . . Meeting in a comfortable, relaxed environment opens communication between parents, child and teacher, and can set the tone for a positive home-school relationship (Fox-Barnett & Meyer, 1992, page 45).

Child-sensitive home visits, where the teacher does not arrive as an educator of parents, but rather spends time specifically with the child in her home, communicates to the family that their child is of primary concern and reinforces the child's feeling of self-worth (page 46). Home visits can make an enormous difference to the quality of the relationship between teacher and parent and teacher and child. However, they take time and it is often difficult to find a way to fit them into an already busy schedule. It is a dedicated teacher, indeed, who sees this activity as worthwhile and finds a way to visit the children at home at some point in the school year.

The Beginning or Novice Teacher

If you are a beginning or novice teacher, be compassionate with yourself as you learn to negotiate your relationships with families of the children in your class. Especially during your first year, you find yourself overwhelmed with *learning the ropes,* and understanding the school's culture, rules and regulations. Many of you are just happy to survive the first year and are unable to think further than surviving the day-to-day assignments of organizing and managing a classroom and getting paperwork completed for the administration (Katz, 1995). As we have discussed throughout this chapter, working with families is one of the most challenging aspects of teaching. Overcoming our biases and navigating between the subjective, emotional attachments of parents and the objective professional stance as a teacher are not easy tasks. It takes skill and practice, time, and experience and can be painful as we learn the best way to communicate appropriately and productively with families.

As you experiment with some of the suggested activities for parent participation and involvement, take it slowly and carefully. Learn which activities will be supportive and encouraging for you as a beginning teacher and try not to take on too much at once. Some teachers are comfortable sharing themselves with parents right from the beginning. Others will take a bit longer. Remember, you also come with a family. Just as the children in your class do. Your family's cultural norms are bound to be different to many of the children's families in your classroom. If, in the first year, you try one or two activities and they are successful with parents, the following year will be easier and you can add in more. Remember, if you are afraid of parents who seem defensive and passionate about the care and education of their child, they are most likely even more afraid of you! And, their children are more precious to them than anything else in the world.

However long it takes, and whatever obstacles might rise up to greet you as you develop authentic, caring, professional and respectful relationships with families, teacher-parent cooperation is a most valuable contribution to children's emotional well-being and academic achievement in the long run.

References

Fox-Barnett, M., & Meyer, T. (1992). The teacher's playing at my house this week! *Young Children, July, Vol. 47. Number 5. 45–50.*

Gestwicki, C. (2007). *Home, School, and Community Relations.* Clifton Park, New York: Thomson Delmar Learning.

Jacobson, T. (2003). *Confronting Our Discomfort: Clearing the Way for Anti-Bias in Early Childhood.* Portsmouth, New Hampshire: Heinemann.

Katz, L. (1995). "The Developmental Stages of Teachers" in *Talks with Teachers of Young Children: A Collection.* Stamford, CT: Ablex.

Kohn, A. (2006). *The Homework Myth: Why Our Kids Get Too Much of a Bad Thing.* Cambridge, MA: Da Capo Press.

McShepard, R., Goler, T., & Batson, M.C. (2007). The rap on culture: How anti-education messages in media, at home, and on the street hold back African American youth. *PolicyBridge, May 2007. www.policy-bridge.org*

CHAPTER SEVEN

Your Best Friend or Your Worst Enemy

Youth Popular Culture,
Pedagogy, and Curriculum in
Urban Classrooms

Jeff Duncan-Andrade

This chapter discusses the potential of youth popular culture to create an engaging and empowering twenty-first-century curriculum in schools. Specifically, this chapter investigates three key questions around the issue of developing a culturally relevant curriculum for students traditionally disenfranchised by U.S. schools: 1) What popular cultural literacies are urban youth investing themselves in?; 2) Why are they investing themselves in these areas?; and 3) How can schools more effectively incorporate those literacies into the school culture? I begin with the proposition that teachers should make better use of their access to youth cultural interests. Next, this chapter draws on education theory and interviews with students from an urban high school to examine the relevance of youth popular culture to curricular design. The chapter concludes with a call for educators to build on the momentum of the 1980s multicultural education movement by developing pedagogical strategies and curricula that draw on youth cultural literacies. Ultimately, this chapter aims to synthesize data and theory as a means of discussing promising ways to teach urban students.

Popular Culture and Pedagogy

It is important to begin with a discussion of the term "youth popular culture" and its relevance in relation to pedagogy. Broadly defined, youth popular culture includes the various cultural activities in which young people invest their time, including but not limited to: music, television, movies, video games, sport, Internet, text messaging, style, and language practices. Central to a discussion of youth popular culture is the point that culture is not just a process of consumption (critical or passive); it is also a process of production, of individual and collective interpretation (meaning making) through representations of styles, **discursive practices**, **semiotics**, and texts. The complexity of this relationship between cultural consumption and production warrants some attention here in order to more fully understand youth popular culture as a pedagogical tool. Recent theoretical notions of the purpose and role of popular culture in society suggest that it is a "rapidly shifting . . . argument and debate about a society and its own culture" (Hall, 1992). Williams (1980) argues that any discussion of culture must pay attention to the dynamic nature of culture as a set of "activities of men [and women] in real social and economic relationships, containing fundamental contradictions and variations and therefore always in a state of dynamic process" (Williams, 1991; p. 410). West's (1999) "new cultural politics of difference" and Hall's (1992) discussion of popular culture echo Williams' insistence that modern discussions of culture recognize popular culture as a simultaneous site of resistance and commodification. For West (1999) there is "new kind of cultural worker in the making, associated with a new politics of difference" (West, 1999; p. 119). This cultural worker grapples

Discursive practices

Rational argument to support a position.

Semiotics

The study of signs and symbols.

with what West calls "an inescapable double-bind" as their cultural participation and production "is a gesture that is simultaneously progressive and co-opted" (p. 120). This description of a new century popular cultural participant fits with Hall's insistence that the struggle over cultural **hegemony** is "waged as much in popular culture as anywhere else" (p. 468) and that space is inherently a contradictory space. Nowhere is the contradictory nature of popular culture more clear than in youth popular culture—a socio-politically charged space because of its increasing influence on the cultural sensibilities of the culture industry. Its increasing focus on youth has spurred debate over the implications of popular culture for the field of education, particularly around issues of pedagogy. To better understand the competing pedagogical ideologies, it is worth drawing from Grossberg (1994) at length. He suggests that there are four types of pedagogical practices, all of which differently engage the value of popular culture in education. Grossberg's first model, "hierarchical practice," is one where the teacher is judge and jury of truth. He is careful to recognize that there are times when it is appropriate for teachers to take this sort of authoritative stance, but that the problem emerges when . . .

> the teacher assumes that he or she understands the real meanings of particular texts and practices, the real relations of power embodied within them, and the real interests of the different social groups brought together in the classroom or in the broader society (Grossberg, 1994).

This culturally imperialistic approach to teaching, what Freire (1970) referred to as the "banking concept of education," is symbolic of a set of material relations of power where teachers control the creation, interpretation, legitimation, and dissemination of knowledge and students are expected to "patiently receive, memorize, and repeat" (p. 53) that information. Grossberg's second model, "dialogic practice" attempts to avoid a teacher-centered system of knowledge control by creating opportunities for the silenced to speak for themselves. To be sure, it is

Hegemony
The domination of one group over another.

important that educators actively engage their students in Hall's argument and debate over cultural sensibilities. However, as Grossberg points out, educators seeking to give voice to the voiceless, often wrongly presume that these groups have not already created these spaces for themselves (p. 16). They fail to recognize that historically marginalized student groups often develop sophisticated ways of cultural participation that schools do not acknowledge or legitimate (MacLeod, 1987; Willis, 1981), and that these cultural activities are often responses to structural and material conditions of inequality. Similar to dialogic practice, Grossberg's "praxical pedagogy" can underestimate the cultural activity that is already taking place in the lives of students. The praxical pedagogy model draws heavily from critical pedagogy's aim to develop agency among marginalized groups to change their material conditions. It moves from critical dialogue for understanding toward a pedagogy of action where students are given tools to "intervene into their own history" (p. 16). Grossberg points out that this approach can be doubly problematic. First, it can lead teachers to operate from the deficit perspective that students are coming to the classroom as "empty vessels" (Freire, 1970), lacking the skills and experiences that would allow them to be active agents for change. Secondly, teachers run the risk of replicating the shortcomings of hierarchical pedagogy if they presume that there is a fixed set of skills that will empower students to engage in critical action. Teachers must be aware that a scripted approach to developing agency in young people discounts critical cultural activities that are already there and overlooks the fact that oppressive conditions require context-specific solutions.

Youth Popular Culture and Curriculum

To manage the complexity of fulfilling the role of instructional leader, while avoiding a replication of oppressive relations of power, Grossberg suggests that teachers "locate places from which [they] can

construct and disseminate knowledge in relation to the materiality of power, conflict, and oppression" (p. 17). He describes a fourth pedagogical model, a "pedagogy of articulation and risk" that avoids the pitfalls of the first three models while maintaining some claims to authority and a commitment to developing the capacity of students as critical civic participants. It is a pedagogy that " . . . neither starts with nor works within a set of texts but, rather, deals with the formations of the popular, the cartographies of taste, stability, and mobility within which students are located" (p. 18). This fourth space admits to an understanding of the complexity of culture and the role of the pedagogue in navigating that complexity. A pedagogy of articulation and risk recognizes that popular culture is a preeminent site of contestation for cultural hegemonic practices (Hall, 1996). It denies false **binaries** which suggest that students are at once either passive or critical recipients and producers of culture. Finally, it bears false witness to the paralyzing notion that cultural hegemony is a zero-sum game by insisting that cultural activity is "always about shifting the balance of power in the relations of culture" (p. 468).

Binaries

Either / or conceptualizations. Right or wrong.

Rethinking the Value of Youth Popular Culture in Schools

Teachers are often the group of outsiders most familiar with youth popular culture, from style to media to language practices. This rich database of information is, at best, untapped by schools. At worst, schools reject and debase youth culture as academically irrelevant and socially reprehensible. This adversarial position, often taken by teachers, contributes to many students' perceptions that school is at odds with their personal and cultural interests. Regardless of teachers' and school officials' good intentions, the choice to make youth culture one of the central battlegrounds over cultural sensibilities creates needless and destructive cultural distances instead of opening access to knowledge and supporting, trusting relationships. To understand the potential of youth culture as a pedagogical scaffold, it is important to explore two dimensions of it: 1) youth culture as an avenue that can provide teachers with access to knowledge of and relationships with their students; and 2) youth culture as an avenue that can provide youth with access to the broader society's valued knowledge. A final caveat that is important to include in all discussions of teachers' accessing youth culture for pedagogical and democratic ends: Nothing said here suggests that the teacher abrogate her or his own cultural predilections or "standards" in favor of what may be, almost by definition, transient styles, language, and so forth. Not all cultural discontinuities can be or should be resolved. Perhaps the most important lesson here is that the cultures present in classrooms and under examination here should be seen as additive rather than as zero sum.

With the growing pervasiveness and persuasiveness of twenty-first-century youth culture, most particularly the media (television, music, video games, movies, magazines), traditional school curriculum, coupled with traditional pedagogies, stands little chance of capturing the hearts and minds of young people. Traditional teacher education has approached this attention to "hearts and minds" from psychological (largely behavioral) perspectives. Some educational theorists have become increasingly more critical of this treatment of learning as a largely individual matter, "culture" as an impediment to learning (Hull, Rose, Fraser, & Castellano, 1991; McDermott & Varenne, 1995; Valdes, 1996). Building on criticisms of cultural deficit models, an increasing number of studies have focused on culture as additive, encouraging schools to make better use of students' cultures (Moll et al., 1992; Valenzuela, 1999). This "culture as additive" scholarship emphasizes that the ready access that schools have to students' cultures can be an important tool for teachers attempting to create more engaging educational environments.[1] Basic teacherly sensibilities, honed through attention to

the lives of students sometimes referred to as "caring" (Noddings, 1992) give teachers tremendous access to youth cultural interests. Through an ongoing analysis of these popular cultural interests, teachers will be better able to design curriculum that keeps pace with modern media's cultural production machine. This knowledge of youth culture will also permit teachers to provide their students with productive critiques of the more negative elements. Without this grounding, teachers are left to moralizing sermons and culturally isolating out of hand dismissals that have been problematized by the aforementioned literature that critiques cultural deficit models. Why is this a useful goal for classroom teachers? Many educators agree that schools should give young people access to critical thinking skills. The place where the ideological road splits is over the question of how to best accomplish this goal. For most, critical thinking means that students can engage in analysis and critique of a set of texts similar to those examined in the teacher's schooling experience. In this model, academic literacy is imparted using time-honored curricula (often referred to as the **canon**) and pedagogical strategies. This method of schooling positions students as empty vessels and teachers as the depositers of knowledge into these vessels, described by Freire (1970) as the "banking concept of education." Valenzuela (1999) refers to this pedagogical approach as "aesthetic caring," and differentiates between this sort of schooling and "educación," an approach that foregrounds an ethic of "authentic caring." According to Valenzuela (1999), "schooling" emphasizes an aesthetic caring for students, one that brokers caring as a tradeoff; that is, students are cared for in proportion to their willingness to exchange their own cultural sensibilities for the dominant cultural preferences of the school. Teachers who promote "education" (or educación)[2] over schooling employ an ethic of authentic caring; that is, they create a classroom culture that draws from the cultural sensibilities of young people as a point of

Canon

A comprehensive sample of important works such as key figures in American literature.

strength for increasing intellectual development (Valenzuela, 1999; see also Moll et al., 1992). Critical theorists such as Apple (1990) argue that these competing pedagogical ideologies are the result of the fact that education is inherently a "political act." For that reason, Apple suggests that a liberatory education should focus on the development of critical literacies and sensibilities that challenge traditional ways of schooling. Likewise, Delpit (1988) and Darling-Hammond (1997, 1998) both remind us that power and politics are being brokered every day in schools. From this more critical perspective on schooling, teachers recognize school as an institution that mitigates the distribution of power and the development of identity; they also stake a claim to their capacity as agents of change, disrupting the business-as-usual approach to pedagogy and curriculum. The tool for this raised consciousness is self-critical reflexivity. This process challenges one's own political and cultural subjectivities as they are manifested in the choices made about what is taught and how it is taught. Ultimately, the goal of such a process is to better understand what works for kids, why it is working, and how schools can become more adept at incorporating those things into the classroom and the larger school culture.

The Relevance of Youth Popular Culture for Curriculum Design

According to Nielsen's "Report on Television" Nielsen Media Research (1998) the average child watches three hours of television a day. The Kaiser Foundation (1999) reports that this engagement with electronic media more than doubles to six and one half hours per day when various forms of electronic media are included (i.e., television, movies, video games). This increasingly intense investment of U.S. youth in the media has led the American Academy of Pediatricians (2001) to issue a policy statement regarding the impact of this issue on children's health. The policy statement lists several

recommendations for parents and educators, including the following:

- View television programs along with children and discuss the content.
- Use controversial programming as a stepping-off point to initiate discussions about family values, violence, sex and sexuality, and drugs.
- Support efforts to establish comprehensive media-education programs in schools (Committee on Public Education, 2001).

More recent studies of youth and the media indicate that the hours spent with electronic media are even higher among poor students of color (Goodman, 2003; Nielson Media Research, 1998). Given this data and the Academy of Pediatrician's recommendations for addressing the growing relevance of the media in the lives of young people, two questions seem particularly relevant for teachers to investigate when pursuing a pedagogy and curriculum that addresses the cultural needs of urban children: 1) What are students investing themselves in? and 2) How are they investing themselves in these areas? The answers, although dynamic enough to require on-going inquiry, are readily available to educators if they talk with and observe their students.

A Teacher's Perspective on Youth Culture

While teaching high school English in Oakland, California, I spent significant amounts of my time studying the popular culture of my students. I sought to make their engagement with popular cultural texts (particularly films, music, and television) a centerpiece of intellectual inquiry in the classroom. One tool I used to become informed about the usefulness of youth popular cultural texts was interviews with students. I typically interviewed students from across the academic performance spectrum to allow for multiple perspectives. The interviews used in this piece are from three of my African-American male twelfth-grade students.[3] Isaiah was a consistent honor-roll student who attended Howard University after graduation. Shaun was a student whose grade point average hovered around 2.5 for most of his high school career; he briefly attended Hayward State University before dropping out to work full time. Yancey was a student who struggled to be consistent in school, but was able to do just enough to pass most of his courses; he managed to gather enough credits to graduate and was considering a local junior college.

What is good popular culture?

ANDRADE: Do you think that using things out of popular culture can allow students to learn the skills they'll need to do well on the AP and the SAT type of tests, to write critically, and develop the ability to find spaces in canonical literature that they can relate to? Or, is there just nothing there in the canonical literature for them to relate to?

YANCEY: I think if you show someone how to handle popular culture, if they can understand that, then I think they can understand canonical. Yeah. They can definitely relate that as one and take it on a, take it together [putting his hands together to make a ball]. I mean, I think that's what your question was.

ANDRADE: To take the popular culture together with traditional literature?

SHAUN: Yup.

YANCEY: Yeah.

SHAUN [POINTING AT YANCEY]: I agree with him.

YANCEY: Yeah, I agree. That, that if you can understand popular culture, if you're taught how to understand it as popular culture, that if you're taught to look at it in a certain way and analyze it in a certain way . . .

SHAUN [INTERJECTING]: Critique it, yup.

YANCEY: . . . then I think, definitely, you can take that knowledge and analyze anything.

My students' sensibilities about the pedagogical power of popular culture in classrooms is not a particularly novel idea—theoretical positions on the value of this instructional approach date back to the early twentieth century (Dewey, 1938). In his insightful text on the importance of incorporating learned experiences into the curriculum, Dewey (1938) argues: "...[it is important to] emphasize the fact, first, that young people in traditional schools do have experiences... It sets a problem to the educator. It is [her] his business to arrange for the kind of experiences which, while they do not repel the student, but rather engage his activities, are nevertheless, more than immediately enjoyable since they promote having desirable future experiences' (p. 27).

Modern critical literacy theorists have continued to make the case for the value of critical examinations of youth cultural literacies (Duncan-Andrade & Morrell, in press; Gee, 2004; Giroux, 1983, 1997; Kress, 2003; Lee, 1993; Morrell, 2004; Morrell & Duncan-Andrade, 2003). Critical educational theorists have also maintained that school curricula and pedagogy should more profoundly reflect the popular cultural interests and needs of students (Giroux et al., 1996; Giroux & Simon, 1989; Morrell & Duncan-Andrade, 2002, 2003). For Giroux and Simon (1989), this challenge of using popular culture in classrooms can place teachers at an intellectual and pedagogical crossroads.

"Popular culture and social difference can be taken up by educators either as a pleasurable form of knowledge—power...or such practices can be understood as the terrain on which we meet our students in a pedagogical encounter informed by a project of possibility that enables rather than disables collective prosperity, and social justice" (Giroux & Simon, 1989). Recent classroom-based studies support the merit of the latter of these two roads, that is, educational practices that engage urban students of color in critical intellectual interactions with youth popular cultural forms: When challenged by a critical educator, students begin to understand that the more profound dimension of their freedom lies exactly in the recognition of constraints that can be overcome. They can discover for themselves, in the process of becoming more and more critical, that it is impossible to deny the constitutive power of their consciousness in the social practice in which they participate. The radical pedagogy is dialectical and has as its goal to enable students to become critical of the hegemonic practices that have shaped their experiences and perceptions in hopes of freeing themselves from the bonds of these dominating ideologies. In order for this to happen, learners must be involved in transformative discourse, which legitimizes the wishes, decisions, and dreams of the people involved (Morrell & Duncan-Andrade, 2003). This sort of empowering pedagogy, focused on developing students' capacities as agents of critical awareness and social change, must consist of a critical youth cultural literacy—one that deconstructs the formation of cultural sensibilities resultant from "the power of postmodern literacies such as film and television" (McLaren & Hammer, 1996).

Sadly, my experience is that teachers who do use popular culture often do so in ways that unwittingly reinforce the already present cultural hierarchy. They do this by using the popular cultural texts (usually movies, music, or sport) as a reward—given out to students after the "important work" in the class has been done. In the English classroom, this most commonly manifests itself in the form of a movie at the end of a curriculum unit. This usually translates into one or two days of "fun time" where kids don't have to learn and teachers don't have to teach. The film is never treated as a text to be studied, and what's worse is that this leads to a tacit agreement between student and teacher that youth popular culture is simply a school's tool of pacification unworthy of intellectual interrogation. Young people are never taught to see their engagement with media as a form of literacy development,

nor are they taught how to enhance and refine that development. For some time I have found this misuse of youth culture to be troubling and culturally imperialistic on the part of our educational system. It presumes that for the vast majority of students' free time—upwards of 60 hours per week—students are intellectually unengaged. While this may be true in some senses, I would argue that schools have some culpability in this disengagement with media. Rather than providing young people with the tools for a critical media literacy, we have villainized their culture of media literacy and unwittingly set off a war between the legitimate knowledge of schools and the nefarious knowledge of youth culture. This is a silly war for educators to fight for a number of reasons: 1) It wrongly presumes the higher cultural and intellectual order of printed texts, an argument for which we have no evidence other than our own imperialistic cultural sensibilities; 2) It wrongly presumes that we could not teach the same higher-order thinking skills across academic content areas, using a rich combination of media texts[4] and printed texts; 3) It wrongly presumes that to turn to a pedagogy and curriculum that emphasizes the use of youth popular cultural texts will insure that children will never learn to love reading printed texts and therefore be denied important literacy skills and the richness of the literary canon; 4) It wrongly presumes that education is not supposed to be fun for young people but is, instead, a rite of passage into adulthood where their childlike sensibilities are removed and replaced with the more upstanding sensibilities of adults; and 5) It wrongly presumes that popular cultural texts are more engaging for young people because they are simplistic and nurture a more visceral interaction.

The Nielsen studies (1998, 2000) make it clear that our children are reading texts and that they are doing it with the voracity we might well attribute to budding literary scholars. These studies only further confirm Luke's (1997) preceding argument that there is an "urgent need for educators to engage constructively with media, popular and youth culture to better understand how these discourses structure childhood, adolescence and students' knowledge" (Luke, 1997, p. xx). The problem with moving this project forward is that many educators do not see youth cultural texts as texts at all. But, young people do.

ANDRADE: What types of popular cultural texts do you feel are powerful for their ability to teach young people?

SHAUN: Well, there was one article, not a article, but you know there is this magazine called *The Source*. You know that. I mean *The Source* will give you some information to make you think about the world. That's how I look at it. *The Source* is kinda biased too though—they biased toward the East Coast over the West. So, I couldn't just say *The Source*. But, I mean, *The Source* do have some powerful stuff in it—you just gotta go through and look for it, and look, and look. 'Cause I mean some of them articles you don't really care for, but I don't really care, it doesn't matter to me. I mean, I don't really care what hooriders are doing after they tour. But, they do talk and get deep, I mean, like the letters. I think we should go into the letters in here sometimes.

ANDRADE: What about music? Do you think there's music that's deep?

SHAUN: A lot. A lot of music is deep. Damn near every single tape Tupac has made you could sit there and write any kind of critique, analyzation. Goodie MOB, who else? Fatal.

ISAIAH: KRS One.

SHAUN: KRS One. Yeah, that's, ooh!

YANCEY: That's a deep boy right there.

ANDRADE: What's deep about KRS One or Goodie MOB or Tupac?

SHAUN: They sit there and tell you what's going on in their lives. And every time they talk about some-

thing that's going on in their life, you can always relate it back to your life [Isaiah and Yancey shake their heads in affirmation], that's how I look at it. And, like certain songs on an album, like what song, 'cause I remember we had that assignment where you pick your own song. I had so many rap songs I had up in my head that it was ridiculous [Yancey and Isaiah laugh and nod their heads as to affirm the feeling]. I had like Tupac, and I had Dogg Pound, I had, man, I must have printed out like three different, what ya ma call it, playlists.

ISAIAH: Yeah, lyrics.

SHAUN: Yeah, lyrics. I must have printed out at least three different ones and just sat there and had to look at them, see which one I thought was the deepest, which one I could write the most on. There was so many out there. The one song that really stuck out to me, that I still be thinkin' about right now is, "Reality" by Dogg Pound. I like that song. That song, man, every time I listen to it, it just make me think.

YANCEY: Well, I would relate music as, basically poetry. It's too many that I could probably name off, but I know most of the time when I listen to music, like I would say, you know, sometimes I'll just listen to the beats and listen to the music, not pertaining to the words. But when I do decide, ok, let me pay attention to this artist and see where he's coming from and see what he's saying, they're real deep. I mean, they dig in there! It's just like watching *The Godfather*. It's like, "wow!" It's like, this is just not, you know, "hey baby, let's go groove" . . .

SHAUN [INTERJECTING]: [smirking at the stereotypes of music] "kick it."

YANCEY: . . . or whatever. It's politics in there. It talks about, you know, [pounding his fist into his hand for emphasis] society and, and the drugs and . . .

SHAUN [INTERJECTING]: Struggle! The struggle!

YANCEY: . . . yeah, the struggle there is, and that people don't see [Shaun nods his head in agreement].

The media, you know, what the media decides to not so much talk about and cover up, it's all out in the music, you know. It's just like books you know, people that read books probably have a better understanding than people that just watch the news or watch T.V. of how hard it is to live in the United States. I think the people that have been through they've been there and they've done that and the way they tell it's like they bring you right in their face and it's like you begin to understand a lot more. And you're like, it's just like "wow!" It's real deep.

SHAUN: The reason I say he [KRS One] is deep is because he talks onto subjects that people usually don't want to talk about. Let me think of one song [pause] (to himself): I've got so many songs in my head.

Rather than seeing artists such as KRS One or Tupac Shakur as the creators of intellectually meritous texts, we categorize them and other youth cultural texts, such as electronic media and music, as central contributors to national health concerns over youth violence and adolescent obesity (Malkin, 2003; Steele, 1990). I wonder if we would be attributing these same national health crises to books if children were spending the same amount of time on the couch reading as they are currently spending engaging with electronic media? Would we argue that children are dropping out of school and using foul language because they read J. D. Salinger's *Catcher in the Rye* a dozen times over? Would we argue that children were committing patricide because they played Hamlet in the school play? It is difficult to picture a scenario where we reproach a child for reading too much, but we are quick to chastise children for spending too much time in front of electronic media. This speaks to a conservative national mentality so entrenched in historical notions of literacy that it is dismissive of the potential of youth popular cultural litera-

cies to be one of the richest sources for critical literacy development to emerge in our lifetimes (Gee, 2004; Kress, 2003; Luke, 1999). What is worse is that while we do not deny the impact of the media on young people—Shaun has "so many songs" in his head—we shirk our responsibility as educators to engage young people in the project of critical media literacy development, an endeavor that will better equip them to engage these influential texts. Young people are well aware of the power present in popular cultural texts. They are also confident that teachers could use these texts to teach them the academic literacy skills that schools purport to want to develop in their students.

YANCEY: I would pertain KRS One, basically a hundred percent, to *Savage Inequalities*. I would relate those two real closely to one another. For Kozol in *Savage Inequalities*, he's basically just talking about our school system and the way it's corrupted by the government and how our society is built and how there is such a false in the word "United" States; how it's such a free and liberal country. If I didn't read *Savage Inequalities*, I think listening to KRS One basically would tell me everything, basically relate because he breaks it down the same and it's got a beat to it so you're more interested perhaps. You know, you might be grooving to it and it could be digging deep. But, I relate those two hand in hand. [Smirking] Students probably could teach the teachers.

ANDRADE: What type of impact do you think that would have on students . . .

SHAUN: (exhaling loudly, smiling, and laughing) gshh-hhh . . .

ANDRADE: . . . if there was a KRS One class or a rap in literature class or something like that?

SHAUN: Well, uh, just like, I know what you're saying. But I mean at Cal Berkeley don't they have like a Tupac class?

ANDRADE: Yeah.

SHAUN: I bet you that attendance is like a hundred percent isn't it? It's like I know if they was to have one of those classes here, it wouldn't be no, I don't think there'd be that many people cuttin.' I bet you the class'd be overfull and to the point that people are still in line in the office tryin' to get in. And the reason I say that is because, if they had a Goodie M.O.B., 2Pac, or KRS One class, that's automatic. People already know about them, and they already listen to them, so they already have influence over people. So that's just going to make them want to come to the class even more to learn what they are talking about. And it's going to make them, how you say, just for the fact that it's them teaching, I think they're gonna give them a little more respect than they're gonna give to a regular teacher. I'm not sayin' that regular teachers don't get respect, I'm just sayin' they'd be more obedient in class, that's how I'd say it.

ANDRADE: Do you think that, those classes, those works, those authors could teach kids the same skills that teachers currently try to teach kids using Shakespeare, Chaucer?

SHAUN: Yeah, most definitely I do. Because, the way they'll do it I think it'll get the kids' attention more than what the teachers are doing. Because Shakespeare and *The Odyssey*, not tryin' to hooride, but those kinds of books, people I mean, I wouldn't have read that unless you assigned it and that's on the real. I wouldn't have went in there and grabbed it and looked at it or nuttin.' I would have just passed it, "whew," and moved onto something else. I mean *The Odyssey*, that just automatically make you, not even that, how you say, just the width, just how big the books look, automatically when you see it. I'm not tryin' to say that's the reason I'm gonna turn a book down just cause of the width. I'll grab a skinny book and be like "nah." I'm just saying, I mean, I grab a fat book and read it if it's interesting. It's like the book I got at the house reading now, is . . . about Death Row. It's about how corrupt Suge Knight was and how he did all this, and I know hecka stuff that I didn't never know about Suge Knight and all that stuff. And that pages. I'm only on like a hundred pages now. And I'm still goin' to certain chapters and readin' it all over just cause I'm interested in that kinda stuff.

Worth noting is that both Shaun and Yancey reference printed texts in their discussion about the value of popular cultural texts. They are not arguing for the banishment of printed texts. They are arguing for a more culturally relevant curriculum, one that encourages them to bring to bear the youth cultural knowledge that they possess. Perhaps the recent test score scare tactics that encourage educators to believe we are dealing with a growing population of illiterate children are wide of the mark. Perhaps the student resistance to printed texts that we are seeing in schools is a conscious response by students to what Valenzuela has called "aesthetic caring" (Valenzuela, 1999). Kohl has characterized this as a student's decision to "not learn" (Kohl, 1994). This way of looking at student performance in schools drastically changes our notions of what is actually causing trends of failure. It encourages educators to do away with deficit notions of diminished intellectual capacity on the part of the student by considering acts of resistance to the curriculum as a form of student agency, that not learning is a statement on the part of students to say that they will not be subjected to a curriculum and pedagogy that is dismissive of them and their cultural knowledge. Both Yancey and Shaun suggest that educators need to rethink their position on "official knowledge" (Apple, 1993):

YANCEY: I think, definitely, I think those types of artists such as KRS One, Goodie M.O.B., so on and so forth should definitely be accepted into our school system. For the simple reason that they basically have the same they're writing, I mean, they're putting it down on paper and they're just saying it with a beat and rhyming it out to you. But, that shouldn't mean . . .

SHAUN [INTERJECTING]: That's even more complex.

YANCEY: . . . yeah, basically. It shouldn't even be looked upon differently. I don't know. I think that maybe our, uh, the way the school system is set up they're maybe intimidated by bringing such a thing out. That the students that might actually want to learn this and be able to get something out of it to use in each day of our lives now, to be able to push, strive to excellence through that literature. I think they see it as being, I think they see it as kids will probably understand that better so why don't we make it difficult for them. And if they can make it through this difficult process then they can make it through another difficult process. And, I mean, I disagree with that.

SHAUN: Uh huh. Yup.

YANCEY: I think that just because it perceives to be music and it looks easy to understand. You can take music to a whole different level. I mean, it's on you, on how you teach it, how you take upon it, how dig you deep, I mean, how far down you dig into the music. If you listen to just, you know, the beat and you just let it go through your ears and you're just dancing to it, that's another story. But, if you're sitting there and you're actually writing what he says down and, or she says down, and you look at it and you study it, you can get a lot out of that.

SHAUN: Fo' sho'!

These student perspectives resonate with an increasing body of research (Duncan-Andrade & Morrell, in press; Finn, 1999; Moll et al., 1992; Morrell & Duncan-Andrade, 2003; Valenzuela, 1999) that has found that urban students, particularly urban students of color, are mis-portrayed as being intellectually disengaged. In fact, what we find in discussions with urban youngsters is not necessarily that they want less time in classrooms; rather they want classrooms that are more worth spending time in.

ANDRADE: What would you change about this class, or the unit, or the way that the class incorporates popular culture and the canon?

SHAUN: I remember before when someone said that the class should be longer. And I agree with him that the class should be longer because when we are in class and we're discussing, I mean like when we watch a film like *The Godfather* or something, we'd watch it for like the first 15 or 20 minutes of class and then we've only got like 30 minutes left to discuss it. But, if we're going to discuss *The Godfather* it's going to take longer than 30 minutes to discuss a little, like, one and a half scenes. So, I mean, that's why I think class needs to be at least two hours long.

YANCEY: I would agree to class being longer, as to this class. But, seeing, pertaining that to my other classes . . .

SHAUN [INTERJECTING]: Yeah, that's true.

YANCEY: . . . I think I would definitely suffer to be able to sit in one of those other classes for two hours, for the simple fact that I think the teacher basically doesn't have enough curriculum set up for us to participate in. So, basically, all you're doing is, I mean going in there to be sitting there, and you know . . .

SHAUN [INTERJECTING]: Waste of time.

YANCEY: . . . there's nuttin' to do, basically. I've literally dropped a class, completely, because of that situation. Where I would walk into the class and the teacher had nothing set up and it's basically talk time, you know, social time, social hour. And, to make it two hours, for all classes, I think is, it would be good, but they would have to definitely evaluate each class a lot more and justify as to why that class should be longer. For the simple fact that if I was to be in that class for two hours, simply just falling behind when I could be in such a class where the teacher is prepared to teach you and you're ready to get knowledge . . .

SHAUN: Information.

YANCEY: Basically.

ISAIAH: Yeah, I mean I've had the fortunate experience of being in your class all but one year since the eighth grade. Prior to that it was more or less you read, you know what I'm saying, you read short stories, novels, etcetera and it's just a story. You basically just summarize the plot, you know, and the characters, and "why did Peter do such and such," you know. I think it's very important that, the way we take it in here is much more in depth analysis of the text and that it's texts that mean something to us. And it is, I mean, as far as just understanding it not just from the words, but also for the implications of it in a person or the individual's circumstance . . . I mean I understand what other teachers do in their classes as far as doing a book report and what that consists of. I mean it's not about just knowing what a character did or just the basic plot, but the implications of their actions and a character's motives. That's very important in understanding any text, and most teachers don't do that.

In my experience, these three students' comments reflect the sentiments of many urban students in their desire for a more intellectually rigorous literacy curriculum that employs youth popular culture as a bridge to traditional literacy skills. To be sure, young people want the opportunity to represent their own cultural knowledge, but they are also clamoring for pedagogies that employ this knowledge as a scaffold into skills that allow for more complex literary analyses. To some degree, this request is quite the opposite of current curriculum and pedagogy trends in urban public schools.

Back(Wards) to Basics

Steven Goodman, a renowned educator of urban youth in New York City, critiques conservative cultural and literacy theorists for their unwillingness to recognize the cultural and linguistic assets urban youth develop in their homes and communities. He highlights the work of E. D. Hirsch, Jr. (2001) as a prime example of the increasingly powerful conservative voice in urban school literacy programs, a voice that is calling for a return to drill-and practice exercises that frequently cause "low income urban students to become even more detached and disengaged from school because it widens the disconnect between what students are exposed to out of school and what they are force-fed in school" (Goodman, 2003). Rather than approaching the problem from Hirsch's deficit model which calls for educators to see poor students, particularly students of color, as culturally deficient, more progressive literacy theorists see the problem with the school-based literacy gap as resting largely on the shoulders of the school (Finn, 1999; Gee, 2004; Lee, 1993; Mahiri, 1998; Morrell & Duncan-Andrade, 2003). These perspectives on literacy recognize that there is only one correct form. The debate for progressives is not over whether school-based literacy is important, but over how it scaffolds into school-based literacies.

Rethinking Cultural Relevance in Classroom Literacy

The 1980s gave rise to a multicultural education movement that called cultural awareness to the front of educational debate. The positive impact that emerged out of this discourse cannot be overstated. It has made teachers around the nation more sensitive to the needs of students of color, particularly in the selection of curriculum. James Banks, often at the center of this dialogue, insists on the need for a multicultural pedagogy and curriculum: "Teachers should also select content from diverse ethnic groups so that students from various cultures will see their images in the curriculum. Educational equity will exist for all students when teachers become sensitive to the cultural diversity in their classrooms, vary their teaching styles so as to appeal to a diverse student population, and modify their curricula to include ethnic content (Banks, 1994)." Sadly, twenty years after Banks originally published this call for more ethnic content in the curriculum, many educators continue to employ culture as a proxy for race. So, while the curriculum has become more multiethnic, the pedagogical method of delivering this content remains virtually unchanged.

Educators must expand multicultural education to include a broader definition of culture. This will mean developing curriculum, as well as pedagogy, that empowers students to critically engage the electronic media and other forms of youth popular culture (i.e., music, style, sport). Inside of these cultural spaces, students often display the same academic literacy skills (critique, analysis, memorization, recitation, oral presentation) that we are asking them to produce in the classroom. A multicultural curriculum and pedagogy should be using youth culture to scaffold these skills into academic literacy.

Making Youth Culture Part of a Multicultural Education

Urban students come to the classroom with many of the skills that teachers expect to teach them. They can analyze text. They can develop and support an argument. They understand concepts of theme, characterization, rhyme, rhythm, meter and tone. They display these skill sets almost every day when they talk about things that are relevant to them as teenagers—this is what I refer to as youth culture. To bridge this gap between youth culture and the culture of the classroom, teachers must learn about the interests of their students and find ways to value

them in their classroom pedagogy. A classroom would not have to become a live version of MTV to incorporate youth culture in the pedagogy. The goal is to help students to understand that the texts they choose to access are really quite similar to the texts that they often reject as irrelevant. At its core, this approach to pedagogy believes that a rigorous multicultural curriculum should be a marriage of the student's culture and canonical culture. Not surprisingly, students intuitively understand the potential of this sort of pedagogical scaffold.

SHAUN: If you learn one way to cook on a stove, you can always go to another stove and learn to cook. That's just like if you learn popular culture, you can come back and learn how to use canonical culture. Because learning, basically all you have to do is use you 'mind and be interested in what you are learning. Because if you are bored in class you are just going to doze off in class and sleep (aside: cause some teachers will let you sleep I ain't even gonna lie.). If it's interesting though, you'll stay up and you'll participate and you'll try to get some points of information in. But no matter what you'll always try to learn. But I think if you are allowed to learn from that pop culture and then that teacher tried to bring you into the canonical, or the regular text, I think if you are paying attention in this one (pop culture) and they can relate it to the other then the person will learn both ways. I can say for myself that I did that in this class.

SHAUN: (Makes use of a vivid metaphor to articulate a common sense principle of learning theory) If the curriculum and pedagogy are interesting to young people, they'll be excited about learning. Students want a classroom culture that reflects expanded definitions of literacy. They want literacy instruction that emphasizes more meaningful learning activities that allow them to develop academic literacy skills that are transferable to their daily lives:

ANDRADE: Drawing from your experience with *The Godfather* Trilogy in this class, would you suggest that teachers use film as text in their classrooms?

YANCEY: For me, definitely. Because before, a film like *The Godfather* was more or less like a movie for entertainment. But, now, I can watch *The Godfather* over and over again and I know I'll find something new. And I'll be like, wow, I didn't know that. I didn't know that connected. You know, it's that deep thought in there, that when you're watching it, you're really thinking about like simple, like I'm talking about simple, I mean like some hand gestures. Every movement is like a big issue in that film that you can definitely relate it to something. Before that, before you explained it to us and analyzed it with us and showed it to us, when you're talking about it my lips drop. I'll be like, "huh?" Sometimes it'll be like extreme, but, no doubt about it, it makes sense. So, you know, we just learned to take it from there.

SHAUN: Cause when you be talking about the movie, cause at first we'll watch a scene and you'll stop it. And you'll ask us a question, like "you got any questions?" And you'll see everybody in class don't want to say nothing so they'll just sit there all quiet. And then you start sparking conversation and then everybody just starts getting into it. Especially like, oh what's that scene, like in the very first scene of *The Godfather* when he says, [impersonating the voice of Vito's character] "I believe in America" [Yancey and Isaiah laugh]. I never really even like tripped off that part of the movie. I just watched it and knew that dude was gonna die sooner or later. That's all I'm knowin,' like when he gonna die, when he gonna die? But then after you watched it in here, and you were talking about belief in America and then the movie showed how when he was a little kid and how America was all corrupt and how all this stuff comes back on him. It was just like, damn, I never noticed that. It's always something new.

YANCEY: Yeah, I was able to get a lot from the film. I would just add something simple to it like a symbol that I never thought of when I would watch films. Like how they're particularly, they got, like when *The Godfather* started out. It started out that scene where it didn't show the face of the Godfather, it showed his back and his hand. And, [laughing] I thought, hey, the cameraman was just doin' that just to be doin' it. But, there's a much bigger issue behind that. And now, I mean [smiling] I be wantin' to go watch any little movies that come out and try to find that little story in every film . . .

YANCEY: I want to add on a little bit more. I think also from this class, that um, it's given me like, I mean, I know when I see like people talk about films or even a book, instead of just seeing it for what it's like, I guess the cover I would say. Or, when you're just watching a film, you're just watching it for entertainment or reading a book for entertainment. I have the want, it's like a challenge to me, to figure out what the writer of that book or the producer of the film is thinking or what his motive is, as to why he's doing this, like why, why. That question "why" always revolving through my head. Like, "why is this happening" or "why is this particular story talking about this subject"— where does it connect to it?

For both Shaun and Yancey, the use of popular film[5] and music as legitimate academic texts provided a variety of opportunities to develop skills of analysis and discussion. More importantly though, it has added to their media literacy tool kit, "challenging" them to change the way they interact with the media in their lives. New literacy theorists (Duncan-Andrade & Morrell, in press; Gee, 2004; Gutiérrez, Rymes & Larson, 1995; Gutiérrez & Stone, 2002; Kress, 2003; Lee, 1993; Morrell, 2004; Morrell & Duncan-Andrade, 2003) have crafted broader definitions of literacy activities that would support a pedagogical approach that challenges traditionalist notions of literacy being tied exclusively to print. A curriculum that draws from youth culture would embrace these expanding definitions of literacy by viewing students as producers of and participants in various cultural literacies, such as image, style, and discursive practices. This more inclusive approach to literacy instruction recognizes students as cultural producers with their own spheres of emerging literacy participation. This pedagogy of articulation and risk (Grossberg, 1994) values and learns from the cultural literacies students bring to the classroom and assists them as they expand those literacies and develop new ones. Teachers should aim to develop young people's critical literacy, but they should also recognize students as producers of literacy and support that production. For Freire, this is the ultimate form of critical pedagogy; that is, engaging young people in critical dialogues over various literacies, providing space for production of these literacies, and then valuing those products enough to engage in critical dialogue over them. If, indeed, urban schools hope to advance the spirit of critical pedagogy and the multicultural education movement, then they would do well to listen to young people and make better use of youth cultural literacies in their pedagogy and curriculum.

Notes

1. The issue of student disengagement is well documented (Finn, 1999; Kohl, 1994; MacLeod, 1987). This paper is not an attempt to duplicate that work but, instead, aims to discuss promising solutions to the problem.
2. Valenzuela highlights the difference in the U.S. use of the term "education," which often means "schooling" for Mexican children, and the Mexican term *educacion* which elicits the expectation of a more holistic, authentically caring relationship.
3. Pseudonyms are used for all three students.
4. Important to consider here are the types of media texts that are employed in the classroom. Students can be just as disengaged with dated and culturally irrelevant films and documentaries as they are with traditional texts.

5. The Godfather Trilogy, although stretching back into the 1970s, remains popular with students, particularly because of ongoing popular cultural references to the mafia and the godfather (see HBO's hit series "The Sopranos" and Snoop Dogg's album "The Doggfather").

References

American Academy of Pediatricians Committee on Public Education (2001). *Children, Adolescents and Television*. Elk Grove Village, IL, American Academy of Pediatrics: 423–426.

Apple, M. (1990). *Ideology and Curriculum*. New York, Routledge.

———. (1993). *Official Knowledge: Democratic Education in a Conservative Age*. New York: Routledge.

Banks, J. A. (1994). Ethnicity, Class, Cognitive, and Motivational Styles: Research and Teaching Implications. In J. Kretovicks & E. J. Nussel (eds.), *Transforming Urban Education* (pp. 277–290). Boston: Allyn and Bacon.

Committee on Public Education. (2001). *Children, Adolescents and Television* (Policy Statement No. Volume 107, Number 2). Elk Grove Village, IL: American Academy of Pediatrics.

Darling-Hammond, L. (1998). *New Standards, Old Inequalities: The Current Challenge for African American Education*. Chicago: National Urban League.

———. (1997). *The Right to Learn: A Blueprint for Creating Schools That Work*. San Francisco: Jossey-Bass Publishers.

Delpit, L. (1988). "The Silenced Dialogue: Power and Pedagogy in Education Other People's Children." *Harvard Educational Review, 58*(3): 1280–298.

Dewey, J. (1938). *Experience and Education*. New York: Simon and Schuster.

Duncan-Andrade, J., and Morrell, E. (in press). E "race" ing, Enabling: Toward a Critical Media Pedagogy in Urban Secondary Classrooms. In G. Duncan (ed.), *Teaching and Researching Across Color Lines: Literacies, Pedagogies, and the Politics of Difference*. Lanham, MD: Rowman and Littlefield.

Finn, P. (1999). *Literacy with an Attitude: Educating Working Class Children in their Own Self Interest*. New York: SUNY Press.

Freire, P. (1970). Pedagogy of the Oppressed. New York: Continuum.

Gee, J. (2004). *What Video Games Have to Teach Us About Learning and Literacy*. New York: Palgrave.

Giroux, H. (1997). *Channel Surfing: Race Talk and the Destruction of Today's Youth*. New York: St. Martin's Press.

———. (1983). *Theory and Resistance in Education: A Pedagogy for the Opposition*. South Hadley, MA: Bergin and Garvey.

Giroux, H., Lankshear, C., McLaren, P., and Peters, M. (eds.). (1996). *Counter Narratives: Cultural Studies and Critical Pedagogies in Postmodern Spaces*. New York: Routledge.

Giroux, H. and Simon, R. (1989). Schooling, Popular Culture, and a Pedagogy of Possibility. In H. Giroux & R. Simon (eds.), *Popular Culture, Schooling and Everyday Life*. Granby, MA: Bergin and Garvey Publishers.

Goodman, S. (2003). *Teaching Youth Media: A Critical Guide to Literacy, Video Production and Social Change*. New York: Teachers College Press.

Grossberg, L. (1994). Bringin' It All Back Home—Pedagogy and Cultural Studies. In H. Giroux & P. McLaren (eds.), *Between Borders: Pedagogy and the Politics of Cultural Studies*. New York: Routledge. Youth Popular Culture and Curriculum 335.

Gutiérrez, K., Rymes, B., and Larson, J. (1995). Script, Counterscript, and Underlife in the Classroom: James Brown versus *Brown v. Board of Education*. *Harvard Educational Review, 65*(3), 445–471.

Gutiérrez, K. and Stone, L. (2002). Hypermediating Literacy Activity: How Learning Contexts Get Reorganized. In O. Saracho & B. Spodek (eds.), *Contemporary Perspectives in Early Childhood Education,* 2(pp. 25–51). Greenwich, Conn: Information Age Publishing.

Hall, S. (1996). What Is This "Black" in Black Popular Culture? In D. K.-H. C. Morley (ed.), *Critical Dialogues in Cultural Studies* (pp. 465–475). New York: Routledge.

———. (1992). Race, Culture and Communications: Looking Backward and Forward at Cultural Studies. *Rethinking Marxism,* 5, 10–18.

Hirsch, E. D. (2001). "Overcoming the Language Gap: Make Better Use of Literacy Time Block." *American Educator* (Summer).

Hull, G., Rose, M., Fraser, K. L., and Castellano, M. (1991). Remediation as Social Construct: Perspectives from an Analysis of Classroom Discourse. *College Composition and Communication*, 42(3), 299–329.

Kaiser Foundation, D. Roberts, et al. (1999). *Kids and Media at the New Millennium: A Comprehensive National Analysis of Children's Media Use*. Menlo Park, CA, Henry J. Kaiser Family Foundation Report.

Kohl, H. (1994). *I Won't Learn from You*. New York: The New Press.

Kress, G. (2003). *Literacy in the New Media Age*. New York: Routledge.

Lee, C. (1993). *Signifying as a Scaffold for Literary Interpretation*. Urbana, IL: NCTE.

Luke, C. (1999). What Next? Toddler Netizens, Playstation Thumb, Technoliteracies. *Contemporary Issues in Early Childhood*, 1(1), 95–100.

———. (1997). *Technological Literacy*. Canaberra: Language Australia Publications.

MacLeod, J. (1987). *Ain't No Makin' It*. Boulder, CO: Westview Press.

Mahiri, J. (1998). *Shooting for Excellence: African American Youth Culture in New Century Schools*. New York: Teachers College Press.

Malkin, M. (2003, January 14). Hip Hop Hogwash. *New York Post*.

McDermott, R. and Varenne, H. (1995). Culture as Disability. *Anthropology and Education Quarterly*, 26(3), 324–348.

McLaren, P. and Hammer, R. (1996). Media Knowledges, Warrior Citizenry and Postmodern Literacies. In H.Giroux, C. Lankshear, P. McLaren & M. Peters (eds.), *Counternarratives: Cultural Studies and Critical Pedagogies in Postmodern Spaces*. New York: Routledge.

Moll, L., Amanti, C., Neff, D., and Gonzalez, N. (1992). Funds of Knowledge for Teaching: Using a Qualitative Approach to Connect Homes and Classrooms. *Theory into Practice*, 31, 132–141.

Morrell, E. (2004). *Linking Literacy and Popular Culture: Finding Connections for Lifelong Learning*. Norwood, MA: Christopher-Gordon.

Morrell, E. and Duncan-Andrade, J. (2003). What Youth Do Learn in School: Using Hip Hop as a Bridge to Canonical Poetry. In J. Mahiri (ed.), *What They Don't Learn in School: Literacy in the Lives of Urban Youth*. New York: Peter Lang.

———. (2002). Toward a Critical Classroom Discourse: Promoting Academic Literacy Through Engaging Hip-Hop Culture with Urban Youth. *English Journal*, 91(6), 88–92.

Nielson Media Research. (1998). *Report on Television*. New York: Nielson Media Research.

Noddings, N. (1992). *The Challenge to Care in Schools*. New York: Teachers College Press.

Steele, S. (1990). *The Content of Our Character: A New Vision of Race in America*. New York: St. Martin's Press.

Valdes, G. (1996). *Con Respeto*. New York: Teachers College Press.

Valenzuela, A. (1999). *Subtractive Schooling: U.S.-Mexican Youth and the Politics of Caring*. New York: SUNY Press.

West, C. (1999). *The New Cultural Politics of Difference. The Cornel West Reader*. New York: Basic Books: 119–139.

Williams, R. (1991). Base and Superstructure in Marxist Cultural Theory. In C. Mukerji & M. Schudson (eds.), *Rethinking Popular Culture: Contemporary Perspectives in Cultural Studies*, (pp. 407–423). Berkeley, CA: University of California Press.

Willis, P. (1981). *Learning to Labor*. New York: Columbia University Press. Youth Popular Culture and Curriculum 337.

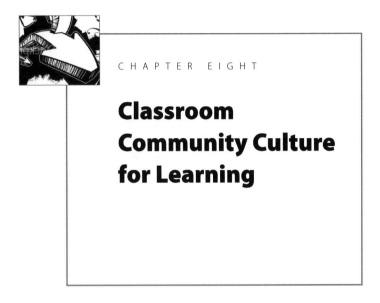

CHAPTER EIGHT

Classroom Community Culture for Learning

Suzanne Gallagher and Greg S. Goodman

Only in Hollywood visions of school does classroom chaos and blatant teacher disrespect dissolve and turn to loving relations based upon mutual positive regard. Looking back at a movie such as *To Sir with Love* and continuing up to the more recent film *Freedom Writers,* we view gross mismatches of teacher-cultures of control versus the post-modern youth culture that stereotypically appears unmanageable, oppositional, and disrespectful. As these scripts go, the 30 minutes of agony teachers such as *Freedom Writers'* Erin Gruwell endure are typically followed by 90 minutes of resolution and teaching bliss. Students are transformed, and lessons are learned. Just do as Gruwell does, and you'll have students metaphorically eating out of your hand. What was so hard to understand about that?

The stereotypical script of the teacher movie and its conflict of students versus teacher makes for a good plotline, but the reality of today's classroom is missing. Our students are not paid actors, and we, unfortunately, are not pulling in seven digits for our performances. As teacher-viewers, we're always in awe of the quick transformations the movies bring to kids who have been at war with systems more invested in forcing compliance and control than in promoting liberation and individual free expression of thought, life-style or action! The conflict for professional educators is that we are real teachers who have taught in actual schools, not virtual ones! Our problem is real. If we don't control our students properly, we're seen as loose, anti-disciplinarians, and we are jeopardizing the authority of the other teachers in our building. If we let our students "have fun" or appear to have fun, they will expect that in every class. How will other teachers view us when their students say, "Mr/s. . . . doesn't make us raise our hands if we want to comment in class"? Many traditional teachers equate rigid, regimented adherence to rules regarding turn-taking with authority. Their every move seems to communicate, "I'm in control here!" For you, the pre-service teacher, don't be fooled by Hollywood scripts. The reality of the classroom for many teachers and students is that the climax of the story is a tragedy, not a romance.

Classroom management

A term to describe discipline and classroom culture features.

Embedded in real scenarios of **classroom management** are issues related to authority, power, control, and leadership. Without question, the teacher is vested with authority as the instructional leader in the classroom. However, critical constructivists view the role of the teacher/instructional leader in a different light than is reflected by the traditional control and authority models. For critical constructivists, the emphasis is on building a classroom community culture. To show how these models differ, let us first examine some of the traditional classroom management approaches.

Traditional Models

Teacher centered

The teacher is the director of all activities in the room.

In our many years of teaching experience, we have seen the promotion of a wide array of techniques touted to promote classroom management. The major focus of these techniques is **teacher centered**; the focus is on what the teacher does to the classroom environment in order to effect the desired behavior in the students. This is a good example of technical rationality (Gallagher, 2003). These techniques may be thought to have some merit in that they can produce the desired behavior in students (Marzano, 2007), and there is clear evidence to reinforce the importance of having clear rules and expectations (Stage & Quiroz, 1997). Teachers reinforce this notion as they witness students learning to conform and to follow directions (Evertson & Neal, 2006). An emphasis on reward for compliant behavior and punishment for infractions is the general mode. As in authoritarian parenting styles, the teacher has complete authority over students. Control and domination is often the cardinal rule in many traditionally structured classrooms.

Most teachers experiment with the practices of classroom management until they find a formula that brings them success. And the winning of control is reinforced in the majority of cases. The goal from this perspective is the same regardless of your stance concerning ethics or social justice: maintaining control of the classroom. However, the moral and ethical issues under-girding the rationale for classroom control play a significant role in the professional's practice. If your reason for control is to mask poor teaching and to quell the rebelliousness spurred by boredom and the concomitant anger your students feel toward you, no classroom management system will work effectively or be justifiable in the eyes of students. Conversely, if you understand that a certain amount of order will provide an environment where you can teach and your curriculum and process are in sync with student interest and ability, that is the best classroom management system and the need to deal with student misbehavior is only rarely needed.

Although it is hard to imagine in our present time, within the real world of the public schools corporal punishment is still legal in 28 states. This antiquated form of punishing students, paddling them on their buttocks with a wooden object, is still permissible under statute of law in the majority of states. Obviously, corporal punishment should never be invoked; however, this form of punishment is mentioned to give you, the student of educational psychology, some foundational knowledge of the crude beginnings of managing student behavior. Using fear and physical domination to control behavior is not only primitive, it is psychologically and physically damaging of students. These laws are criminal, and they need to be stricken from educational statutes, as was done in Pennsylvania during the fall of 2005.

Even in states where corporal punishment is not outlawed, most school districts have sanctions against this form of punishment. However, a behavior that is more apt to be found is psychological belittling or verbal expressions of disrespect of students. The National Educators Association (NEA) has a code of ethics that pre-service teachers need to study and all teachers need to adhere to. One of the principles of ethical behavior is the commitment to students. It reads: Teachers "shall not intentionally expose the student to embarrassment or disparagement" (http://www.nea.org/aboutnea/code.html).

Effective Learning Environments

Effective learning environments are ones that are pro-social and positively reflect a respect for both the participants and the process of education. As we have emphasized earlier in the works by Beachum and McCray and by Duncan-Andrade, harmony is achieved when there is an acceptance of the students by the teacher and mutual positive regard for the teacher by the students. Teacher leadership and authority are enhanced by the mutually respectful

culture of the classroom (Marzano, 2007). This includes both the positive and negative aspects of culture the students represent and the often gnarly and cacophonous chorus of complaints, criticisms, and commentary that attend their lives. Despite the marketing of *Teen* magazine, the experience of adolescence is not an endless series of glorious encounters with clothing and cosmetics! Adolescence is a time of tremendous growth and personal discovery. Much of this experience is dramatically portrayed within the harsh reality of teenage crisis and conflict.

The concept of positive mutual regard has been a mainstay of humanistic psychology since Carl Rogers coined the term in the early 1950s. Rogers espoused a profound belief in the power of individuals to adapt and become themselves. On valuing the worth and dignity of each person, Rogers said, "The primary point of importance . . . is the attitude held by the counselor (read: teacher) toward the worth and significance of the individual" (1951, p. 20). These words still resonate with constructivist educators. What has changed is the time and situation students and teachers must confront. Building a safe space for student learning based upon this attitude of mutual positive regard is the art of an excellent teacher.

Traditional classroom management approaches have also focused on the relationship between effective teaching practices and the lack of behavioral infractions by students. In contrast, we present the concept of **learning-centered** environments where students share in the responsibility for learning and building community in the classroom (Evertson & Neal, 2006). The major focus from this perspective, is that students construct meaning in social environments. Students are engaged in meaningful, productive activities with others, and they share authority and responsibility with teachers.

Learning-centered
Classrooms where students are constructing meaning and knowledge.

We need to be clear that in a learning-centered classroom the teacher never abdicates authority or responsibility for the class process or content;

the teacher "still manages the class in the sense of establishing the environment and creating learning opportunities for students" (Evertson & Neal, 2006, p. 11). However, in this environment the students have responsibility as well. In the day-to-day life in these classrooms, student voices are respected and taken seriously. Through the modeling of the teachers in this environment students learn respect for others, valuing of others, and a more democratic working out of problems. This is akin to what is termed authoritative style, akin to the parenting style of the same name.

Building a Classroom Culture

In a climate of respect and responsibility students are much less likely to be motivated to disrupt or misbehave. Classroom management systems often suggest that an ounce of prevention is worth a pound of cure. Following the advice of author Kolencik, by accepting and effectively dealing with feelings, many behavioral infractions can be avoided.

In the development of the best classroom management system, one of the first foci the teacher will address is the rules and procedures of the classroom. Expert classroom manager, Harry Wong, thinks that training students in the procedures and rules of the classroom is the most important aspect of making an effective learning environment. Wong has made a fortune promoting his system of procedural routines and rules governing classroom behaviors. From greeting the students at the door with a handshake and a "good morning" salutation to the commencement of an immediate task for the student's engagement, every bit of the student's experience is orchestrated. Wong and Wong (1997) leave no room for fooling around! Having sold 3,000,000 copies of their book, *The First Days of School,* we'd say there is a lot of demand for a bomb-proof system.

One critique of Wong's system is that it is too regimented, and there is little room for individual deviation from the procedures or control. Students

who grow up experiencing such excessive control tend to lack individual initiative and make good followers. If the leadership is good, this may not be problematic. However, when the leaders are suspect, good followers are just as much a part of the problem.

Rules need to be a part of every classroom, and the developmental needs of each grade will require slightly different interpretations of the same principles. A major theme of critical constructivism is to build respect for the diverse cultural community within each classroom and to encourage the development of social consciousness for living in a democratic society. Leadership is the gift that good teachers model for their students. In a learning-centered classroom students are considered capable and competent to assist the teacher in providing leadership and formulating classroom rules. As they mature, our students have gained experience with classroom living, and we believe they often have a very good understanding of what works and what doesn't. Teachers need to take the time to reflect on their students' beliefs about good classroom practices and to continually re-examine their own beliefs on what rules support effective practice.

Rules need to be part of the life of the classroom from the beginning of the year or semester. Establishing them early is time well spent in helping the students get acclimated to the classroom. Waiting until unhelpful instances occur takes the rules out of the community-building category and makes it appear as a kind of negative disciplinary action. The best policy is to state rules in a positive voice and to avoid negative wording. "Treat others with respect" is more effective than "no put downs." Say what you want, not what you don't want.

Consistency is an important aspect of rules becoming a support in the classroom atmosphere. Implementing rules and the reinforcing procedures require constant attention. Students figure out very quickly if the classroom rules are merely bulletin board decorations or if they really are serious procedures needing their recognition and cooperation.

Enforcement of the rules also requires delicate negotiation. Using the authority as the teacher, consequences for rule violations need to be appropriate and never excessive. Excessive use of punishment can lead to the demise of the teacher's authority. Fairness is the rule, and understatement of power use is preferable to over-application. The over-application of punishment could be an act of hegemony; the excessive exertion of power and control over a weaker person or subject. Hegemony requires the subjugated to give the power to the person in control or the subjugator. This is not the relationship a teacher wishes to have over students. Hegemony is a misuse of power through subjugation of subordinates, and it debilitates the students' sense of personal agency and control over their own behavior.

Before doling out harsh consequences and/or punishments for misbehavior, the teacher is advised to seek alternative methods for correcting the behavior. Giving the students a chance to self-monitor their behavior is better than relying on the teacher to change the students' actions. Sometimes a cue, "What are we supposed to be doing right now?," is sufficient to redirect a student. Perhaps praising a proximal student for good behavior can stimulate reciprocal positive behavior. Telling the student in a clear voice to stop doing the misdeed and start doing the correct action is very effective. The last action to take is the consequence stage. It should be clear when consequences are meted out that every opportunity to self-correct had been attempted. We work for the successful inclusion of every student.

Dreikurs' Logical Consequences

One of our criticisms of many behavior management systems is the absurdity of their logic. Sometimes the consequences for student misbehavior reflect a lack of thoughtfulness. For example, the

consequence of smoking in school is often suspension or permanent removal such as expulsion. Smoking is (or can lead to) an addiction, and controlling one's urge to smoke often requires tremendous self-discipline. Self-discipline is not gained when one is sent home for a day or two or more. When students are away from school, they can smoke whenever they want. Behavioral psychologists would call this a positive **reinforcer**, because the suspension has the effect of supporting or continuing the behavior, not extinguishing or ending it. Reinforcers are consequences of behavior that perpetuate or support the continuance of the behavior. Teachers often confuse the meaning of this technical term of behavioral psychology. Just because we assume the act we do is a punishment for the child, for example, sending the child out of our room, the child may like to be removed, and he will continue his misbehavior when he returns to class to be reinforced yet again by being forced to leave. The test of reinforcers is to see if they cause repetition of the behavior. If the behavior is maintained or increases, it has been reinforced. Simple as this appears on the surface, the actual implementation of a behavior modification plan is complex and challenging.

Reinforcer

Any behavior or action that causes a behavior to be maintained.

Because behavioral psychology is highly clinical, training in its application is rigorous. Despite its technical difficulty, it has viable applications within some settings; for example it is often used in special education as teachers work with students who have severe mental and psychological issues such as autism, emotional and mental disabilities. Because of the highly technical nature of behavioral psychology, implementation of these techniques requires extensive training before they can be an effective tool for teachers. As a result, the techniques of behavioral psychology are better used in conjunction with cognitively based psychological principles such as the system Rudolph Dreikurs (1982) developed.

Rudolph Dreikurs (1982) proposed that students misbehave to meet the needs of one of four mistaken goals: attention, power, revenge, or inadequacy. By understanding the reason for the child's misbehavior, the teacher can redirect the child to accomplish his or her real goal of being accepted and or loved by others. According to Dreikurs, if the students cannot meet their goals in a positive manner, they will revert to misbehavior to avenge or correct the denial of that acceptance.

Dreikurs and other cognitive and behavioral psychologists made a major contribution to the processes of classroom management in the discovery of the use of logical consequences. The philosophic foundation of this approach is that children need to learn how to behave appropriately, and that logical consequences can be a better teacher than the use of *aversive punishment*. Logical consequences have to do with what is happening now. Punishment deals with the past. To go back to the example of our smoker, what would be a logical consequence of smoking in school? There does not have to be one answer. The child can help to develop a relationship between what was done and what needs to happen to restore order or harmony. Possible consequences could be counseling with the school nurse on the effects of smoking. Watching a film on the relationship of smoking to disease. Joining a stop smoking group with the school counselor. Coming to a special Saturday school session where students visited the cancer ward at the hospital and visited patients to provide company.

The goal of logical consequences is to teach corrective actions. The tone of the process is collaborative, not harsh and stimulated by anger or rejection. Many students lack understanding of social conventions. They do not know the right thing to do. This is not necessarily their fault. Over the years we have witnessed many forms of student misbehavior, and depending on the developmental level of the student, each misbehavior may have a different communicative intent ranging from no message at all to a very significant act. For example, a first grader may raise a middle finger to another student in "the" gesticulation of disrespect. However, when queried by the principal about the event, the child

may not know what that gesticulation means, and the reason they committed the act was imitation of an older sibling's actions. The same behavior in a junior high student may be conducted to make a joke or just to tease another student. The communicative intent was not to express anger or rage but to take a risk and show some bravado. Last, the finger may be used by a high school student as a clear message of contempt. The message is, "I'm angry and this is what you can do!" The logical consequence for the specific behavior needs to address the communicative intent in order to be an effective agent of behavior change. The student needs to cognitively connect behavior to the consequence to learn to adjust and find a more appropriate response.

The system of logical consequences makes tremendous sense for adults, but what about the children it is supposed to affect? Education critic Alfie Kohn (1999) suggests that this process may actually make more sense to the adults than to the children. Children may just see the logical consequence as a thinly disguised punishment. They are not happy to say, "I'm sorry," when in fact they are not sorry at all. Developing compassion is not always an easy or straight-forward process. Often the hurt that killed the compassion is deeper than classroom teachers' capacity or skill to address in a brief intervention.

Critical Constructivist Model:
A Culture of Mutual Enhancement

Critical constructivists base their classroom community culture on the egalitarian principles of mutual enhancement (Miller, 2003) and social justice (Kincheloe, 2005). Mutual enhancement is a feminist concept, and within critical constructivists' classrooms it means that both the teacher and the students receive benefit from the interactive processes of teaching and learning. Developed by Jean Miller of the Wellesley Center for Women, mutual enhancement does not imply that the teacher gives up any of their authority or leadership, as we said above. Rather mutual enhancement means that there is an air of equanimity and universal respect that imbues the classroom culture. In an analogy to therapy, both the client and the therapist benefit from the interaction. Growth occurs for both individuals. In the classroom, learning and growth occur for both the students and the teacher. To differentiate between traditional forms of top-down control and domination, it is more accurate to identify critical constructivist educational leadership as creating a classroom community culture.

A classroom community culture is a set of rules and understandings that are specific to the individuals included in the group and reflective of the values and identities of the world these individuals inhabit. A perfect metaphor for understanding this issue is imbedded in the Ebonics debate. Ebonics, derived from the words "ebony" and "phonics," is a specific language of the urban African American community; it reflects members' situated experience. This language is strongly tied to identity and membership pride. The critical constructivist understands and accepts Ebonics as a communicative tool and includes these neologisms along with other attributes of the families or neighborhood within the classroom community culture. In this context, the teacher is embracing the diversity of the students and affirming the values of those individuals in a truly democratic praxis of the classroom.

Mutual enhancement applies to classroom community culture as it extends to the social atmosphere within the classroom. In a classroom based upon the principles of mutual enhancement, a spirit of shared social responsibilities allows for inclusion and equality. These classrooms develop dispositions of openness to diversity and explorations of other identities. Learning activities promote mixing it up and sparking conversations about differences and similarities.

Mutual enhancement allows for the growth of one's self and promotes the acceptance of others. This is especially meaningful when the "other" is comprised of those who have been marginalized because of minority identifications and eco-

nomic disparities. Mutual enhancement dovetails with critical constructivist philosophy and practice as a further application of *social justice* initiatives. Social justice takes on many meanings in the modern schools, but among the most important is the legitimate recognition of the diversity distributed within the school. Legitimizing diversity is opposed to token, simplistic cinquo do mayo trivializations. One-day food festivals are not examples of socially just pedagogy (Banks, 2006). Valid programs to promote social justice in the classroom and on the campus provide ubiquitous benefit to the school community. Social justice in school means many important things to groups intimate with experiences of oppression and persecution. For example, Gay/lesbian/bisexual and transgendered (GLBT) youth experience horrific persecution in the public school (Gray, 2004). Although the vast majority of today's students on public school and college campuses have gained the knowledge to radically reduce racist attitudes and behavior, we continue to witness overt forms of anti-gay behaviors in and across campuses. Continuing efforts to build a culture of complete acceptance of all diversity is the goal of social justice educators.

Of utmost concern to critical constructivist educators is the implementation of policies to promote social justice in both the classroom and in the community. Working to promote social justice in your classroom is negated within a school where the conversation of social justice gets no air time. When school administrators ignore disproportionate numbers of suspension or expulsion among specific targeted groups, their actions may reflect **institutionalized racism**. Against a backdrop of bigotry, the efforts you make in your classroom will work to expose the larger problems, but they may not come close to meeting your needs to achieve a socially just culture for your students.

The entire school must buy in to promoting socially just education and social culture. We are convinced that if proper attention to issues of

Institutionalized racism

Rules, laws or actions that unfairly affect a specific population.

social justice were in place at Littleton, Colorado's Columbine High School, the persecution of two students (whom we refuse to recognize by name) would not have been allowed nor would it have escalated to their hate-based killing of faculty and students. On dynamic, rapidly changing campuses across this country, critical constructivist educators are continually taking the pulse of their student body and reinventing their responses to revolutionize the process (Kincheloe, 2005).

Rules to Live by . . .

Certainly rules and procedures are a natural part of any group experience, and the classroom is no different as a social group. Rules and procedures need to mirror the philosophies of mutual enhancement and social justice. With any system of rules, those responsible for the rule adoption must support the goals of the governing system. There must be buy-in by all the members of the community. These rules are not just window-dressing or pseudo symbols of our beliefs. The rules exemplify our core beliefs, and what could be considered the culture's **Tao**.

Tao

An Eastern philosophy characterized by values of acceptance and awareness.

The best rule systems are the simplest to learn; however, they may not be the easiest to implement. In our classroom, we choose just two rules. The first is a "Respect" rule. This means that everyone is treated with respect within the classroom, and no one is devalued for any reason. This is in concert with the concept of mutual enhancement. In a respect-governed classroom, there is no hegemony or subjugation of anyone. The goals of gaining knowledge and learning pro-social behaviors are clearly evident.

Implementing the respect rule requires significant reconceptualizing of social relations for many students. Coming from homes and neighborhoods where "doing the dozens" is the game: yo mama. Leaving this put-down interaction out of the classroom needs to be viewed as positive and additive, not negative or rejecting. Although this may seem to contradict the acceptance of community culture,

that is too reductive an explanation. The dozens is a game to build strength and test resolve. Putting someone down with clever word play continues until the loser reveals vulnerability and exposes emotion. The goal is stay strong: don't give in or show hurt.

We agree with the goal of building strength. However, the strength needs to flow from positive, collaborative contributions, not competitive and destructive gaming. The point of the dozens is to stand up to the hegemony of stereotypic representations of poverty, racism, and other put downs. We contribute that the paradox of refuting the process by handing double doses of disrespect to one's classmate or schoolmate may reveal a validation of those derogatory remarks when the loser succumbs to the pain. As Jeff Duncan-Andrade argues about Hip-Hop culture in "Best Friend/Worst Enemy," elements of the anger and alienation youth experience can be used a positive force and deliver energy to transform the rage into something Freire would call love.

Another rule of our classroom is confidentiality; everything that is said in the classroom is potentially sensitive and personal information, and what is said in the classroom needs to stay in the classroom. Therefore, if a personal conversation is going on and a student mentions her parent's divorce (perhaps as it relates to the plot of a novel or theme of a poem), that student does not need to fear that the entire school will be discussing her personal life after school. This rule is hard to monitor, but it pays big dividends for supporting the development of trust within the classroom. Students know when they are being talked about, and they resent gossip just as much as any adult. Protecting confidentiality is a cornerstone of respecting the individual and his or her privileged information.

Reducing Hate Crimes and Violence in the School and Community

We live in the most violent society in the industrialized world. Since 9/11, there have been over 100,000 murders committed in America (Herbert, 2007).

Sadly, Americans are so inured by the violence that news of such outrageous violence is more often met with resignation and denial than more appropriate emotions like repulsion. Violence is ubiquitously enmeshed in our culture's movies, television, and entertainments (paint ball, smack-downs, and gang initiations). Movies such as *Really Bad Things* and *Pulp Fiction* make parodies of the violence through grotesque overuse, but these "jokes" are more reflective of the malaise in our culture than they are successful strokes of sarcasm. Cornel West (1995) accurately sums this up saying, "Post-modern culture is more and more a market culture dominated by gangster mentalities and self-destructive wantonness" (p. 559).

None of American violence is spared on our children. Schools are often sites of violence, and this is too common news.

> Violence in America is too frequently appearing in schoolyards. . . . According to a Justice Department report on juvenile justice and delinquency, "American kids are the most violent. Teenagers have 'alarmingly high' rates of violence compared with those of youths in other nations, a comparison that also holds for adult crime rates. An American teenager is ten times more likely to commit murder than a Canadian teenager" (Hinds, 2000, p. 3) (Goodman, 2004, p. 5)

The first job of the critical constructivist educator is to create a culture where students are safe to learn. Accomplishing this feat is the single most critical aspect of the school community, and we do not want to imply that this is anything shy of huge. Making a safe school is a long-term project, and it requires the buy-in of all of the community's citizens. Everyone must not only see the value in maintaining safety and decorum but the need to commit to the daily maintenance of the values that can support harmony.

One of our favorite slogans from the sixties admonished, "If you want peace, then support justice!" The values of social justice undergird safe schools. Critical constructivist schools are organizations that fairly represent all of the constituents of the community. Staff represent the student body in cultural identity and shared understandings. Realia and other school artifacts demonstrate the contributions of students, staff, and parents. As you walk through these schools, you will see yourself represented in the people and things in evidence.

Safety is also protected by participation. The engagement of all of the members of the community in the preservation of the community values speaks louder than words. Walking the talk of critical constructivism is accomplished by participating in active conversations about racism, class, and sexual identities. From "Teaching Tolerance" to others of the myriad social justice initiatives available through the National Association of Multicultural Educators (N.A.M.E. org), the Southern Poverty Law Center (teachingtolerance.org), or the Tolerance Museum, there are many ways to revive the movement to provide social justice programs in your school.

Creating a classroom community culture with affirming values can diminish the need for safety and discipline concerns. However, teaching will always require vigilance and the need to courageously respond to the demands of challenging situations. Prevention and intervention programs, police and metal detectors, dogs and security cameras will remain in many of our schools, but these things cannot replace the courage it takes to personally confront violent acts and other criminal behaviors. Teachers practice their profession within real communities, and as we work to build a new world, we still confront violent vestiges of our dark side. By applying critical constructivist social justice praxis, we are moving toward a harmonious and idealized reinvention of ourselves. Following Freire (1970), "To teach is to be a prisoner of hope" (p. 91). The teacher in each of us hopes that you are excited to take up this challenge to reinvent our schools and the communities they serve.

References

Banks, J. A. (2006). *Diversity and citizenship education: Global perspectives*. San Francisco, CA: Jossey-Bass.

Dreikurs, R. (1982). *Maintaining sanity in the classroom.* New York: Harper Collins

Evertson, C. M., & Neal, K. W. (2006). http://www.eric.ed.gov/ ERICWebPortal/Home.portal?_nfpb=true&_pageLabel=ERICSearch Result&_urlType=action&newSearch=true&ERICExtSearch_ SearchType_0=au&ERICExtSearch_SearchValue_0=%22Neal+Kristen +W.%22 Looking into learning-centered classrooms: Implications for classroom management. [Working Paper]. Washington, DC: NEA [ERIC Document Reproduction Service No. ED495820]

Freire, P. (1970). *Pedagogy of the oppressed.* New York: Contiuum.

Gallagher, S. (2003). *Educational psychology: Disrupting the dominant discourse.* New York: Peter Lang Publishing.

Goodman, G. (2004). *Reducing hate crimes and violence among American youth: Creating transformational agency through critical praxis.* New York: Peter Lang Publishing.

Gray, M. (2004). Finding pride and the struggle for freedom to assemble. In G. Goodman & K. Carey (Eds.) *Critical multicultural conversations.* Cresskill, NJ: Hampton Press.

Herbert, B. (2007). 100,000 gone since 2001. *New York Times.* August 14, p. D 18.

Hinds, Michael deCourcy (2000). *Violent kids: Can we change the trend?* Dubuque, IA: Edward J. Arnone Publisher.

Kincheloe, J. (2005). *Critical constructivism.* New York: Peter Lang Publishing.

Kohn, A. (1999). *The schools our children deserve: Moving beyond traditional classrooms and "tougher standards."* Boston, MA: Houghton Mifflin.

Marzano, R. (2007). *The art and science of teaching: A comprehensive framework for effective instruction.* Alexandria, Virginia: Association for Supervision and Curriculum Development.

Miller, J.B. (2003). Telling the truth about power. In *Research and Action Report 25* (1 Fall/Winter). Wellesley, MA: Wellesley College for Women.

Rogers, C. (1951). *Client-centered therapy.* Boston, MA: Houghton Mifflin Company.

Stage, S.A. & Quiroz, D.R. (1997). A meta-analysis of interventions to decrease disruptive classroom behavior in public education settings. *School Psychology Review, 26*(3), 333–368.

West, C. (1995). Race matters. In *Race, class, and gender: An anthology,* edited by Margaret L. Anderson and Patricia Hill Collins. New York: Wadsworth Publishing.

Wong, H. & Wong, R. (1997). *The first days of school.* Fresno, CA: Harry K. Wong Publications.

CHAPTER NINE

Affective and Motivational Factors for Learning and Achievement

Patricia Kolencik

"The curriculum is so much necessary raw materials, but warmth is the vital element for the growing plant and the soul."
Carl Jung (1875–1961) Swiss psychiatrist

"The extent to which emotional upsets can interfere with mental life is no news to teachers. Students who are anxious, angry, or depressed don't learn; people who are caught in these states do not take in information efficiently or deal with it well."
Daniel Goleman, *Emotional Intelligence*

How are you feeling? Pause for a moment and reflect on your feelings. Are you feeling excited, happy, enthusiastic, energized, elated, content, secure, confident, comfortable, worry free, loved, intelligent, competent, trusting, beautiful, buoyant, creative, honored, respected, revered, sexy, fabulous, gregarious, on top of the world?

Or are you feeling lonely, unsatisfied, hurt, depressed, down-trodden, unintelligent, incomplete, disrespected, unqualified, defeated, unwanted, disconnected, ashamed, unappreciated?

The way that we feel and our perceptions of ourselves in relationship to our feelings have a huge effect upon our functioning within our relationships, our careers, and our education (Bandura, 2001). In this chapter, you will investigate several important aspects of students' **affective** or attitudinal learning. The purpose of this investigation is to help you to make connections between the mind (the combination of thoughts and feelings) and your students' emotional, physical, and cognitive development (Watson-Gegeo & Welshman-Gegeo, 2004). According to Watson-Gegeo and Gegeo:

Affect

Related to a person's feelings

> Until now, it has been assumed that the higher cognitive functions are independent of other mental processes, such as feelings, intuition, and so forth—in fact, that they must be kept separate from the latter, less rational mental processes. However, research has shown that emotion (for instance) is essential to making logical, rational judgments, including moral decisions (Damasio, 1994), and that emotion "links closely with **cognition** to shape action, thought , and long-term development" (Fischer, Kennedy, Cheng, 1998, pp. 22–23) p. 243.

Cognition

Thinking.

To assist in discovering how these key personal growth components link together as one mind, we will be examining various theories of emotional intelligence and motivation. From this examination, you will be able to understand that if your students come to class with negative emotional **baggage** and troubled minds, they will not function optimally. Through your examination of current research on emotion's role in learning, you will come to comprehend the multitude of factors that influence students' motivation to study, learn, and achieve in the diverse classroom (Damasio, 1994). In addition, you will explore the salient aspects of

Baggage

Feelings from one's past experience.

a supported affective learning environment which works to increase student motivation and promote the understanding of the emotional needs of your students.

The following essential questions guide the foci of this chapter:

1. What roles do emotions (affect) play in learning?
2. What is emotional intelligence?
3. What is motivation?
4. What are the two types of motivation?
5. What are the principal theories of motivation?
6. What psycho-social and familial factors affect motivation?

What Roles Do Emotions (Affect) Play in Learning?

Consider these scenarios:

- A twelve-year-old went on a rampage and vandalized a car in the parking lot. The reason: His classmates called him a "sissy" and he wanted to impress them.
- A student reports her classmate is contemplating suicide.
- A fight breaks out between rival gang members
- A student's father dies.
- A student who has just moved to the school is being bullied.
- A student is misbehaving in class and is reprimanded by the teacher. A power struggle ensues.
- A student cheats on an exam.
- A student calls another student "gay."

All of these scenarios: 1) involve examples of relevant emotions such as anger, anxiety, fear, frustration, confusion, bewilderment, disillusionment, uncertainty, and helplessness that students experience on a daily basis; 2) illustrate that learning is

Affective domain

The person's constellation of intrapersonal and interpersonal feelings.

not a smooth process but rather a complex emotional process; and 3) are tied to the **affective domain** in the learning process and contribute to the student's motivation to learn.

Of all the aspects of human growth and cognitive development affecting the learning process, no other is as pervasive and significant as the affective domain (Damasio, 1994). How parents, teachers, and other adults display or deny expression of feelings and react to their own emotional experiences can provide key lessons in their students' developing and regulating personal emotional competence. Because of the critical role of emotions upon learning, it is important for teachers to be aware of the importance of feelings and to be able to discuss interpersonal and intrapersonal issues with their students. Students learn about the nature and expression of emotion from their day-to-day interaction with other individuals. These daily interactions can help students learn to understand and cope with their emotional experiences or they can have inverse, negative consequences.

Even when they are not explicitly stated, affective objectives are pervasive in school work (Smith & Ragan, 1999). Although educators may not always be aware of it, teachers are continuously involved in some form of affective learning. Students look to teachers as models for the development of coping skills, manners, self-discipline, fairness, generosity, courage, compassion, and a host of other interpersonal and intrapersonal qualities. In some cases, affective or attitudinal learning can be one of the main objectives of instruction. Anti-drug campaigns and teaching tolerance for diversity are two examples of this type of emotionally connected instruction.

In the wake of school violence and other risks to student safety, many schools are beginning to take a more active role in students' emotional development (Goodman, 2002). The Collaborative for Academic, Social and Emotional Learning (CASEL) at the University of Illinois at Chicago has devel-

oped five competency areas of social and emotional learning. The five competencies are social-awareness, self-awareness, self-management, relationship skills, and responsible decision making (CASEL, 2005). Schools are developing programs such as PATHS (Promoting Alternative Thinking) (1995) and School Connect (2006) that use these social and emotional learning competencies as the framework to integrate these skills into the curriculum. The book, *The Freedom Writers Diary* (Freedom Writers & Filipovic, 1999), inspired by English teacher Erin Gruwell, is another example of a curricular movement used to help students understand and express their emotions about prejudice, intolerance, racism, and respect for diversity.

Let us now take a deeper look at students' emotions (affect) and its impact on cognitive learning. Affect is the fuel that students bring to the classroom, connecting them to the "why" of learning. As a teacher, you must be cognizant of the fact that students' interest and excitement about the content they are learning are integral factors in the teaching and learning process. How do you feel about learning content knowledge? Are your feelings positive? Are you excited, interested, and curious about learning? Or are your feelings negative? Are you angry or bored? Your attitude about learning is influenced by emotion which researchers call hot cognition (Hoffman, 1991; Miller, 2002; Pintrich, Marx & Boyle, 1993). For example, you may get excited when you read about a new scientific advancement that could lead to a cure for cancer. Or you may feel sad when you read about a tsunami that killed hundreds or people. Your reaction to these scenarios is directed by your emotions; thus, affect is deeply interwoven into cognitive learning. Students are more likely to pay attention, to learn, and to remember events, images, and readings that provoke a strong emotional response such as excitement, sadness, or anger (Alexander & Murphy, 1998; Cowley & Underwood, 1998). Facts and concepts that are related to the student's personal or situational interests are the most meaningful and create high interest (Renninger, Hidi, & Krapp, 1992; Schraw & Lehman, 2001).

The concept of hot cognition tells us that students are more likely to attend to and remember things that not only stimulate their thinking but also elicit emotional reactions. When the student's emotions are engaged, the brain codes the content by triggering the release of chemicals that single out and mark the experience as important and meaningful (Jensen, 1997). Students will learn more when they become both cognitively and emotionally involved in classroom subject matter. Learning is enhanced when the teachers help their students see the importance of content knowledge by revealing its relevance to them.

One of the most powerful strategies that teachers can use in the classroom to build upon students' interests is to connect new content to students' prior knowledge and experiences (Marzano, 1998). This process is sometimes referred to as scaffolding (Ormrod, 2006). A scaffold is a structure used to support student learning. By both personally and emotionally linking new content to what students already know and understand, teachers provide a scaffold for connecting prior knowledge to the present curriculum (Vygotsky, 1978).

In addition to scaffolding, the following constructivist learning strategies are effective ways to assist the teacher in making these connections and emotionally enhancing learning.

1. Allow students to choose projects or read novels based on their interests.
2. Use primary source materials with interesting content or detail such as personal letters and diaries in history.
3. Predict what will happen in an experiment.
4. Have students design and conduct interviews and surveys to learn about each other's interests.

5. Keep a classroom library stocked with books that connect to students' interests and hobbies.
6. Use graphic organizers and concept maps such as a K-W-L chart as instructional devices.
7. Provide opportunities for students to write their own ideas and feelings about the learning through journaling, learning logs, or discussions.
8. Provide an agenda for the day or the class so that students know what to expect.
9. Jensen (1998) states, "In order for learning to be considered relevant, it must relate to something the learner already knows. It must activate a learner's existing neural networks. The more relevance, the greater the meaning" (p. 84). By making the learning relevant to the students from the beginning of the lesson, the teacher opens the door for better understanding by the students. For example, to begin a unit on estimation, a teacher might bring a jar of marbles to class and ask students to guess the number of marbles in the jar and then discuss ideas about how to estimate the number. By beginning a lesson with a motivational opener like this estimation example, the teacher taps into two every important student emotions—curiosity and fun. Thus, successful, effective teachers capitalize on students' interests and curiosity to create a positive learning climate.

What Is Emotional Intelligence?

Because emotions are an integral part of a student's total personality, an understanding of the nature of emotional intelligence and how it affects learning is of vital importance to teachers. Teaching is about the head and the heart: the mind. In other words, the teaching and learning process is not just about imparting didactic knowledge in fundamental content skills. Teaching is also about emotional intelligence (Goleman, 1995), a type of social intelligence that involves the ability to monitor one's own and others' emotions, to discriminate among them, and to use the information to guide one's thinking and actions." (Goleman, 1995, p. 95). The work of Goleman (1995) indicates that motivation is a critical component for school success.

Building on the earlier concepts of "intrapersonal" and "interpersonal" intelligences framed by Howard Gardner's Multiple Intelligences theory (1993), Daniel Goleman (1995) in his book *Emotional Intelligence,* documented that "emotional intelligence (EQ)" is a greater predictor of academic and life success than is IQ (intelligent quotient) as measured by standardized intelligence tests and may be as important as any other type of learning that takes place in school. Goleman introduced the concept of "emotional literacy," a term designating the notion that students' emotional and social skills can be cultivated and developed from infancy throughout an entire lifetime. He calls for a "schooling of emotions" and advocates that teachers play a critical role in developing students' emotional (EQ) as well as intellectual (IQ) talents. Goleman (1995) identifies four areas in emotional competency: 1) identifying, expressing, and understanding emotions; 2) controlling and managing emotions; 3) recognizing emotions toward others; and, 4) managing relationships. Researchers such as Goleman (1995), Gardner (1993), Robert Slavin (1989, 1995, 1996) and Ellen Langer (1989, 1997), have begun to recognize and value this emotional dimension of human intelligence and describe the profound and diverse impact that emotions have on one's lifestyle. These researchers posit that people with emotional literacy skills are more likely to be successful in their professional and personal lives.

How does this theory of emotional intelligence influence teaching and learning? Teachers need to know that their ability to handle students' affective competency skills has a direct impact on instructional delivery, classroom management, and their relationship with students. Effective teachers know that students who have emotional self-control and possess social competency skills are attentive, focused, productive, empathic, and self-motivated. Effective teachers also know that students who lack social competency skills are often distracted from learning, are rejected by peers, and have a history of dropping out of school (Salovey & Mayer 2004).

Emotional intelligence influences teachers' ability to treat students equitably. Teachers should be able to recognize the individual differences that distinguish one student from another. Taking account of these differences makes for sound instructional practice. Teachers need to have the skills to adjust their practice based on observation and knowledge of students' emotional intelligence to foster students' self-esteem, motivation, character, civic responsibility, and their respect for individual cultural, religious, and racial differences.

Successful teachers are adept at dealing with students, both children and adolescents, as they confront personal emotional challenges, sensitive issues, and life-threatening problems as they grow into emotionally mature adults. Many of the challenges and difficulties teachers face concern how to cope with their students' wide variety of needs—some of which are essential for physical survival and others of which are important for psychological well-being—and, how to help young people to grow up as soundly and as trouble free as possible (Eisenberg & Fabes, 1998). For example, if you teach inner-city students whose lives on the street are surrounded by emotions—many of which are negative—you, as a teacher, will want to teach students some self-management skills to help them battle these distressed feelings.

Emotional intelligence is related to discipline problems, dropout rates, low esteem and dozens of other learning and life skill problems. Difficulties in handling emotional experiences may impede students' ability to satisfy their need to feel respected, secure, and socially connected. Thus, teachers need to create a caring, positive and safe learning climate and foster discussion skills that help students actively and respectfully listen to their peers. In the classroom, teachers can function as a role model on how to exhibit and express emotions. Through their own actions, teachers can help students express emotions in socially appropriate ways. Effective teachers model ways of regulating emotions, such as calming down before reacting to a hectic situation or seeking support when stressed or frustrated. Often we teach more by what we do than by what we say.

Teachers can also boost students' social and emotional competency skills by imbedding affective education into the daily academic learning agenda. Suggestions for student involvement include having students create classroom guidelines for dealing with student misbehaviors in the classroom and using class meetings to share feelings about important events or experiences and to build community. Effective teachers also integrate books, stories, plays, poetry, and videos to stimulate discussions of emotional experiences. For example, students could explore the historical effects of racism and learn about institutions, legislation, and movements that sought to right these wrongs.

Simonson and Maushak (2001) have drawn on findings from a number of studies to create a series of guidelines for effective design of affective instruction. These are:

- Make the instruction realistic, relevant, and technically stimulating
- Present new information
- Present persuasive messages in a credible manner
- Elicit purposeful emotional involvement
- Involve the learner in planning, production or delivery of the message
- Provide post-instruction discussion or critique opportunities.

Smith and Ragan (1999) focus on the behavioral aspect of affective learning and emphasize the importance of three key instructional approaches:

- Demonstration of the desired behavior by a respected role model
- Practice of the desired behavior, often through role playing
- Reinforcement of the desired behavior

Teachers need not view academic learning and social and emotional learning at opposite ends but rather bolster support on a daily basis for this affective learning domain. When both academic learning and emotional learning support each other, students are more apt to be engaged and motivated in learning.

Emotion and motivation cannot be considered separately. What and how much is learned is influenced by a student's motivation. And like a revolving door, motivation for learning is influenced by the student's emotional states, beliefs, interests, goals, and habits of thinking.

What Is Motivation?

Why are you reading this chapter? Are you interested in learning more about the topic of motivation to increase your knowledge for future use in the classroom? Are you reading the chapter because there will be a test on this material in the future? Do you need this course to complete your teacher certification requirements? The answers to these questions deal with your "motivation" to study.

Motivation is an elusive concept. Motivation is usually defined as an intrinsic or extrinsic process that arouses, directs, and maintains behavior and relates to the drive to do something. Motivation causes us to get up in the morning and go to school or to work. Motivation drives us to study new things and encourages us to try again when we fail.

Because motivation is an obscure concept, a basic question about motivation always arises, "Where does it come from—within or outside the individual? Consider this example, why do students raise their hand in class? Do they raise their hand because of their interest in the subject matter or because of their interest in earning a good grade? The answer is probably more complicated than either alternative. Nonetheless, motivation is something students must find for themselves, thus, presenting different motivational challenges to classroom teachers.

Teachers, however, can play a powerful role in motivating students through their words and actions. If the teacher is moody or unpleasant or tries to make assignments unnecessarily hard, student motivation and learning will decrease. Effective teachers are caring and provide security—two controlling motivators. If teachers want to motivate students, they must demonstrate sincere concern for student welfare and make them feel as secure as possible.

Effective teachers use a variety of methods so that all students want to learn *most* of the time. Establishing rapport by showing sincerity and humility, teaching with a sense of humor, maintaining a cheerful, positive attitude, making lessons motivating, increasing student accountability by encouraging and expecting quality work, preparing activities that are authentic, purposeful and connected to real life, and treating students with respect are all effective techniques that can be used to motivate most students to learn. An essential part of teaching is helping students find their own good reasons to learn.

What Are the Two Types of Motivation?

Researchers have identified two types of motivation: intrinsic motivation and extrinsic motivation.

Intrinsic motivation is an innate drive, i.e., it is a process nurtured by feelings and needs from within. Students will do something for the sheer joy of doing it or because they want to discover something, answer a question, or experience the feeling of self-accomplishment. For example, you may want to read this chapter because you value learning and want to be knowledgeable about skills

you will need as a teacher to understand students' motives for learning. Thus, personal factors such as needs, interests, and curiosity explain the concept of intrinsic motivation, motivation associated with activities nurtured by drives and needs within oneself that are their own reward.

Sometimes students' behavior is directed by outside forces. This type of behavior or process is known as extrinsic motivation. Extrinsic motivation is created by external factors such as rewards and punishments. When students do something in order to earn a grade, avoid punishment, or please the teacher or the parent, they care only about their sole gain and nothing about the task at hand. For example, you detest psychology and read this chapter to earn an A on the test next week. You are motivated to pass the certification requirements and/or to keep your scholarship. Thus, you are motivated by factors external to yourself and possibly unrelated to the task you are performing.

Extrinsic motivators, such as good grades, a teacher's or parent's praise, extra privileges, public recognition, competition, even stickers or candy, are often expected or relied on by students. Often times, these external motivators get in the way of learning because they are sometimes overused or abused. However, many experts believe that extrinsic motivators can be every effective in helping students develop intrinsic motivation to learn or behave.

On the other hand, Kohn (1999) in his book, *Punished by Rewards: The Trouble with Gold Stars, Incentive Plans, A's, Praise and Other Bribes,* argues that extrinsic motivators, including good grades, some types of praise, and stickers, are ineffective and counterproductive to the quality of the learning process. Kohn (1999) contends, "No kid deserves to be manipulated with extrinsics so as to comply with what someone else wants." He states that rewards can have the inverse effect of motivating and take away someone's desire to learn.

Whether or not you agree or disagree with Kohn, the lynchpin to keep in mind is that students are often not as deeply engaged in learning as teachers would like them to be. McCune et al. (1999) found that "students will be more likely to engage in learning activities when they attribute success or failure to things they can control, like their own effort or lack or it, rather than to forces over which they have little or no control, such as their ability, luck, or outside forces" (p. 39). Therefore, an effective teacher recognizes that students vary in their motivation levels. An effective teacher knows how to support intrinsically motivated students and seeks the variety of strategies necessary to provide extrinsic motivation to students who need it. "Students learn when they have a reason and an effective teacher helps students find their own good reasons to learn" (Brandt, 1995, p. 87). Conversely, whether student motivation is intrinsic or extrinsic, teachers must ensure that their students' needs in the context of Malsow's Hierarchy of Needs for physical survival, safety, belongingness, love, and esteem are met.

What Are the Theories of Motivation?

Of all the questions teachers have concerning affect, the most commonly evoked query is: "How can I motivate my students to learn?" Good teachers know that students who feel motivated to learn are a joy to teach. But how do our students become motivated, and what can you do to maintain this desire to learn? Theorists, researchers, and psychologists have explored the following principles related to the effect motivation has on students' learning and behavior.

Motivation is defined as a feeling of a force that directs behavior toward specific goals for which people strive (Maehr, & Meyer, 1997; Graham & Weiner, 1996; Pintrich, Marx, & Boyle, 1993). This feeling affects the choices that students make—whether to watch a football game or write an assigned research paper; whether to take an active role and try out for

the lead in a school play or assume a passive role and sit in the audience and watch.

Motivation can also be self-sustaining. Often this powerful force leads to increased effort and energy. Motivation increases the amount of intensity and the level of involvement that students expend in activities directly related to their needs and goals (Csikszentmihalyi & Nakamura, 1989); therefore, motivation often determines whether students pursue a learning task enthusiastically and wholeheartedly or apathetically and lackadaisically. For example, why do some students start their homework right away while others procrastinate?

Motivation increases initiation of and persistence in activities. Students are more likely to begin a task that they actually *want* to do. They are more likely to continue that task until they've completed it, even when they are occasionally interrupted or frustrated in their efforts to do so (Larson, 2000). For example, why do some students read the entire chapter in the textbook while others read just a few pages? Some of the answer may be that motivation enhances cognitive processing. Motivation affects what and how information is processed (Pintrich & Schunk, 2002). Motivated students are more likely to pay attention and take pleasure in performing the learning activity. Paying attention and learning for enjoyment results in students' long-term retention and critical understanding of the material in order to construct meaning rather than simply memorizing the facts to pass an upcoming test.

Perhaps most important of all, motivation leads to improved performance. When goal-directed behavior, energy and effort, initiation, persistence, reinforcement, and cognitive processing are all combined, students are totally motivated to learn. These students tend to be the highest achievers (Gottfried, 1990; Schiefele, Krapp & Winteler, 1992; Walbert & Uguroglu, 1980); just the opposite is true of students who are least motivated. The unmotivated, our lowest achievers, are frequently at high risk for dropping out of school before they graduate

(Goodman, 2002; Hardre & Reeve, 2001; Hymel, Comfort, Schonert-Reichl & McDougall, 1996; Valerand, Fortier, & Guay, 1997).

Factors That Affect Motivation

To illustrate the practical applications of these principles in a typical classroom setting, I present two student case profiles. These case studies may help you to understand two key emotional and motivational factors: learned helplessness and anxiety. These two psychological phenomena exert significant influence on the teaching and learning process.

Case 1:

Michael won't even start the assignment—as usual. He just keeps saying, "I don't understand, or "This is too hard." When he answers the teacher's questions correctly, he "guessed" and he "doesn't really know." Michael spends most of his time staring into space; he is falling farther and farther behind. Michael has trouble starting the assignment right from the beginning. He feels defeated and helpless and maintains that nothing he does matters. "I will always fail because I am stupid," continues Michael.

Case 2:

Sarah pretends to be working on her assignment but spends most of her time making fun of the assignment, because she is afraid to try. She fears that she will look foolish in front of her peers and believes that everyone will think she is "dumb." In terms of the principles of motivation, Sarah makes poor choices, procrastinates, avoids engagement, and gives up easily because she is so concerned about how others will judge her. She freezes on tests and "forgets" everything she knows when she has to answer questions in class. Her parents are very high achievers and expect her to become a successful adult, too, but her prospects for this future look dim.

In Case 1, Miguel's actions can be termed learned helplessness, a condition that affects motivation over time. Learned helplessness is based on an experience in which the student feels he or she has no control and is doomed to failure. Students who experience repeated failures might develop a "defensive pessimism" to protect themselves from negative feedback (Martin, Marsh, & Debus, 2001). Learned helplessness can result from a child's upbringing (Hokoda & Fincham, 1995) but also from inconsistent, unpredictable use of rewards and punishments by teachers. Focusing on learning goals (goals of students who are motivated primarily by desire for knowledge acquisition and self-improvement) rather than performance goals (goals of students who are motivated primarily by a desire to gain recognition from others and to earn good grades) can reduce learned helplessness. All students can attain learning goals if they can connect to a personal goal for themselves (Dweck, 1986). Teachers can prevent or reduce learned helplessness by setting consistent, high expectations and accentuating positive outcomes of learning, providing students with opportunities to succeed in small strides, and by giving immediate, encouraging feedback.

In Case 2, Sarah was experiencing debilitating anxiety which was seriously inhibiting her learning and performance. This was particularly problematic during tests. One of the main sources of anxiety in school is the fear of failure and, with it, loss of self-esteem (Hill & Wigfield, 1984). Sarah's feelings of anxiety arose from what she thought and how she felt while she worked. Sarah was experiencing anxiety because she faced situations in which she believed she had little or no chance of succeeding. Her sources of anxiety resulted from concern about what others would think of her and her worry about the future—not meeting her parents' expectations of pursuing a meaningful career. Thus, Sarah's anxiety distracted her attention from the task at hand and blocked her performance.

Teachers can apply many strategies to reduce the negative impact of anxiety on learning and performance by creating a learning environment that is safe and accepting with clear, positive expectations. Teachers should also provide unambiguous instruction and frequent feedback. Another tool for reducing anxiety is to provide students with rubrics for self-evaluation and to give frequent opportunities for self-reflection. In testing situations, teachers can employ a number of strategies to help anxious students perform well. For example, teachers can give students additional time to complete a test and check their work. Tests that begin with easy problems and have standard, simple responses are better for anxious students. Test-anxious students can be trained in test-taking skills and relaxation techniques, both which can have a positive impact on their test performance (Spielberger & Vagg, 1995).

Teachers who have the best success are the ones who deeply care about their students. This caring covers not only the academic competency their students' achieve, but it extends to the whole child. A caring and compassionate teacher knows that the feelings that the child experiences are an integral part of his or her life. These feelings play a dominant role in the interpersonal and intrapersonal world of the student. Without careful and sensitive attention to these feelings, the child may not be able to fully learn and develop. By giving the gifts of love and understanding, teachers can often accomplish educational miracles within their classrooms (Eben, 2006).

References

Alexander, P. A., & Murphy, P. K. (1998). The research base for APA's Learner-Centered Psychological Principles. In N. Lambert & B. McCombs (Eds.), *How students learn: Reforming schools through learner-centered education* (pp. 33–60). Washington, D.C: American Psychological Association.

Bandura, A. (2001). Social cognitive theory: An agentic perspective. *Annual Review of Psychology, 52,* 1–26.

Brandt, R. (1995). Why people learn. *Educational Leadership.* 53, (1). Available www.ascd.org.

Collaborative for Academic, Social, and Emotional Learning. (2005). *Social emotional learning (SEL) competencies.* Chicago: IL: Author. Availalble: www.casel.org/about_sel/SELskills.php./

Cowley, G., & Underwood, A. (1998, June 15). Memory. *Newsweek, 131* (24), 48–54.

Csikszentmihalyi, M., & Nakamura, J. (1989). The dynamics of intrinsic motivation: A study of adolescence. In C. Ames & R. Ames (Eds.), *Research on motivation in education: Vols. 3: Goals and cognition.* San Digeo, CA: Academic Press.

Damasio, A. (1994). *Descartes' error: Emotion, reason, and the human brain.* New York: Grosset/Putnam.

Dweck, C. S. (1986). Motivational processes affecting learning. *American Psychologist, 41,* 1040–1048.

Eben, J. (2006). *How many wins have you had today?* Fresno, CA: Hergenroeder Press.

Eisenberger, N., & Fabes, R. A. (1998). Prosocial development. In W. Damon (Series Ed.) & N. Eisenberg (Vol. Ed). *Handbook of child psychology* (5th ed. Vol.3, pp.701–778. New York: Wiley.

Fischer, K.W., Kennedy, B., Cheng, C-L. (1998). Culture and biology in emotional development. In D. Sharma & K.W. Fischer (Eds.), Socioemotional development across cultures. *New Directions for Child Development, 81,* 21–43.

Freedom Writers & Filipovic, Z. (1999). *Freedom writers diary: How a teacher and 150 teens used writing to change themselves and the world around them.* New York: Broadway Books.

Gardner, H. (1993). *Multiple intelligences: The Theory in Practice.* New York: Basic.

Goleman, D. (1995). *Emotional intelligence.* New York: Bantam.

Goodman, G. (2002). *Reducing hate crimes and violence among American youth: Creating transformational agency through critical praxis.* New York: Peter Lang.

Gottfried, A. E. (1990). Academic intrinsic motivation in young elementary school children. *Journal of Educational Psychology, 82,* 525–538.

Graham, S. & Weiner, B. (1996). Theories and principle of motivation. In D. C. Berliner & R. C. Calfee (Eds.), *Handbook of education psychology.* New York: Macmillan.

Hardre, P. L., & Reeve, J. (2001). *A motivational model of rural high students' dropout intentions.* Paper presented at the annual meeting of the American Educational Research Association, Seattle, WA.

Hill, K., & Wigfield, A. (1984). Test anxiety: A major educational problem and what can be done about it. *Elementary School Journal, 85,* 105–126.

Hoffman, M. L. (1991). Empathy, social cognition, and moral action. In W. M. Kurtines & J. L. Gewirtz (Eds.), *Moral behavior and development: Vol. 1: Theory* (pp. 275–301). Hillsdale, NJ: Erlbaum.

Hokoda, A., & Fincham, F. D. (1995). Origins of children's helpless and mastery achievement patterns in the family. *Journal of Education Psychology, 87,* 375–385.

Hymel, S., Comfort, C., Schonert-Reichl, K., & McDougall, P. (1996). Academic failure and school dropout: the influence of peers. In J. Juvonen & K. R. Wentzel (Eds.), *Social motivation: Understanding children's school adjustment* (pp. 313–345). Cambridge, England: Cambridge University Press.

Jensen, E. (1997). *Completing the puzzle: The brain-compatible approach to learning* (2nd ed.). Del Mar, CA: Turning Point.

Jensen, E. (1998). *Introduction to brain-compatible learning.* Del Mar, CA: Turning Point.

Kohn, A. (1999). *Punished by rewards: The trouble with gold stars, incentive plans, A's praise and other bribes.* Boston: Houghton Mifflin.

Langer, E. (1997). *The power of mindful learning.* New York: Addison-Wesley.

———. (1989). *Mindfulness.* New York: Addison-Wesley.

Larson, R. W. (2000). Toward a psychology of positive youth development. *American Psychologist, 55,* pp.170–183.

McCune, S. L., Stephens, D. E., & Lowe, M. E. (1999). *Barron's how to prepare for the ExCET* (2nd ed.*).* Haupauge: NY: Barron's Educational Series.

Maehr, M. L. & Meyer, H. A. (1997). Understanding motivation and schooling: Where we've been, where we are, where we need to go. *Educational Psychology Review, 9 (4),* 371–409.

Martin, A. J., Marsh, H. W., & Debus, R. L. (2001). Self-handicapping and defensive pessimism: Exploring a model of predicators and outcomes from a self-protection perspective. *Journal of Educational Psychology. 93* (1), 87–102.

Marzano, R.J. (1998). *A theory-based meta-analysis of research on instruction.* Aurora, CO: Mid-Continent Regional Educational Laboratory.

Miller, P.H. (2002). *Theories of developmental psychology* (4th ed.). New York: Worth.

Ormrod, S. (2006). *Essentials of educational psychology.* Upper Saddle River, N.J.: Prentice Hall.

Pintrich, P. R., Marx, R. W., & Boyle, R. A. (1993). Beyond cold conceptual change: the role of motivational beliefs and classroom contextual factors in the process of conceptual change. *Review of Educational Research, 63,* 167–199.

Pintrich, P.R. & Schunk, D. H. (2002). *Motivation in education: Theory, research, and applications* (2nd ed.). Upper Saddle Rier, NJ: Merrill/ Prentice Hall.

Renninger, K. A., Hidi, S., & Krapp, A. (Eds.) (1992). *The role of interest in learning and development.* Hillsdale, NJ: Erlbaum.

Salovey, P.& Mayer, J. D. (2004*). emotional intelligence: Key readings on the mayer and salovey model.* New York: Dude.

Schiefele, U., Krapp, A., & Winteler, A. (1992). Interest as a predictor of academic achievement: a meta-analysis of research. In K. A. Renninger, S. Hidi, & A. Krapp (Eds.), *The role of interest in learning and development.* Hillsdale, NJ: Erlbaum.

Schraw, G. & Lehman, S. (2001). Situational interest: A review of the literature and directions for future research. *Educational Psychology Review, 13,* 23–52.

Simonson, M. and Maushak, N. (2001). Instructional technology and attitude change. In D. Jonassen (Ed.), *Handbook of research for educational communications and technology* (pp. 984–1016). Mahwah, NJ: Lawrence Erlbaum Associates.

Slavin, R. (1995). *Cooperative learning: Theory, research, and practice.* Boston: Allyn & Bacon.

Slavin, R. (1996). *Every child, every school: Success for all.* Thousand Oaks, CA: Corwin Press.

Slavin, R., Karweit, N. & Madden, N. (1989). *Effective programs for students at risk.* Boston: Allyn & Bacon.

Smith, P. & Ragan, T.J. (1999). *Instructional design.* New York: John Wiley & Sons.

Spielberger,C. & Vagg, P. (Eds.) (1995). *Test anxiety: Theory, assessment, and treatment.* Washington, D.C: Taylor & Francis.

Valerand, R. J., Fortier,M. S., & Guay, F. (1997). Self-determination and persistence in a real-life setting: Toward a motivational model of high school dropout. *Journal of Personality and Social Psychology, 72,* 1161–1176.

Vygotsky, L. (1978). *Mind in society: The development of higher psychological processes.* Cambridge, MA: Harvard University Press.

Walbert, H. J., & Uguroglu, M. (1980). Motivation and educational productivity: Theories, results, and implications. In L. J. Fyans, Jr. (Ed.), *Achievement motivation: Recent trends in theory and research.* New York: Plenum Press.

Watson-Gegeo, K. & Gegeo, D. (2004). Deep culture: Pushing the epistemological boundaries. In G. Goodman & K. Carey (Eds.), *Critical multicultural conversations.* Cresskill, N.J.: Hampton Press.

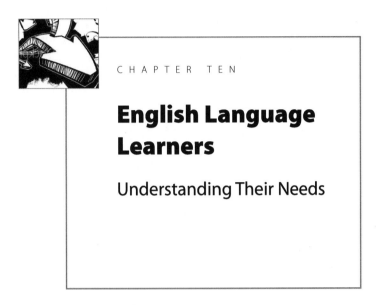

CHAPTER TEN

English Language Learners

Understanding Their Needs

Binbin Jiang

English language learners (ELLs) are students whose native languages are not English but are learning English in our schools. ELLs make up over 5 million students, among whom 80% are Spanish speaking, nearly 10.3 percent of public school enrollment. By the year 2025, ELLs under age 18 are projected to be approximately 50% of the American population (American Federation of Teachers, 2006). It will be virtually impossible for a professional educator to serve in any public or private school setting in which the students are not racially, culturally or linguistically diverse. To better prepare each future educator so that she/he can work effectively with this population of students in schools, I will address the linguistic, social, psychological and cultural factors that affect the schooling experience and academic success of these English language learners.

Specific attention will be paid to how children and youth acquire a second language in school, and how long it takes to acquire conversational and academic language in a second language. It is important to understand the role first language literacy and prior formal schooling have on the student's progress in a second language. Prior social and cultural experiences can have a significant affect on issues of second language learning. The combination of social and psychological factors effect ELLs in their learning of the English language. I will conclude this chapter with a discussion of how cultural differences affect ELLs' academic success and present principles for teachers use in effectively working with these unique learners in schools.

While ELLs may be all ages, come from a wide range of ethnic backgrounds, hail from different economic situations, and may have come to this country for a variety of reasons, they all share the common need to learn English. Throughout the history of American education many different terms have been used to describe or characterize children whose second language is English: students with limited English proficiency (LEPs); students for whom English is a second language (ESLs); or second language learners (SLLs). Currently educators most commonly refer to these children as English language learners (ELLs). This shift in language represents a more accurate reflection of the process of language acquisition.

Krashen's Second Language Learning Theory & Stages of Second Language Acquisition

How do ELLs learn English and become competent in the use of English language? There are many theories about second language learning; however, Stephan Krashen's theory (1981) has been among the most influential in helping educators understand this process. Krashen's theory includes five major components: a language **acquisition**/ learning hypothesis; the natural order hypothesis; the mon-

Acquisition
The process of gaining language.

itor hypothesis; the comprehensible input hypothesis; and the affective filter hypothesis.

The acquisition-learning hypothesis distinguishes between informal learning of a language (acquisition) and formal learning of academic language within the classroom setting. Acquisition is similar in many ways to the process children use in acquiring their first language and is largely subconscious. Learning the academic language is generally the product of formal instruction. The context for first language acquisition is at home and in real-life situations in which children feel free and safe. Conversely, the context for learning academic language is usually in the classroom in which learners are given specific instructions on certain aspects of the target language; for example, vocabulary, pronunciation of words, grammar, listening, speaking, reading and writing. The implication is that teachers who create an atmosphere where students feel free, and safe, to experiment using the target language can successfully promote more active learning. As a second language learner, I learned English language grammar and how to understand, speak, read and write in English in the formal classroom context where I grew up in China. However, when I came to the United States where English is used in everyday life and professional contexts, I have acquired more native-like English usage. This experience is especially critical in understanding the **idiomatic expressions** of conversational English.

Idiomatic expressions

Metaphors used in common speech; "I bombed the test."

The natural order hypothesis states that we acquire the rules of a language in a predictable sequence. For example, an understanding of the plural of nouns is acquired more quickly than rules of the third-person singular verb ending of "s." According to Krashen, (1992), "The natural order appears to be immune to deliberate teaching; we cannot change the natural order by explanation, drills and exercises" (p. 2). Another example that Krashen gives is that adults learning a second language acquire the progressive "-ing" marker earlier than the third person singular "-s" even though we do more patterned drills and exercises on the latter. This hypothesis tells us that constant correction of grammatical errors to beginning learners of a second language is not especially helpful.

Krashen's monitor hypothesis suggests that language learned in the classroom serves only to "edit" or "monitor" what the students pick up or acquire. When the student produces language, it may contain errors. A student can "monitor" to make some self-corrections, but his focus will conflict with a focus on fluency and the content of the message. This hypothesis reminds teachers that second language learners are often trying to produce something that is correct using the rules they have learned to plan and monitor the sentence or paragraph before they actually say or write it. Consequently, teachers need to give students sufficient time to think and not require answers from them before they are ready in the second language. For instance, when I was learning the past tense in English, it took me a very long time to acquire the use of past tense as there are no verb tenses in Chinese (my native language). For a long time, I would actually search for the past tense of the verb in my mind to fit into the sentence before I actually spoke it. The process of searching for the past tense is the monitor or editor function in language learning.

Comprehensible input hypothesis claims that people acquire language when they receive comprehensible input which is slightly beyond their current level of understanding. For example, people learn the rules of language in a natural order, learning rule 1, then rule 2 and so on. When the first rule is learned, they are ready to learn the next. According to Krashen (1992):

> More generally, if "i" represents the last rule we have acquired, and "i+1" the next rule we have acquired . . . we move from "i" to "i+1" by understanding input containing "i+1." We are able to do this with the help of our previously acquired linguistic competence, as well as extra-linguistic

knowledge, which includes our knowledge of the world and our knowledge of the situation. In other words, we use context. (p. 4)

The point is that the input (i) must be slightly beyond the learners' ability level (i+1) so that acquisition will take place. Krashen (1992) states that "teaching methods containing more comprehensible input have been shown to be more effective than 'traditional' methods . . . for both beginning and intermediate language teaching" (p. 3). In teaching my beginning adult ELLs, I try to speak slowly, use simple sentence structure, and use visual aids and repetition to make the input comprehensible for the students. I relate to this aspect of second language learning because of a negative experience I had caused by a lack of understanding English. While I was a college freshman majoring in English in China, I experienced comprehension input difficulty in an American history class taught by an American professor. Because I did not have the background knowledge nor the vocabulary necessary to understand the content of the class, his lectures in English were way beyond my comprehension. In addition, the professor used the normal native speaker's speed when lecturing. If he had known about the concept of comprehensible input, I probably would have had a more effective learning experience in that course.

The affective filter hypothesis claims that learners put up a resistance to learning in certain situations. This mental block prevents them "from utilizing input fully for further language acquisition" when they are "in a less than optimal affective state" (Krashen, 1992, p.9). An optimal state for second language learning is one in which learners have a low level of anxiety, high motivation, self-esteem and confidence. For example, when language learners feel nervous or embarrassed, they can receive comprehensible input but still not acquire the language as their affective filter is high. On the other hand, a student with high motivation can cause the affective filter to be lowered. This hypothesis indicates that students will not acquire a language if their stress level or boredom level is too high. Therefore, we must create a comfortable classroom context and provide materials that will sustain students' curiosity while we teach the necessary content.

Krashen (1985) summarized the five interrelated hypotheses in his book, *Inquiries and Insights,* in one sentence: "We acquire language when we obtain comprehensible input in a low-anxiety situation, when we are presented with interesting messages, and when we understand these messages" (p. 94). In other words, language is acquired in a natural order when students are given comprehensible input in a risk-free environment.

To put Krashen's second language acquisition theory into practice, Krashen and Terrell (1983) developed the Natural Approach teaching method. Based on the Natural Approach method, there are four basic stages or levels that all new learners of English progress through to acquire the target language. It is important to note that the length of time each student spends at a particular stage may vary greatly. In addition, ELLs in the same class may be at different stages/levels of their English proficiency. Knowing the characteristics of each stage/level can be very useful to content area teachers who work with ELLs as they assess which stage/level each ELL is at in order to communicate effectively with each of them and to select appropriate teaching strategies.

The first stage is known as the pre-production/silent period. During this time, students have anywhere from 10 hours to six months of exposure to English, and their vocabulary includes approximately 500 receptive words (words they can understand but don't use yet). They do not usually produce much verbal language at this time, but they communicate using gestures and actions. During this stage, students only understand language that has been made comprehensible. They often rely on modeling, visual stimuli such as pictures and

objects, context clues, key words and use listening strategies to understand meaning. These language learners frequently communicate through pointing and physical gestures. For students in this stage of language learning, the teacher should provide activities geared to tap their knowledge but not to force production (speaking). These students benefit from classroom activities that allow them to respond by imitating, drawing, pointing, and matching.

After having spent anywhere from three months to a year immersed in learning English, students begin to acquire a small yet active vocabulary of approximately 100 words. This is referred to as stage two: the early production period. During this time, students grow to have a receptive vocabulary level of approximately 1,000 words, and they begin to feel ready to speak in one- or two-word phrases. At this stage of language learning, students can demonstrate their comprehension of material by giving short responses to easy yes/no questions and either/or questions. They can also respond to simple who, what, when, where questions. They may benefit from classroom activities that employ language they can understand, require them to name and group objects, and call for responses to simple questions.

Stage Three: Speech Emergence

After somewhere between one and three years of exposure to English, students' development of proficiency increases exponentially. This is known as the speech emergence stage. During this time, they use phrases and sentences, and their active vocabulary grows to about 3,000 words with nearly 7,000 words of receptive vocabulary. There is a noticeable increase in listening comprehension. Students will try to speak in phrases and start to use complete sentences. They often mix basic phrases and sentences in both languages. They will begin to use the social language necessary in the classroom. Ask students at this stage how and why questions that elicit short responses. They will be able to participate in many of the mainstream academic subjects. They may benefit from classroom activities that encourage them to experiment with language and develop and expand their vocabulary.

After about three to four years of exposure to English, students have accumulated approximately 6,000 active words and 12,000 receptive words. This is known as the Nearly Fluent/Intermediate Fluency stage of language acquisition. Students understand most of what is said in the classroom, and they are developing good comprehension skills. They can express their ideas comprehensibly in both oral and written communication. These students expand on their basic sentences and extend their language abilities to employ more complex sentence structures and make fewer errors when speaking. Functionally, they will be able to read most grade-level material. Teachers may ask these students open-ended questions that allow more complicated responses and the use of complex sentences. These sophisticated second language learners may benefit from classroom literacy activities and instruction in vocabulary and grammar.

Cummins' View of Second Language Proficiency

According to Cummins (1981), there are two important types of language proficiency. Cummins identified these levels of comprehension as Basic Interpersonal Communication Skills (BICS) and Cognitive Academic Language Proficiency (CALP). BICS refers to skills or proficiency in conversational English used in informal interpersonal communications such as at the dinner table or on the school playground. In contrast, CALP is the skill or proficiency in the academic language or formal language used in classrooms and in textbooks. It is the complex syntax of English including forms, rules, and relationships of formal oral and written English. According to Collier's (1989) study, it takes approximately two years for a student to achieve proficiency in BICS, but generally five to seven years to achieve proficiency in CALP.

In concert with Krashen and Terrell's four stages of the language development, students begin to develop their BICS at the Pre-Production Stage and reach BICS during the Speech Emergence Stage. At this stage/level, they also begin their initial development of CALP. At the Intermediate Fluency Stage, students continue to develop their CALP and begin to demonstrate their development in CALP through listening, speaking, reading and writing in English. In other words, a student who is fluent in English on the playground is likely to require five to seven years to acquire the level of proficiency needed for successful academic learning. The implication for teachers is not to overlook the fact that academic language can still be challenging and adversely affect the student's academic performance even though she/he is fluent in everyday conversations.

Cummins' Common Underlying Proficiency (CUP) Model of Bilingual Proficiency indicates that bilingual students develop proficiency in two languages but with the same underlying proficiency. The implication of this model is that proficiencies developed in one language are transferable to another. According to Cummins, "Concepts are most readily developed in the first language and, once developed, are accessible through the second language. In other words, what we learn in one language transfers into the new language" (Freeman & Freeman, 1992, p. 176). For instance, in my Chinese literature class in high school, I learned the literary terminology and the related concepts applied to literature, such as flashback, theme characterization, and foreshadowing. When these terms were encountered in English, the concepts were already understood, and, thus, I was able to transfer the knowledge learned in Chinese to English.

Evidence for transfer of language skills also comes from research done by Cummins (1979a). He examined the relationship between bilingual children's academic skills in the primary and second language. Correlations between the first language (L1) and the second language (L2) proficiency were statistically significant which may imply that children who read well in L1 were likely to read well in L2 (Cummins, 1979b).

In my own research (Jiang, 1999, Jiang & Kuehn, 2001), I have also examined the relationship between bilingual students' academic language skills in L1 and L2. Although, my focus was on adult learners, I found similar results regarding the relationship between a bilingual's academic proficiency in L1 and L2 and the issue of transfer (Bossers, 1991; Canale, Frenette, and Belanger, 1988; Carson and Kuehn, 1994; Cummins, 1984; Hoover, 1983; Verhoeven, 1991).

As people learn languages, they develop certain skills that may naturally transfer from L1 to L2. The level of proficiency reached in L1 does influence the development of their proficiency in L2 (Odlin, 1986). Empirical studies have indicated that the "transfer of ability to L2 can only occur if individuals have already acquired that ability in their L1" (Carson and Kuehn, 1994, p. 260).

The Role of First Language Literacy and Formal Schooling

As I have discussed so far, students who have had prior formal schooling and L1 language proficiency in their native country will be more likely to transfer their knowledge and skills to the L2 learning experiences. This experience and prior success can make their transition and learning in the L2 context much smoother. Conversely, the students who have not had formal schooling and L1 literacy will not have the knowledge and skill from their L1 to transfer. These students can encounter more difficulties and challenges, and it may take them much more time and effort to learn English. These two groups of students are distinguished by Faltis and Coulter (2007) as immigrant students with parallel and nonparallel schooling experiences.

According to Faltis and Coulter, immigrant students with parallel schooling experiences typically enter school at grade level or above and may have had prior exposure to English in school or at home

with tutors. These students tend to have smooth transitions into school culture and they often excel academically. Research conducted by Suárez-Orozco & Suárez-Orozco (2001) provides documentation that Salvadoran immigrant children with parallel schooling experiences do succeed academically in school once they gain oral and written proficiency in English.

Zhou (1998) also discusses "parachute kids" in Southern California. These are transnational immigrant children and youth from high-achieving families in China and Taiwan who "drop in" to American schools and live with relatives. These immigrant children and young adults have parallel formal schooling experiences, and they also experience academic success and smoother transition.

Conversely, immigrant students with non-parallel schooling experiences and long-term English learners encounter the most difficulty in the schooling experience in the U.S. and present the greatest challenges for schools and classroom teachers. Non-parallel immigrant students are typically at least two grade levels below where they should be for their age group (Faltis & Coulter, 2007). Gibson (1998) has found that these students also face a number of other obstacles in school. In addition to entering school knowing little or no English, they often have to deal with conflicts between family values and school values. Another challenge many of these students face when they enter school is their minimal knowledge of and experience with computer technology. Computers have become an essential tool for the successful schooling for secondary students (Suárez-Orozco, 2005).

Long-term English learners are immigrant students who have been in English learning programs for at least five years, and they remain English learners. These are students who are below grade level in reading and writing, and they are mostly unable to participate in and benefit from mainstream English-only classrooms unless they can be given individualized instructional practices (Freeman & Freeman,

2002). Specifically, these students need a schooling environment that is inclusive and supportive of their specific language and literacy needs.

Sociocultural Issues Related to Language Learning

In both positive and negative ways, elements related to social status and to the students' cultural background contribute considerable influence to the success of ESL students' learning. In their discussion of Labov's (1972) findings, Diaz-Rico and Weed (1995) reached the following conclusion:

> As students learn a second language, their success is dependent on such extra-linguistic factors as the pattern of acculturation for their community; the status of their primary language in relation to English; their own speech community's view of the English language and the English-speaking community; the dialect of English they are hearing and learning and its relationship to standard English; the patterns of social and cultural language usage in the community (Labov, 1972); and the compatibility between the home culture and the cultural patterns and organization of schools (Diaz-Rico and Weed, pp. 40–41). Language is important "in defining the shape of thought." (Hakuta, 1986, p. 79).

Similarly, Ogbu (1986, 1991) discusses the different reasons that immigrants come to the United States and the factors that can lead to social integration or isolation. He describes these groups as immigrant minorities and involuntary minorities who often experience discrimination and autonomous minorities who stay separate from the majority culture (Freeman & Freeman, 1994). New immigrants view the "economic, political, and social barriers against them as more or less temporary problems" which they will "overcome with the passage of time, hard work, or more education" while involuntary minorities view these conditions as "permanent problems" which they "may have little hope of overcoming . . ." (pp. 222–3). Ogbu is famous for coining the term **involuntary immigrants** to define

Involuntary immigrants

People who come to a country against their will.

those who came to America against their will; for example, slaves.

While Ogbu (1981) looks at minority students in relation to the social and cultural factors that affect their success and failure in general, Schumann examines specific social factors that affect ESL students' acquisition of L2. Schumann uses the term assimilation to describe voluntary immigrants, and the term acculturation to describe immigrants who are in-between since they adapt to the new culture but continue to maintain their own. Schumann defines preservation as the behavior of involuntary immigrants who remain isolated and retain their own culture and reject the new culture.

Schumann (1978) posits, "Assimilation fosters minimal social distance and preservation causes it to be maximal. Hence, second language learning is enhanced by assimilation and hampered by preservation. Acculturation falls in the middle." (p. 78).

Social and Psychological Factors

Schumann (1978) developed a model for analysis of the instances in which learners "create both a psychological distance and social distance from speakers of the second language community" (Gass and Selinker, 1994, p. 236). The significance of these differences formed the basis for Schumann's Acculturation Model. Schumann characterized the relationship between the acculturation model and second language acquisition as follows: "Second language acquisition is just one aspect of acculturation and the degree to which a learner acculturates to the target-language group will control the degree to which he acquires the second language . . ." (McLaughlin, 1987, p. 110). From this point of view, second language acquisition is determined by the degree of social and psychological distance between the learner and the target language culture.

Schumann identified eight influential factors in determining social distance. Social dominance refers to the power relations between speakers of the two languages. The L2 learner may be in a subordinate position that may be related to economic or cultural status. The greater the dominance of the speakers of the target language, the greater difficulty the learners will have in acquiring that language. When there is more equality between the two groups, the second language will be easier to acquire.

The integration pattern refers to the full, partial, or limited integration of the L2 learner and depends upon the degree of his or her assimilation and acculturation into the new culture and the degree of the preservation of the L2 learner's native culture. Preservation is linked to an individual's desire to maintain aspects of his or her native culture while living within the new culture. When cultural groups band together this is considered enclosure. Enclosure refers to the confinement of the L2 learner to the native culture and environment. Size of the group has a significant effect, and it refers to the number of a particular cultural group that create or maintain norms.

Cohesiveness is an outgrowth of all of the earlier stages, and it refers to the unity surrounding a specific non-mainstream culture. For example, my Hmong students have enough unity within their group that their need to assimilate with the target language group is alleviated. Cultural congruence is maintained with the cohesiveness, and this refers to the points of correspondence and the harmonious agreement among cultures.

Attitude refers to the positive, negative, or neutral attitudes between the groups, more often being negative or neutral. The intended length of stay for the L2 learner also affects the way in which the target language is learned. For example, someone who plans to stay in a country for a short length of time only may have little reason or motivation to become proficient in the target language.

Psychological distance, according to Schumann (1978), results from the affective influence of certain psychological factors: language shock, culture shock, motivation, and ego boundaries (Ellis, 1986).

Whereas language shock can lead to doubt and confusion, culture shock can lead to disorientation, stress, fear, and other negative attitudes. A person with high motivation to learn the target language and to learn the culture would probably not suffer from language or culture shock. However, that learner may still have ego boundaries which cause inhibition, defensiveness, and self-consciousness that slow down the process of language acquisition. According to Freeman and Freeman (1994), "In situations where social distance neither strongly promotes nor inhibits language acquisition, psychological distance may play a crucial role" (p. 83).

Cultural Differences Affecting ELL's Academic Success

Because schools are a microcosm of society, many of the same social, cultural, and psychological factors affecting students in society will affect them within the school culture. This can also affect their academic success. For example, students who are not native English speakers must socialize with those who are on campus and in the classroom. More importantly, they must integrate into the school community in order to better understand the school system's organizational structure, policies, and expectations. Second language learners need to integrate within the diverse school population and the classroom in order to better develop the learning and social strategies needed for success.

Teachers also must become sensitive to the second language students' needs and provide support to help them adapt to the new school culture. Part of the responsibility that teachers have is to understand that differences in language and culture are often subtle, but they affect students' classroom participation in several ways. Understanding these will help teachers to respond in ways that will help both ELLs and other students to learn.

Cultural differences can mean different rules for classroom behavior. Zehler (1994) recommended the following advice for teachers to be sensitive to the cultural differences among the ELLs in schools.

Students from other cultures may behave differently than what is expected in the American classrooms as they may have different views of how to be a student based on their own cultural norms. For example, in some countries, it is disrespectful to ask questions of a teacher or speak in class. As a result, students from these countries may appear to be reluctant to ask any questions or participate in class discussions. However, as they adjust to the American school culture, they may gradually become acculturated and begin to follow their American peers' behavior.

Cultural differences can also affect students' understanding of content. New knowledge is constructed based on what is already known by an individual learner. Research in reading indicates that reading comprehension involves both understanding the words on the page and one's relevant background knowledge of the topic. However, textbooks used in schools often appear to have been written by authors who assume all students have the same background knowledge. In fact, many ELLs may not fully understand these texts because of a lack of background knowledge or lack of schooling experience in this country. Consequently, they will be less likely to fully comprehend or remember the content material. Students whose experience is not in the mainstream, therefore, will often need additional explanation and examples to help them bridge the gap between the new material and their existing knowledge bases.

Cultural differences can also affect interpersonal relations. Misinterpretation of respect, appreciation and showing interest may occur because of the interaction of multiple cultures in the classroom. It is common practice in some Asian and Latin American cultures for students not to look at the teacher in the eye to show respect when the teacher is talking. Unfortunately, this could be interpreted as the student's lack of attention or as a sign of disrespect if the teacher does not know the culture of the ELL. The way in which praise

is given may also be different. For some cultural groups, praise to an individual student is not given in public. In contrast, a quiet word of praise to the student is the norm for them. Teachers need to learn about different cultural practices and be sensitive to student reactions while also helping students to learn about American culture.

As a former ELL and as an educator working with ELLs and training teachers for ELLs for over 17 years in the United States and other countries, I have identified developed six principles for integrating instructional practices (Jiang & DeVillar, 2005). As an example, I will use a particular class that I taught with 30 beginning level (Between Pre-production and Early Production in Krashen & Terrell's model) ELLs in an adult school in California (Jiang, 2004). In my classroom, nine different languages were spoken and many different cultures (Laotion, Hmong, Vietnamese, Miao, Hispanic, Ethiopian, etc.) were present. To illustrate how each principle was implemented for helping these students to succeed in their learning and cultural adjustment in the United States, I will describe each principle in detail.

The first principle involves building the classroom community and culture. As ELLs experience linguistic, psychological, cultural, and other challenges in school while they are striving to learn both English and content knowledge, they need support and understanding from the teacher and their peers. Building a classroom community in which everyone cares about and learns from one another will provide the opportunity for ELLs to feel safe and comfortable to learn and to be willing share their experiences with others. For any teacher with a diverse student population, the American students can also benefit from learning about diverse cultures and be exposed to other languages that will help them to appreciate cultural and linguistic diversity and to broaden their understanding of the world. One way of building a classroom community is through getting to know one another by sharing everyone's experiences, talents, and families.

In my class, I started by sharing about myself, my family and the reasons why I was in the United States. This set the example for my students to tell about their lives, families and the reasons for coming to the U.S. They also brought pictures of their family, cultural artifacts and foods to share with their classmates. Through these sharing experiences, they began to understand and respect one another which mark the beginning of building the classroom community.

This cultural sharing helped the class members to have more pride in their own culture and increased their self-esteem and self-confidence. It also motivated students to learn English in order to share with others. These connections resulted in higher attendance rates. Through the code of visual aid, they understood more clearly the content of the discussion and participated in it through verbal and non-verbal communications. Cultural sharing contributed to the development of a positive environment of a community of learners. These students learned to greet each other in one another's native languages as a sign of appreciation of all the cultures represented in the community. This sensitivity helped students to feel more comfortable and to share more deeply personal experiences. It became obvious that they cared about one another.

This cultural sharing activity was also a valuable experience for me. For me to learn about the lives, history and oppression that my students had experienced in their homelands, it helped me to see more relevant themes for future learning units. As a participant and co-learner in the cultural sharing conversations, my respect and understanding for each class member grew as they opened up to our class community by sharing their beautiful culture traditions, their struggles through the war and hardships, and their talents and knowledge about the parts of the world that I did not know before. These students broadened my perspective on how social, cultural, and historical factors could affect individual learners.

Collaborative group work is another strong tool for promoting student learning. Because of my interest in students' sharing of their cultures, their experiences, and their talents, I took pictures of all the activities we had in class and brought the photos back to class. The students were excited to see themselves in the pictures. In order to celebrate and keep these wonderful memories, we decided to put the pictures on the bulletin board. I further thought it would be even more meaningful if the students could document their own activities.

According to the social learning principles of Vygotsky (1962, 1978), students working together can help gain access to new areas of learning beyond those they are able to accomplish alone. In other words, effective, long-term learning takes place when learners engage in mutually meaningful activities. It is productive for them to work in dyads or small groups, take an active role in the learning process, collaborate with one another, and exercise choice during their activities. As students collaborate, they learn to externalize their thoughts in order to communicate with each other, to solve problems, and to construct concepts, thus learning (D. E. Freeman and Y. Freeman, 1994). In order to facilitate such learning, teachers become mediators, helping students through their interaction to reach higher levels of proficiency. Vygotsky refers to the distance between the individual level of students and the potential level students can reach in collaborative interaction in the Zone of Proximal Development. According to his theory, learners working together have the potential to reach higher levels of development.

Learning to function in groups also helps students to function in society: "In communities of learners, students appear to learn how to coordinate with, support, and lead others, to become responsible and organized in their management of their own learning, and to be able to build on their previous interest to learn in new areas and to sustain motivation to learn" (Rogoff, Matusov, and White, 1996, p.

410). In other words, "Learning must be an active, social, discovery process, guided by the teacher, rather than a transmission process controlled by the teacher . . ." and "A learner is a thinker and an engaged participant; each role informs and transforms the other" (DeVillar, 1999, p.45).

Using these principles, I arranged the students into several groups. As members of the class community, they were willing to help each other in their collaborative group work. Each student contributed what he or she could to the writing within their particular group. For example, one person would take the role of scribe and editor; others helped with the vocabulary, or assisted with the spelling of a word. Other students would assist with the structures of the sentences. They enjoyed helping with the layout, for example, by determining where to integrate the photographs with the writing. Then, each group shared its text-and-image work with the whole class before placing their individual project on the bulletin board. The level of pride exhibited by students was very high.

The activity of using the pictures (or the codes) from the culture sharing continued to produce results. Most significantly, this activity transformed into more dialogue and action because of the collaborative group work. Students were learning to write about themselves and their activities and learning to read by reading each other's writings. By working together to learn to read and to write in English, they took active steps towards overcoming their language difficulties and towards making positive changes in their own lives.

Freire, the father of critical pedagogy, advocates a dialogical approach in which every member of the community becomes a co-learner in the critical learning process. "The students—no longer docile listeners—are now critical co-investigators in dialogue with the teacher" (Freire, 1998, p. 75). Dialogic approach is applicable to immigrant ELLs, in particular, since most of them come from backgrounds that are similar to the participants in

Freire's literacy programs—low socioeconomic status with limited or no access to education in their home countries. After coming to the United States, many of them have experienced emotional and social barriers in learning English, culture shock, lack of self-confidence, homesickness, and a sense of loss and vulnerability in the new environment.

In my teaching with the 30 adult ELLs in my class, I integrated their experiences into our content learning, and they became more active in the learning process. All this engagement made the learning authentic and interesting, thus helping the students learn more effectively. For example, the students enjoyed the weekly cultural sharing time so much that we gradually changed it to the first daily activity. In this activity, students shared experiences of their family and community and their perspectives. However, some students could not understand everything that was being shared because of the lack of vocabulary or their listening proficiency. They suggested that I write what the class contributed on the board so that they could copy and share them with their family. This started our class journal where we integrated listening, speaking, reading and writing within one activity using the content of students' experiences and reflections.

The daily journals provided authentic reading material for not only the class members but also some of the family members because of the relevant content. This activity was one of the favorite activities—for both the students and me—as it engaged the whole class in a writing project to produce a collective journal and evolved through different students' input over time. This practice adhered to the principle that students needed to be immersed in literature of all kinds to help them progress in writing, to become more proficient writers "through exposure to books and print . . ." (Weaver, 1994, p. 98).

Cummins contributes the notion of context-embedded instruction as "interpersonal involvement in a shared reality that reduces the need for explicit linguistic elaboration of the message" (Cummins, 1981, p.11). This is essential to beginning ESL classes, where the instructor can use pictures, realia, activities modeled by the teacher and the language aide, books and prints that have rich illustrations. In the specific adult L2 situation described here, communication was facilitated through the use of appropriate reading materials with pictures, slower and shorter utterances in instruction, and help of a multilingual aide.

In order to make learning more meaningful and authentic to the students, my curriculum closely related the students' learning to their daily lives. When students studied the unit on shopping, they engaged, singly and through group projects, in making up menus, comparing prices for various foods from ads in the local newspaper, and composing related shopping lists. Each group then presented to the rest of the class, telling what they wanted to prepare, what they needed to buy, and where they had decided to purchase the items. Later, when we had potluck lunches, students were able to explain how to make the food they brought, and they provided the name of the dish. In order to make some of these themes more comprehensible to students, we simulated a grocery store with cash registers, canned foods, counters, price tags, and students played various roles.

These context-embedded learning activities provided students with useful tools to become more independent and active in dealing with daily living situations. Daily living problems could be very frustrating to them because they did not know how to communicate. Difficulties could arise with the school about their children's sickness, reporting family emergencies, or even conversing with the clerks at grocery stores. With the improvement of their English literacy, the students gained more confidence in themselves and were willing to take more risks with learning to read and write in English.

A meaningful way in which to introduce and develop students' writing is through immersion in

literature of all kinds. The first book we read together in this class was called *What a Wonderful World* (Weiss et al., 1995). It demonstrated the beauty of the world with beautiful pictures and simple verses. The students enjoyed reading along with me. This reading naturally led us into the discussion of their homeland and their writing and drawings about their homeland. Their work amazed me. They used words with codes they knew to define pictures of their homes, rivers, farm animals, trees, flowers. All of these things were personally meaningful and the images represented their lives and their stories. At the same time, I also realized how much help they needed in order to become literate in English (since most of their writings consisted of only words or phrases) so that they could share their stories and have their voices heard. It taught me again that their lives comprised the best themes for learning to read and write.

As the students developed their literacy skills, they were not only able to share their work with a larger community, but also demonstrated more critical themes in their writing content and creative format. For instance, during the latter half of the school year, students began to write their own journals. One weekend, a Hmong student witnessed a killing near his apartment. With the help of his children, he wrote about the incident and shared his writing with the class. This journal evoked discussions on gang violence in the local community and resulted in the topic of how to keep children from the gang influence and watch for one another in their own neighborhood. This example also illustrated the unlimited potential motivated learners could have in sharing experiences of their lives (even if negative) which could be transformed into actions that would change the learners' lives.

In the month of Lincoln and Washington's birthdays, we read biographical stories about these American presidents. The students learned how these presidents contributed to important events in American history. They also asked many questions about the information contained in the books. The knowledge they gained helped them to pass the citizenship test. We also celebrated President's Day with a group project in which students wrote about the presidents or heroes from their native cultures. They drew pictures of the person and wrote about his or her life and contributions to that particular country.

This project was more challenging to my students than the previous projects since it involved new vocabulary, especially words related to specific historical terms and events. However, with the help of their group members, the aide, and sometimes their family members, we succeeded in completing the project. To showcase the students' efforts, we put these writing projects on display on the classroom bulletin board. This display attracted students' and other teachers' attention from more advanced classes. This achievement, in turn, made my students feel proud about the fact that they could write something that was of so much interest. This was in a sense a community publication and showed the importance recognition plays in building students' self-esteem (Freeman and Freeman, 1994).

Faith in the ELLs

Having faith in your students is the most critical among all of the principles of teaching success. Teachers show faith in their students by organizing teaching and learning in ways that are consistent with all principles for success. Teachers understand that students learn when they are engaged in meaningful activities that relate to their own experiences. They develop learner-centered lessons, drawing on the interests and needs of their students. Teachers realize that many modes of instruction can be used to provide important resources for learning. Teachers also recognize that during social interaction, students learn a great deal from each other, from teachers, and from the community (Freeman & Freeman, 1998).

In my work with this class, I also used encouragement and first language support to demonstrate my faith in their learning of English. One way I gave encouragement to students was by valuing them as contributing members of the class community in my daily interactions with them and in integrating their experiences into the curriculum. First language support was given in the class for most of my students through the use of bilingual material and with the help of the instructional aide. My positive attitude and high expectations toward my students helped some of them to have the self-confidence to overcome learning difficulties. My encouragement of their use of first language in the classroom not only facilitated their learning of English (Lucas et al, 1990) but also increased their pride and confidence in themselves and their cultures. Most importantly, my encouragement reduced their psychological stress and increased their motivation for learning.

Conclusion

All teachers can build a classroom community with culturally diverse learners and provide a safe and risk-free environment so that students are willing to help each other and they are comfortable enough to learn. Using student life experiences as codes in teaching makes learning authentic and interesting. Setting the correct psychological stage, you are helping all the students learn more effectively. Freirean educators also believe that lessons should be learner centered and should have immediate meaning and purpose for learner. One of the best ways to insure this is to promote learning taking place while utilizing social interaction. Learners, themselves, are the ones who actually construct knowledge and thus empower themselves in the collaborative process. Collaborative group work provides scaffolding for the learner (Jiang & DeVillar, 2005), especially for the less advanced student. As students come across difficulties in learning, encouragement is always an important ingredient for turning resistance to success. Using positive psychology and context-embedded instruction makes learning more comprehensible, and it lowers the affective filter of the students.

References

American Federation of Teachers, (2006). Where we stand: English language learners. Retrieved August, 20, 2007 from http://aft. org/pubs-reports/downloads/teachers/ellwws.pdf.

Bossers, B. (1991). On thresholds, ceilings and short-circuits. The relation between L1 reading, L2 reading and L2 knowledge. In *ALLA Review:* 45–60.

Canale, M.; N. Frenette, & M. Belanger. (1988). Evaluation of minority student writing in first and second language. In Fine, J. (Ed.), *Second language discourse: A textbook of current research,* 147–165. Norwood, NJ: Ablex.

Carson, J. E., & P. A. Kuehn. (1994). Evidence of transfer and loss in developing second language writers. In A. H. Cumming (Ed.), *Bilingual Performance in Reading and Writing.* 257–281. Ontario Institute for Studies in Education.

Collier, V. (1989). How long? A synthesis of research on academic achievement in a second language. In *TESOL Quarterly,* 23 (3), 509–532.

Cummins, J. (1979a, October). Cognitive/Academic language proficiency, linguistic interdependence, the optimum age question, and some other matters. In *Working papers on Bilingualism,* 19 (1).

Cummins, J. (1979b). Linguistic interdependence and the educational development of bilingual children. *Bilingual Education Paper Service,* 3 (2). (ERIC Document Reproduction Service No. ED 257312).

Cummins, J. (1981). The role of primary language development in promoting education success for language minority students. In Office for Bilingual Bicultural Education. (Ed.), *Schooling and language minority students: A theoretical framework.* Los Angeles, CA.: Evaluation, Dissemination and Assessment Center (California State University), pp. 3–49.

Cummins, J. (1984). *Bilingualism and special education: Issues in assessment and pedagogy.* San Diego, CA: College-Hill Press Inc.

DeVillar, R.A. (1999). Developing critical literacy through technology in U.S. schools: Reflections and projections. In Finajero, J.V. & R.A. DeVillar, Eds. The power of two languages: Effective dual language use across the curriculum. Millennium Edition. New York: McGraw-Hill School Publishing Company.

Diaz-Rico, L. T., & Weed, K. Z. (1995). *The Cross-cultural language, and academic development handbook.* Boston, MA: Allyn and Bacon.

Ellis, R. (1986). *Understanding second language acquisition.* New York, NY: Oxford University Press.

Faltis, C., & Coulter, C. (2007). *Teaching English learners and immigrant students in secondary school.* Upper Saddle River, NJ: Merrill/ Pearson.

Freeman, D. E. & Y.S. Freeman, (1994). *Between worlds: Access to second language acquisition.* Portsmouth, NH: Heinemann.

Freeman, Y.S. & D.E. Freeman, (1998). *ESL/EFL teaching: Principles of success.* Portsmouth, NH: Heinemann.

Freeman, Y., & Freeman, D. (2002). *Closing the achievement gap: How to reach limited-formal-schooling and long-term English learners.* Portsmouth, NH: Heinemann.

Freire, P. (1998). The banking concept of education. In Freire, A.M.A. & D. Macedo, Eds. *The Paulo Freire Reader.* New York: Continuum.

Gass, S. M., & L. Selinker, Eds. (1994). *Language transfer in language learning.* Philadelphia, PA: John Benjamins North America.

Gibson, M. (1998). Promoting academic success among immigrant students: Is acculturation the issue? *Educational Policy, 12*(6), 615–633.

Hakuta, K. (1986). *Mirror of language.* New York, NY: Basic Books, A Division of Harper Collins Publishers.

Hoover, W. (1983). Reading: A universal process. In S. Hudelson (Ed.), *Learning to read in different languages,* Washington DC: Center for Applied Linguistics, 27–31.

Jiang, B. (2004). Problem-Posing: Freire's transformational method in adult ESL. In G. Goodman & K. Carey (Eds.), *Critical multicultural conversations.* Hampton Press: Cresskill, NJ, 23–38.

———. (1999). *Transfer in the Academic Language Development of Post-secondary ESL students.* Unpublished Dissertation, University of California, Davis and California State University, Fresno.

Jiang, B. & DeVillar, R. (2005). EFL Professional Development in Cross-Cultural Relief: Examining Effects of U.S. Frameworks on Teacher Practice in Mexico. In *Journal of Hispanic Higher Education,* 4 (2), 134–148.

Jiang, B. & Kuehn, P. (2001). Transfer in the Academic Language Development of Post-secondary ESL Students, In R. DeVillar & J. Tinajero (Eds.) *Bilingual Research Journal,* 25 (4), 653–672.

Krashen, S. (1992). *Second language acquisition and second language learning.* New York: Pergamon Press Inc.

Krashen, S & Terrell, T. (1983). *The natural approach: Language acquisition in the classroom.* Hayward, CA: Alemany Press.

Labov, W. (1972). *Sociolinguistic patterns.* Oxford: Basil Blackwell.

McLaughlin, B. (1987). *Theories of second language learning.* London: Edward Arnold.

Odlin, T. (1986). *Language transfer: cross-linguistic influence in language learning.* New York: Cambridge University Press.

Ogbu, J. (1991). Immigrant and involuntary minorities in comparative perspective. In M. Gibson & J. Ogbu (Eds.). *Minority status and school: A Comparative study of immigrant and involuntary minorities.* New York: Garland Publishing Co.

Ogbu, J. U. (1981). School ethnography: A multilevel approach. *Anthropology and Education Quarterly, 12* (1).

Ogbu, J. U., & M.U. Matute-Bianchi, (1986). Understanding sociocultural factors: Knowledge, identity, and school adjustment. In Office for Bilingual Bicultural Education (Ed.), *Beyond language: Social and cultural factors in schooling language minority students.* Los Angeles, CA.: Evaluation, Dissemination and Assessment Center, pp. 73–142.

Rogoff, B., & E. Matusov, & C. White, (1996). Models of teaching and learning: Participation in a community of learners. In D.R. Olson & N. Torrance (Eds.), *The handbook of education and human development.* Oxford: Blackwell.

Schumann, J. (1978). *The acculturation model for second language acquisition.* In Gingras, R. C., Ed., *Second language acquisition & foreign language teaching.* Arlington, Virginia: Center for Applied Linguistics, pp. 27–50.

(1978). *The pidginization process: A model for second language acquisition.* Rowley, Mass. Newbury House.

Suárez-Orozco, M. (2005). Everything you ever wanted to know about assimilation but were afraid to ask. In M. Suárez-Orozco, C. Suárez-Orozco, & D. Baolian Qin (Eds.), *The new immigration: An interdisciplinary reader* (pp. 67–84). New York: Routledge.

Suárez-Orozco, C. & M. Suárez-Orozco. (2001). *Children of immigration.* Cambridge, MA: Harvard University Press.

Verhoeven, L. (1991). Acquisition of biliteracy. In J. H. Hulstin & J. F. Matter (Eds.). In *Reading in two languages.* Amsterdam: AILA. AILA Review, 8, 6–74.

Vygotsky, L. (1978). *Mind in society: The development of higher psychological processes.* Cambridge, MA: Harvard University Press.

———. (1962). *Though and Language.* Translated by Eugenia Hanfmann Gertrude Vakar. Cambridge, MA: MIT Press.

Weaver, C. (1994). *Reading process and practice.* Portsmouth, NH: Heinemann.

Zehler, M. (1994). *Working with English Language Learners: Strategies for Elementary and Middle School Teachers.* NCBE Program Information Guide, 19. Washington, DC: National Clearinghouse for Bilingual Education.

Zhou, M. (1998). "Parachute kids" in Southern California: The educational experience of Chinese children in transnational families. *Educational Policy, 12*(6), 682–704.

CHAPTER ELEVEN

Paying Attention and Assessing Achievement

Positive Applications for the Classroom

Karen T. Carey

Are children making academic achievement? Are we competitive with other countries? Does anyone know what we are doing in our schools? Questions continue to arise about how our children are doing despite the Federal Government's No Child Left Behind Act (2002).

How do we know if anyone is progressing in any academic area? How do you know when you have *learned* something? How do I know if you have learned something? Most of us demonstrate what we have learned. Our actions show what we know, our character, and our views about the world. However, we are rarely evaluated academically by our actions and how we function in our day-to-day activities. Progress is generally assessed in schools through standardized, objective multiple choice item testing, and in actuality these tests tell us very little about the student, the classroom, or the learning that has taken place.

History

During the middle 1800s the state superintendent of instruction in Massachusetts required the assessment of students' skills through written examinations to hold schools accountable (Linn & Gronlund, 2000). Other districts around the country also began to assess students, and following World War I schools began using multiple choice tests to assess students in academic areas. Following World War II the assessment of students in schools became accepted practice in most districts around the country. In 1983, *A Nation at Risk: The Imperative for Educational Reform* was published by the National Commission on Excellence in Education. Several recommendations for the use of tests to enhance students' educational achievement were made by the Commission. *A Nation at Risk* (1983) also advocated further educational overhauls including the certification of a student's credentials, the identification of the need for remedial intervention, and provisions for the opportunity to complete advanced work. The report enticed many to action with concerns about where students in the United States ranked in comparison to other countries and the need for schools districts to demonstrate that all students were learning and progressing. All of this political dialogue resulted in a heightened interest in accountability.

In 2002, the federal government passed the No Child Left Behind (NCLB) Act (2002) requiring each state to develop "world class" **standards** for children in the third through eighth grades. NCLB was to help all children, especially those from impoverished backgrounds and to close the achievement gap between the highest and lowest academic performers. To meet the letter of the law, each state developed assessment measures aligned with the state's curriculum to meet specific standards. NCLB further mandated that educators assess all students in grades three to eight annually. Because they are

Standards
Conventions listing what should be taught.

conducted on a massive scale, the traditional multiple-choice format was selected as the most cost-efficient way to meet the letter of the law. Should schools and/or districts not meet their annual goals set forth by the state as outlined in NCLB, monies are withheld from those sites, and remediations are put in place for the teachers at those schools (No Child Left Behind, 2002). Today, every school district includes some form of traditional **standardized assessment** of students, and many also now require their seniors to pass high school exit exams in order to graduate.

Standardized assessment
Tests scientifically designed to be similar to one another.

Although many good arguments are offered defending school improvement through assessments, there are many critics of this approach to school reform and improvement (Goodman & Carey, 2004). Assessment is a necessary and critical ingredient for student success, but is standardized assessment and punishment for underperformance the answer? According to Apple (2006) the characteristics of NCLB "include a massive centralization of control, a loss of local autonomy, and a redefinition of what counts as good or bad education that is simply reduced to scores on problematic tests of achievement" (p. 25). Perhaps there are better ways to find out how your students are learning and what you need to know to teach them better.

As mentioned above, states are required to develop specific standards, and many have gone as far as to identify the specific curriculum to be used at every grade level. Unfortunately, only in rare instances do the assessment tools selected by the states to be used at the end of year match the curriculum used by classroom teachers. This results in deleterious consequences for students when there is no match between what is taught and what is tested. The only way students' can actually do well on such standardized assessments is if teachers prepare students for these specific tests or if the students possessed the cultural capital to do well on these measures of reading and generally accepted knowledge. Cultural capital is defined as family background, vocabulary, opportunity, and experience (Bourdieu, 1993). But no matter what we think may be assessed, only if the tests and the curriculum are well aligned can teachers be sure that students will be tested on what they have been taught.

Another problem with standardized group tests is that such tests do not allow for any kind of changes in instruction or informed decision-making by teachers. They are "one-shot" evaluations that result in students potentially being stigmatized and teachers made to suffer whatever consequences the politicians and state agencies deem to be necessary. Such assessments tell us little about how students learn, what they need to learn, and the best way to teach students the skills they will need for the future. In order to understand the problem more fully, a brief review of some of the most common group standardized tests follows below.

Standardized Group Tests

The most common standardized group tests currently in use are the California Achievement Tests (CAT), the Iowa Tests of Basic Skills (ITBS), the Metropolitan Achievement Tests (MAT), and the Stanford Achievement Tests (SAT). Despite millions of dollars spent and thousands of hours invested to create unbiased and fair assessments, there are significant problems and deficiencies with all of these tests. Because your students will be taking these tests, it is important to note that many of the negative consequences of these assessments are related to the test instruments themselves, not the teaching that goes on within your school.

The California Achievement Test, Form 6 (CAT6), also known as the Terra-Nova Second Edition (CTB/McGraw-Hill, 2002), includes subtests in reading/language arts, mathematics, science, social studies, word analysis, vocabulary, language

Normed

Tests that are designed to compare one student to another in a controlled distribution.

mechanics, spelling, and mathematics computation. There are 13 levels of the test, one for each grade kindergarten through twelve. The test wa **normed** on over 264,000 children during fall and

spring standardizations and includes students identified as eligible for special education. The problem with the CAT6 is that there is minimal evidence of any type of validity and no evidence of test-retest or alternate form reliability. A further criticism of this assessment tool is that it does not align with California's state standards for instruction even though it bears California's name and by implication implies it relates to instruction in that state (Bell, 2002; CVERC, 2002). For many reasons the use of this test in schools to assess the overall achievement of students must be viewed with extreme caution.

The Iowa Tests of Basic Skills (ITBS) (Hoover, Dunbar, & Frisbie, 2001) consist of ten levels for students in grades kindergarten through eight and were normed in 2000. Subtests include vocabulary, word analysis, reading comprehension, listening, language, mathematics, social studies, science and sources of information for students in grades kindergarten through third, and vocabulary, reading comprehension, spelling, capitalization, punctuation, usage and expression, math concepts and estimation, math problem solving and data interpretation, math computation, social studies, science, maps and diagrams, and reference questions for students from grades three to eight.

Additional standardized achievement tests such as the Tests of Achievement and Proficiency (TAP) (Scannell, 1996) and the Iowa Tests of Educational Development (ITED) (Forsyth, Ansley, Feldt, & Alnot, 2001) are available for students in grades 9–12. Subtests for the TAP include vocabulary, reading comprehension, written expression, math concepts and problem solving, math computation, social studies, science, information processing. The ITED tests vocabulary, reading comprehension, spelling, language: revising written materials, math concepts and problem solving, math computation, analysis of social studies materials, analysis of science materials and sources of information. The TAP was constructed in 1992 and is primarily a norm-referenced test, while the ITED was standardized in 2000 and is a norm-referenced and curriculum referenced test. The ITBS and ITED were normed on approximately 180,000 students. The construct and criterion validity of these tests are lacking and there is no test-retest reliability reported. In sum, the use of these tests must be questioned when technical adequacy is so poor.

The Metropolitan Achievement Tests, Eighth Edition (MAT8) (Harcourt Educational Measurement, 2002) consists of 13 levels from kindergarten through twelfth grades. Subtests include sounds and print, reading vocabulary, reading comprehension, open-ended reading, mathematics, mathematics concepts and problem solving, mathematics computation, open-ended mathematics, language, spelling, open-ended writing, science and social studies. The test was normed on a total of 140,000 students during fall and spring standardizations in the 1999–2000 academic year. Again, as with the other tests discussed, content and construct validity are insufficient for evaluating student progress. Further reducing the test's value, reliabilities reported for internal consistency and test-retest are too low to be used to make individual decisions about students.

The Stanford Achievement Test, Ninth Edition (Harcourt Brace Educational Measurement, 1996) consists of 13 levels and includes five to 13 subtests at each level. Subtests include sounds and letters, word study skills, word reading, sentence reading, reading vocabulary, reading comprehension, mathematics, mathematics problem solving, mathematics: procedures, language, spelling, study skills, listening to words and stories, listening, environment, science, and social science. The test was normed on approximately 250,000 students. Validity is addressed in the manual, and the authors did go to some lengths to insure the test had strong content and construct validity by having the items reviewed by subject matter experts, people of differing cultures and ethnicities, and teachers involved in the

standardization. Reliability is reported for internal consistency and alternate form. However, conclusions concerning individuals based upon results of this assessment need to be viewed with caution.

Of the four tests reviewed, only one appears to have adequate technical adequacy for screening students on academic achievement. However, all of these tests are used by state departments to meet the No Child Left Behind requirements of yearly testing. Without technical adequacy, they tell us virtually nothing. Of gravest concern are the high stakes consequences of such tests upon students and their families, teachers, and schools. Stigmatizing students and penalizing schools based on technically inadequate tests is unethical and unprofessional.

Professional psychometrist's knowledge about good assessment practices has been virtually ignored by the states' school administrators and the federal government's legislative and administrative branches. Large-scale assessments, such as the California Achievement Test, were developed and implemented despite other assessment initiatives that were recommended which, if actually attempted, could benefit students on an individual level. This desire to provide improved outcomes for individual students has led to the more recent developments of performance-based assessments.

Appropriate Assessment

Performance-based assessments allow us to "observe students while they are performing or we examine the products they create and evaluate the level of proficiency demonstrated" (Stiggins, 2001, p. 184). Students are required to perform some activity rather than simply answering or knowing an answer (Linn & Gronlund, 2000). Other types of assessment have grown from this movement as well, including outcomes-based assessment, authentic assessment, and alternative assessment. Outcomes-based assessments refer to the "products" schools produce in terms of the knowledge and experiences students take with them (Ysseldyke & Thurlow, 1993). Authentic assessment identifies the "knowledge, thinking, problem-solving skills, social skills and attitudes exhibited by those in the community, on the job, or in advanced courses as part of their normal work" (Tobari & Borich, 1999, p. 4). Those skills that are necessary outside of the school setting and are needed in the real world are the abilities and knowledge that are stressed. Alternative assessment may be defined as anything other than the traditional model of multiple-choice and other standardized tests.

The assessment of a student's classroom may be the most important part of any evaluation conducted. Teachers are generally concerned about children in their classrooms because these children are having difficulty in the classroom, not in contrived settings. School professionals hired to assist teachers often fail to take the time to observe students in the classroom, interview teachers, or assess the learning environment. Paying attention and assessing academic achievement require more than multiple choice tests. The best and most appropriate ways to assess achievement are the goal of every successful teacher, and we will now examine a few of these tools.

Teacher-Made Assessments

Teacher-made evaluations, sometimes referred to as formative assessments, are the most common form of academic measurement and provide the teacher with student outcomes concerning what they have been exposed to in the classroom. To know how students can perform teacher-made assessments should be experiential and use the material actually taught in the classroom. Unfortunately, many teacher-made assessments have no relevance to learning outcomes and often are only given in order for the teacher to issue the students grades. True-false and multiple choice tests still tend to be the methods of choice for classroom assessments and often only one test is given on a particular area of content. Such assessments do not provide teachers with information needed to modify instruction in order that

students can succeed, and no information related to a student's daily or weekly progress is obtained. Most importantly, teacher-made assessments have generally not been used with any other group of students, or if they have, the data collected are not analyzed in any way to determine if the scores obtained are meaningful, that is, valid or reliable.

Teacher-made assessments can be improved by insuring (a) the assessments match the content covered in class, (b) the assessment provides an adequate representation of the material covered, and (c) each question measures one or more learning objectives (Braus, Wood, & LeFranc, 1993). In addition, teacher-made assessments should evaluate students' abilities to think critically. Critical thinking is best assessed by using some type of performance-based or experiential assessment. Often, classroom assessments tell how students perform (i.e., based on the grades obtained), but information relative to how students arrive at answers can be lacking. Taking the time to analyze students' responses requires extra time on the part of teachers; however, it may in the long run be far more beneficial in terms of the students' actual attainment of knowledge.

Classroom Assessment

The review of common standardized group assessments and teacher-made tests, demonstrates over and over again the problems evidenced with such tools. The question then arises, "How can I appropriately assess the students in the classroom?"

In contrast to the great number of standardized tests in use at this time, a number of far more useful methods can be implemented to provide teachers with the information needed to truly make a difference for their students. While alternative assessments take additional effort, when one considers the wasted time and energy that go into evaluating students in the classroom through the use of standardized tests, these techniques more efficiently provide information that can help teachers make informed educational decisions for all of their students.

Consultation with Other Teachers and Parents

One of the first steps in assessing a student's functioning often involves engaging in consultation and assessment with the child's previous teacher, a teacher's aide, their parent, or some other individual. Consultation is a systematic way to guide problem-solving which involves identifying the problem and then developing interventions approaches to rectify the situation. As discussed in the chapter on parents, the role of the child's care-giver is critical in the development and success of each individual. Often we cannot understand the difficulties the child experiences until we hear the story of the child's life from the parent's perspective. This understanding can build compassion for the child's struggles with learning and socialization (Goodman & Carey, 2004).

Classroom Observations

Classrooms should be viewed as ecosystems that provide support for student learning. The interactions between teacher and student and student to students can provide a wealth of information about how the classroom is functioning and whether successful learning can take place. Evidence supporting the value of psycho-social and pro-social conditions within the classroom is voluminous. For example, Hobbs (1966) wrote, "The group is important to the child. When a group is functioning well, it is extremely difficult for an individual child to behave in a disturbed way" (p. 112).

Classroom observations can result in useful information for developing change strategies concerning students. Well-functioning classrooms have teachers who utilize an age-appropriate curriculum and who teach adaptive behavior skills that can help to prevent behavior problems and increase pro-social interactions (Dunlap & Kern, 1996; Nordquist & Twardosz, 1990). Highly functioning and experienced classroom teachers can assess students as they engage curriculum in a natural environment. In this sensitive setting, any change for individual

students may affect other childrens' and teachers' behaviors. Thus, teachers and others need ways to evaluate what is happening in the classroom setting, and the most effective technique is the use of structured observations.

The best method of evaluation for developing effective interventions is to carefully assess your students to obtain usable data by planning, conducting, and using classroom observations. Using structured observations based on carefully developed problem-solving, the teacher can assist in the identification of selected specific behaviors to observe and help create appropriate interventions. The emotional distancing of the teacher as observer enhances the teacher's objectivity and improves the validity of the intervention.

Teachers need to develop good observation skills. They need to be objective, collect data, and be able to analyze observation data to determine exactly what is occurring in the classroom. When conducting classroom observations, the teacher must decide what to evaluate in the natural environment of the classroom. The best practice is to attempt sampling of behaviors across several classes or units and different days. For many students, time of day is also an important aspect to explore. Some behaviors only occur at certain times of the day, for example, right before lunch. This information can only be obtained through an individualized problem-solving strategy, making sure observations are conducted at specific times. Observing throughout a class period or unit at selected times addresses the teacher's decision related to when to observe. Selecting time checks as observation units require that the 1) sessions must be equivalent in opportunities for the occurrence or nonoccurrence of behavior; and 2) conditions must be the same for all observation periods (Cooper, Heron, & Heward, 1987). From the consultation session, teachers can get an idea of the usual time periods for activities, making it possible to have comparable sessions. Finally, it is important to select an adequate observation length. Behaviors that do not occur often may require longer time periods; behaviors that occur more often may require shorter time periods. Sample behaviors from the observations must be representative and accurate.

Many teachers have developed simple ways of observing without taking away from instructional time. In some cases, students can monitor their own behavior by keeping track of how many problems they complete, how many words they can read, or how often they engage in disruptive behavior. Teachers can "count" behaviors by transferring tokens or pegs or some other small item from one pocket to another or use small note cards in their pockets to record occurrences of events.

Methods for Observing and Recording Behavior

Observation includes "recording the stream of behavior, dividing it into units, and analyzing the units" (Wright, 1967, p. 10). The observation should be a "detailed, sequential, narrative account of behavior and its immediate environmental context as seen by skilled observers" (Wright, 1967, p. 32). Observations need to be guided by specific questions related to the environment, instruction, behaviors, skills, and tasks (Wolery, 1989). There are several useful ways to observe behavior in the classroom. Oftentimes observers conduct so-called observations by simply writing down everything they see (or think they see) and developing impressions about a student's behavior. Conducting observations in this manner is haphazard and subject to bias and incomplete information (Linn & Gronlund, 2000). In order to get an accurate picture of a student's behavior in the classroom, whether it be academic or social-emotional, we must collect objective data on the problem behavior identified during our consultation.

Real-Time Observations

The natural environment allows for on-going observations to be conducted as the behavior actually occurs. If the teacher is unable to record these events, a teacher aide or other adult may be able to make the recordings. Barnett and Carey (1992) recommended that preliminary observations be done using real-time observations to select those behavior and environmental features that are important to note and may add to our understanding of the behavior identified during consultation.

Real-time observations focus on the child's situation (including actions of peers and teachers toward the child) as well as specific child behavior. The procedure shown in Figure 1 requires the teacher or other observer to record the exact times of the beginning and ending of behavior. Activity changes are recorded by time notations, and arrows are used for the observer to note the appropriateness (↑) or inappropriateness (↓) of the child's behavior. Each line of the observation protocol should include only one unit of behavior, and each behavior should be mutually exclusive (one activity is recorded) and exhaustive (all time is accounted for) (Sackett, 1978; Suen & Ary, 1989). Time notations can be made at prespecified intervals such as one minute (Wright, 1967), two minutes (Bijou and colleagues, 1969), or a variation (Barnett & Carey, 1992).

Data derived from real-time observations include:

1. Frequency or Event recording. Frequency equals the number of times behavior occurs in an observation session. Frequency can be useful for describing aggressive behaviors, time on task, or transition times.
2. Rate of Occurrence. Rate of occurrence is the frequency of behavior divided by the length of the observation session. Using the rate of occurrence allows for comparisons of frequency across sessions of different lengths, providing us with measures of reliability and validity. This is use-

FIGURE 1. AN EXAMPLE OF REAL-TIME RECORDING

Setting: Special Day Class for Emotionally Disturbed Students

Time: 8:15–8:35　Child: D

↑	8:15	D. enters classroom and tosses book bag on table. Walks to get chair from stack for his desk. Takes chair back to his desk.
↓	8:16	D. sits down and then runs to the classroom door, shouting for S. Teacher intervenes and attempts to get D. back to his seat
↓	8:17	D. agrees to go back to his seat and as soon as he is seated he runs to the door again and starts shouting for S. Teacher intervenes and asks D. to come with him to the office space in the classroom.
↑	8:19	D. and Teacher go to the office space in the classroom and the Teacher asks, "What is going on, D.?" D. states that he "saw S. earlier but that S. said he wasn't coming to class today."
↑	8:21	Teacher says for "D. not to worry about S., that he would find out what is going on, but that D. needs to get back to his desk and get to work." D agrees and leaves the office area.
↑	8:22	D. returns to his desk, opens his backpack and removes a notebook and a pencil. Other students in the class are working on writing in journals. D. takes out his journal and begins completing the assignment.
↓	8:24	S. enters the room and D. jumps up to greet him. D. states "I thought you weren't coming today." "I thought I would have a good day but now you're here. How am I supposed to get any work done with you here?"
↓	8:25	D. begins to scream at S., telling him he hates him and that he is ruining everything for D. D. hits S.
↓	8:26	Teacher and aide tell D. to not hit S. but D. continues.
↑	8:27	Teacher and aide tell D. again to calm down and D. begins to move away from S. toward the Teacher. Teacher tells D. three times to stay calm which D. does.
↑	8:29	D. moves closer to the Teacher and when he is about three feet away says to the teacher, "I am really sorry, I don't know what happened." Teacher tells D. he must apologize to S.
↑	8:30	D. tells S. that he is sorry and hopes they can still be friends. S. says he is sorry too about telling D. he wouldn't be in class. Teacher encourages them to shake hands and they do.
↑	8:32	Teacher directs D. back to his desk to continue working on his journal. D. follows the Teacher's directions, returns to his seat and begins working.
↑	8:34	D. continues working quietly.
Frequency:		D. engaged in inappropriate behavior five times and appropriate behavior nine times.

Two episodes of shouting.

Two episodes of hitting.

Rate of Occurrence: 2 D. engaged in yelling behavior.

Bout duration: For hitting—lasted for two minutes

Prevalence: Four bouts of behavior.

ful when our time is limited but we need to make comparisons across different days, again to insure reliability.

3. Bout duration. Bout (one occurrence of behavior) duration is the length of time the behavior occurs. Bout duration can be useful for recording states of behavior (tantrum), on-task behavior (paying attention during instruction), or activity engagement (such as art instruction).

4. Prevalence. Prevalence is the proportion of time a bout is found within an observation session. Bout durations are totaled and divided by the session length (expressed in the same time units) and the result is multiplied by 100. Using prevalence allows us to compare states of behavior, such as paying attention in class, across observation sessions of different lengths.

5. Inter-response time (IRT). IRT is the time between bouts and is calculated by recording the time period from the end of a behavior to the beginning of the next behavior. The mean IRT is calculated by dividing the sum of all IRT durations by the number of non-occurrences of behavior. IRT is useful for setting observation intervals, particularly when only limited time is available for several observations.

Antecedent-Behavior-Consequence Analysis

Antecedent-Behavior-Consequence Analysis or ABC Analysis is a basic strategy for the functional analysis of behavior (Bijou, Peterson, & Ault, 1968). All behavior that we engage in is thought to have a function. Functional analysis of behavior refers to what function a behavior serves for a student. Antecedents are events that precede a behavior and may increase or decrease the behavior. Consequences can be either reinforcing, punishing, or neutral depending which type is administered. In general, the setting is first described and then observations are recorded on a three-column form (see Figure 2). Similar to Real-Time Observations, a time column is also included.

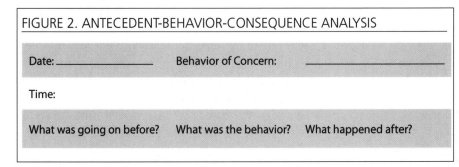

FIGURE 2. ANTECEDENT-BEHAVIOR-CONSEQUENCE ANALYSIS

Date: _____ Behavior of Concern: _____

Time:

What was going on before?   What was the behavior?   What happened after?

Frequency or Event Recording

Frequency recording involves simply tallying the number of times a behavior occurs in an observation session. Only behaviors or events that are predefined are recorded. To use this technique successfully, only behaviors of brief and stable durations, such as activity changes, calling out, or aggressive acts can be recorded. There are many ways to record frequencies and events including simply making tally marks on a piece of paper or using counters of some kind.

Duration recording is the recording of the elapsed time for each occurrence of a behavior, and the total duration or the behavior. This method is used when the concern is the length of time a student engages in a specific behavior. For example, when a student is not paying attention during seatwork, duration recording is the method to use to record how long the student does not pay attention. In addition, the latency of the response can be recorded. Latency is the amount of time before beginning a behavior, such as the length of time it takes a student to begin to pay attention (Barnett & Carey, 1992).

Other Methods

Many other methods exist for observing and recording behaviors. These include discrete skill sequences or task analysis where every component required to complete an activity is first recorded and then the student is observed to determine where she/he has difficulty. Another example is category sampling.

This technique is used for behaviors that can be categorized, such as on-task behavior. All evidence of on-task behavior is recorded even if it takes different forms. Artifacts of student work are good examples of productivity. Permanent products, which may include work and homework completion, give the teacher and parent a specific point of reference for evaluation of student performance. All teachers should take the time to review actual student work products as they can tell us much about teacher's own expectations and how the student performs relative to her/his peers.

Direct observation of the student's attempts at work completion are also effective means of measurement. Trials to criterion define how many times a "response opportunity" is presented before the student performs the task to a specified criterion (Cooper, Heron, & Heward, 1987, p. 74). In other words how long does it take a student to meet some teacher expectation given the opportunity to do so? Levels of assistance include recording the amount of support a student needs to complete a task or participate with peers. Some students need additional support from teachers and/or peers, and knowing how much support is necessary can provide us with information in terms of how to insure the student gets such support. Probes include structuring tasks in such a way that data can be collected. Oftentimes it is not possible to actually observe the behavior in the real world, and we need to "set up" situations for the behavior to occur in order that we can observe it.

Observing More Than One Child

Micro-norms refer to the norms accepted in a classroom. This is also referred to as classroom culture. What is acceptable behavior for this classroom? Each teacher sets behavioral expectations and rules differently. Intra-group or whole group observation can be especially useful for teachers observing students coming to their own classrooms the next academic year. Appropriate comparison students (3–4) must

be selected, and generally observations are conducted using momentary time sampling, where each
student is observed for one interval, before moving
on to the next. Each student is observed engaged in
a task for preset time period (e.g., 10 seconds). Such
data can help us see whether or not the student
identified is actually behaving in ways significantly
different from her/his peers.

Self-Observation

Self-observation is used when we are interested in
the emotions and thoughts of a student. Although
self-observation can be used to assess overt behaviors, it is best utilized when we want to know if the
student is cognizant of her/his behaviors. In order
for self-observation to be effective, the student must
be able to discriminate the occurrence from the
nonoccurrence of a behavior. The results of self-
observations must be recorded by the student. Based
on the data recorded, the student needs to evaluate
him/herself. Generally the student needs to be
trained in order to self-observe.

Although several strategies can be used to
improve accuracy, students are often not accurate
at self-observation. Aids to success include combin-
ing self-observation with other strategies used by
adults to monitor the student's behavior. Agreement
checks can be conducted to improve performance
through the surveillance of the teacher. It is important to recognize that complete accuracy is not
necessary for the student to derive benefit from
self-observation (Kanfer & Gaelick, 1986).

Curriculum-Based Assessment

Although many of the standardized tools currently used to assess students in the classroom are
neither reliable nor valid, a useful tool for developing academic interventions is found in the process
of assessing the student with her/his actual curriculum. Assessing the student on what s/he has
actually learned provides us with information we
can use to change the instruction and see the stu-

dent make *real* gains. Curriculum-based assessment allows for continuous, ongoing observations of the student's performance in the classroom setting. By analyzing the student's level of skill development, we can determine the appropriate level of instruction for that particular student in a specified area (Barnett & Carey, 1992).

According to Barnett et al. (1999) "the information gained from curriculum based assessment includes: (1) current level of performance or functioning; (2) rate of learning new skills; (3) strategies necessary to learn new skills; (4) length of time the new skill is retained; (5) generalization of previously taught skills to a new task; (6) observed behaviors that deter learning; (7) environmental conditions needed to learn new skills (individual, group, peer instruction); (8) motivational techniques used to acquire skills; and (9) skills acquisition in relationship to peers" (p. 66). Curriculum-based assessment has been relegated in the past to students in elementary school. However, this assessment tool can be used with any curriculum that is based on developmentally sequenced tasks and ongoing assessment (weekly or more often). For example, at the high school level where computer literacy classes are now required, the curriculum for these classes is based on an appropriate developmental progression. A student's knowledge of computer literacy can be assessed in such classes by conducting brief probes of his/her knowledge. One example would be asking students to find a particular file on the computer (a task that should take no longer than one minute). By gathering information on this task the teacher would know whether or not the student is able to turn on the computer, find the correct program, use the mouse or keyboard in the appropriate way, go to the correct tool bar icon, and locate the file. Should the student break down at any step along the way, the teacher would know exactly when to begin instruction for that student in order to insure the student continues to make progress. By engaging

in such activities once, twice or three times a week, students are less likely to fall behind their peers.

In many school districts such assessments are relegated to the use of local norms developed to determine student eligibility for special education. However, that is not what we are referring to here. Curriculum-based assessment should be viewed as a part of the seamless process from assessment to intervention. By continually assessing a student's areas of weakness and changing instruction, we can be assured that we are doing everything possible for the student to make academic, behavioral, and social gains.

Summary

This chapter provides teachers with the basic, necessary tools to begin to engage in ubiquitous assessment: continuous assessment of the functioning of themselves and their students within the classroom (Goodman & Carey, 2004). Daily and continuous assessment means going far beyond the one-test requirement of NCLB. Truly understanding the complexities of the classroom and the methods for assessing what happens in the educational setting can provide the teacher with meaningful assessment data to ensure change and growth for all students.

The primary goal of all teachers is the outcome of learning: both academic and social. It is critical to remember that the student is a whole person. The whole person is one that embodies a mind, body and a spirit. This view allows us to see the student beyond his or her test scores and to see them as personal agents with other people with whom the student interacts within their environment.

Furthermore, every teacher has his or her own, unique way of presenting material, structuring the classroom, and using academic time. Some students benefit from a classroom with lots of activity, group work, and noise; others simply do not. Knowing the students with whom we work through our interactions with them, observations of them in the natural environment, interviewing important persons in their lives, and assessing them regularly in the instructional material to which they have been exposed can provide us with the knowledge we need to make instructional and psycho-social decisions in students' best interests. Paying attention and assessing achievement are two important tools for professional mastery. The ubiquitously aware and "with it" teachers are the one's who achieve the best in student outcomes.

References

Achenbach, T. M. (1991). *Manual for the Child Behavior Checklist/4–18.* Burlington, VT: University of Vermont, Department of Psychiatry.

Alessi, G. J., & Kaye, J. H. (1983). *Behavioral assessment for school psychologists.* Washington, DC: National Association of School Psychologists.

Apple, M. W. (2006). *Educating the "right" way: Markets, standards, God, and inequality.* New York: Taylor & Francis Group.

Barnett, D. W., & Carey, K. T. (1992). *Designing interventions for pre-school learning and behavior problems.* San Francisco: Jossey-Bass.

Barnett, D. W., Bell, S. H., & Carey, K. T. (1999). *Designing preschool interventions.* New York: Guilford.

Bell, T. (2002). State adopts new school tests. *San Francisco Chronicle,* 26 April, p. A. 1.

Bijou, S. W., Peterson, R. F., & Ault, M. H. (1968). A method to integrate descriptive and experimental field studies at the level of data and empirical concepts. *Journal of Applied Behavior Analysis, 1,* 175–191.

Bijou, S. W., Peterson, R. F., Harris, F. R., Allen, K. E., & Johnson, M. S. (1969). Methodology for experimental studies of young children in natural settings. *Psychological Record, 19,* 177–210.

Bourdieu, P. (1993). *The field of cultural reproduction.* New York: Columbia University Press.

Braus, J. A., Wood, D., & LeFranc, L.E., (1993). *Environmental education in the schools: Creating a program that works.* Peace Corps.

Brown, L, & Hammill, D. (1990). *Behavior Rating Profile* (2nd ed.). Austin, TX: Pro-Ed.

Carey, K. T. (1989*). The treatment utility potential of two methods of assessing stressful relationships in families: A study of practitioner utility.* Unpublished doctoral dissertation, University of Cincinnati.

Central Valley Educational Research Consortium (CVERC) (2002). *What works: Characteristics of high-performing schools in the Central Valley.* Fresno, CA: California State University, Fresno.

Cooper, J. O., Heron, T. E., & Heward, W. L. (1987). *Applied behavior analysis.* Columbus, OH: Merrill.

CTB/McGraw-Hill (2002). *Terra Nova,* Second Edition. Monterey, CA: Author.

Dunlap, G., & Kern, L. (1996). Modifying instruction activities to promote desirable behavior: A conceptual and practical framework. *School Psychology Quarterly, 11,* 297–312.

Forsyth, R. L., Ansley, T., Feldt, L., & Alnot, S. (2001). *Iowa Tests of Educational Achievement.* Chicago: Riverside Publishing Company.

Goodman, G. & Carey, K.L. (2004). *Ubiquitous assessment: Evaluation techniques for the new millennium.* New York: Peter Lang Publishing.

Gutkin, T. B., & Curtis, M. J. (1990). School-based consultation: Theory and techniques. In C. R. Reynolds & T. B. Gutkin (Eds.). *Handbook of school psychology* (pp. 796–828). New York: Wiley.

Harcourt Brace Educational Measurement. (1996). *Stanford Achievement Test, Ninth Edition.* San Antonio, TX: Psychological Corporation.

Harcourt Educational Measurement, Inc. (2002). Metropolitan Achievement Tests, Eighth Edition. San Antonio, TX: Author.

Hartmann, D. P. (1984). Assessment strategies. In D. H. Barlow & M. Hersen (Eds.). *Single case experimental designs: Strategies for studying behavior change* (2nd ed, pp. 107–139). New York: Pergamon.

Hobbs, N. (1966). Helping disturbed children: Psychological and ecological strategies. *American Psychologist, 21,* 1105–1115.

Hoover, H. D., Dunbar, S. B., & Frisbie, D. A. (2001). *Iowa Tests of Basic Skills.* Chicago: Riverside Publishing Company.

Kanfer, F. H. & Gaelick, L. (1986). Self-management methods. In F. H. Kanfer & A. P. Goldstein (Eds.), *Helping people change: A textbook of methods* (3rd ed., pp. 283–245). New York:Pergamon.

Kaufman, A., & Kaufman, N. (1998). *Kaufman Tests of Educational Achievement-Normative Update-Comprehensive form manual.* Circle Pines, MN: American Guidance Service.

Linn, R. L. & Gronlund, N. E. (2000). *Measurement and assessment in teaching* (Eighth edition). Upper Saddle River, New Jersey: Merrill.

Markwardt, F. (1998). *Peabody Individual Achievement Test-Revised-Normative Update.* Circle Pines, MN: American Guidance Service.

National Commission on Excellence in Education (1983). *A nation at risk: The imperative for educational reform.* Washington, DC: U.S. Government Printing Office.

No Child Left Behind (2002). Public Law 107–110, 1st session (January 8).

Nordquist, V. M., & Twardosz, S. (1990). Preventing behavior problems in early childhood special education classroom through

environmental organization. *Education and Treatment of Children,* *13,* 274–287.

Peterson, D. R. (1968). *The clinical study of social behavior.* New York: Appleton-Century-Crofts.

Psychological Corporation (2001). *Wechsler Individual Achievement Test,* Second Edition. San Antonio, TX: Author.

Reynolds, C. R., & Kamphaus, R. W. (1992*). Behavior Assessment System for Children.* Circle Pines, MN: American Guidance Service.

Sackett, G. P. (1978). Measurement in observational research. In G. P. Sackett (Ed.). *Observing behavior: Vol. 2. Data collection and analysis methods* (pp. 25–43). Baltimore: University Park Press.

Salvia, J. & Ysseldyke, J. E. (2004). *Assessment in special and inclusive education* (9th Ed.). Boston: Houghton Mifflin.

Scannell, D. P. (1996). *Tests of Achievement and Proficiency.* Chicago: Riverside Publishing Company.

Shinn, M. R. (1989). *Curriculum-based measurement: Assessing special children.* New York: Guilford.

Stiggins, R. J. (2001). *Student-involved classroom assessment* (3rd Ed.). New Jersey: Merrill Prentice Hall.

Suen, H. K. & Ary, D. (1989). *Analyzing quantitative behavioral observation data.* Hillsdale, NJ: Erlbaum.

Tindall, G. A. & Marston, D. B. (1990). *Classroom-based assessment: Evaluating instructional outcomes.* Columbus, OH: Merrill.

Tombari, M., & Borich, G. (1999). *Authentic assessment in the classroom: Applications and practice.* New Jersey: Merrill Prentice Hall

Vedder-Dobocq, S. (1990). *An investigation of the utility of the Parenting Stress Index for intervention decisions.* Unpublished doctoral dissertation, University of Cincinnati.

Wolery, M. (1989). Using direct observation in assessment. In D. B. Bailey, Jr. & M. Wolery (Eds.). *Assessing infants and preschoolers with handicaps* (pp. 64–96). Columbus, OH: Merrill.

Wright, H. F. (1967). *Recording and analyzing child behavior.* New York: Harper & Row.

Ysseldyke, J. E., & Christenson, S. L. (2002). *Functional assessment of academic behavior: Creating effective learning environments.* Longmont, CO: Sopris West.

Ysseldyke, J. E., & Thurlow, M. L. (1993). *Self-study guide to the development of educational outcomes and indicators.* Minneapolis, MN: National Center on Educational Outcomes, University of Minnesota.

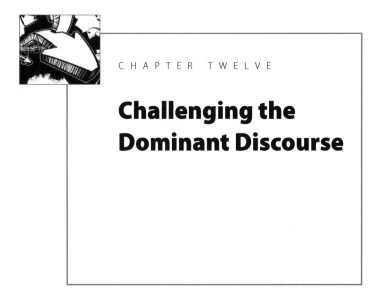

CHAPTER TWELVE

Challenging the Dominant Discourse

Suzanne Gallagher

Introduction

Teaching can be both an exciting experience and a daunting enterprise. Some teachers appear to meet the challenges of the classroom with courage and hope. Others seem to be ruled by the fear that they will lose control, and the students will steal the show, creating chaos and confusion. In fear-based classrooms, challenging the teacher or the curriculum is not allowed. We all have experienced the teachers who appeared to feel annoyed, angry, or threatened when either they or the content of their course was challenged. Some teachers try to dispel any questioning in their class, as if query were a deterrent to the completion of the delivery of more important information. In effect, these teachers are saying: "Stop the stupid questions and let me just teach!," when, in fact, they are acting out of the fear of losing control!

Critical Educators

Individuals who teach for social justice.

Conversely, emotionally objective and psychologically secure educators believe that questioning and challenging are necessary activities because both add a zestful, enlivened quality to the learning process. These are the courageous and **critical educators** who believe that we all need to query the world around us; we need to ask more and better questions to discover the truth and meaning of what we are learning. To me, this is not just a value added dimension of learning and teaching; it is an imperative to learning. I think the following story, which I have told elsewhere (Gallagher, 2003), can illustrate how a student's challenging and questioning of my work led to improving professional development as a teacher.

The story takes place as I was beginning to teach my first course of educational psychology. I was a doctorial student, and I had been studying the field for several years. I was inexperienced in the classroom, but I was eager to share what I had learned with my students. I was especially excited to try out all of the things I had learned about educational psychology on these very first students of mine. Among the techniques I chose to apply to check on their learning of the material was the pop quiz. Pop quizzes are an excellent example of variable-interval schedule of *reinforcement* that follows from a behavioral theory of learning; you'll find schedules of reinforcement covered in almost every educational psychology book. I felt that these surprise quizzes would keep my students studying the materials as we moved along the course, and of course it would keep students coming to class. I further assumed that since students wanted a good grade, they would see the need to study and attend class every day because they never knew when I would pop quiz on them. I also had learned that a more consistent study of material helped students store the information in long-term memory; in other words, spaced study was more effective than "massed" study, e.g., cramming for a test. This all made perfect sense to the educational psychologist within me.

Contrary to my belief, not all of my students shared my enthusiasm for this process. When one of my students asked me why I was giving pop quizzes, I explained my reasoning using bona fide concepts I had learned from graduate-level educational psychology courses. I gave the student perfectly valid reasons why I chose this mode for one of my marking methods. But no matter how I tried, the student was not satisfied. My student felt as though I was trying to control her if she wanted a good mark. I was looking at it from my professor's perspective, but she was letting me know that she had a very different response to what I considered my benign methods. Was I wrong or was I correct? Could my methods assist students in learning the material? Maybe. But they were also over-controlling students and evoking a negative emotion. The student wasn't feeling free to learn, and I began to question the practice.

As a response to this scene with my student, I began to get a sinking feeling that educational psychology had an underside. There was a lot more going on in this discipline than simply advancing the learning and teaching process. The amount of time and energy that teachers spend trying to make students learn educational psychology, for example, and trying to control the environment so that students will learn, needed to be more deeply examined. Rather then using the techniques of educational psychology in a clinical fashion, teachers need to spend the time and energy engaging students in meaningful and interesting aspects of the content and process of our subjects and courses. The teacher's control of the classroom needs to be balanced with cooperation in an atmosphere of mutual enhancement (Miller, 2003). The feminist in me was feeling the need to liberate both myself and my students from the traditional tools of control and domination.

In overt forms among the brave and in covert fashion from the meek, students do challenge teachers and course materials in many ways. Most often this is done in informal places and ways, far away from the ears of the teachers, outside the course spaces: in the dorms, in the hallways, or in the café over coffee. Sometimes the challenge is never even spoken. It's that internalized question that arises in students as they listen or read. There is something that seems not quite right, yet the learner senses that their position or point of view is not worthy of being voiced in class. To combat this disabling of student voices, teachers need to open spaces where challenge is a welcomed dialogue (Freire, 1992). Freire, mentor to many critical educators, supported the notion that good conversation is a key component of any learning process. At its best school is a place where students can ask their questions and mount their arguments in such a way that learning is advanced and understanding of content is deepened.

I like to believe that I would have eventually been drawn to examine this underside of educational psychology at some point along in my study, but I will always be grateful to that student who challenged my conception of the discipline and my authority. As I have grown in my professional career as an educational psychology professor, I have come to realize that there were more questionable practices within the discipline, and I have considered them as both a feminist and as a critical thinker. In this chapter, I will share my challenge to some of educational psychology's tenets, and I will point out some of the undersides of the discipline of educational psychology. I want to expose how the discipline has the power to mark students in such a way that their educational experience can be liberating and, conversely, in ways that could make educational experiences oppressive. Educational psychology is a powerful **discourse**, and those who espouse education as their profession need to be willing to examine it critically.

Discourse
Conversation.

Dominant Discourse

As a beginning student of this aspect of psychology, you may well ask: what is the dominant discourse of educational psychology, and why does it need to be challenged? Educational psychology has long been considered the branch of psychology that deals with issues related to the learning and teaching process. Most generally, the content of educational psychology is presented in exhaustive texts covering the content of the discipline in hundreds of pages of tedious reading. The major goal of such textbooks, or of a class related to educational psychology, is to assist pre-service teachers to teach well. Many people think that good teaching entails learning a variety of scientific discoveries about how learning happens. Students then learn how to apply these scientific discoveries to the practice of teaching. There is a promise implied that if a pre-service teacher learns the stuff of educational psychology, they will become a good teacher. An example found in a textbook says: "Effective teachers know that the principles of educational psychology and educational research will help them guide students' learning" (Santrock, 2008, p. 2). In an online review for another text, students are told that educational psychology "arms students with the current, practical knowledge they need to become effective teachers" (http://www.mhhe.com/socscience/education/edpsych/).

As serious students, we want to learn whatever we can in order to become better teachers and to assist our future students in their learning. We want to be knowledgeable regarding these important facts and concepts, and to prepare ourselves, we want to do well in educational psychology classes. And, of course, we want to pass the test. These are worthy goals, and if we approach the material of the textbook or course uncritically, we may attain our goals; yet, as teachers we may miss the mark. We miss the mark if in our application of this knowledge we are not required to ask questions, and we don't allow for the development of critical thinkers.

The Role of Discourse

When we talk about discourse we mean what is said in written or verbal form and also what is discussed in the name of the discipline. Formal or critical discussion is the discourse of a particular subject. According to feminists Karen Watson-Gegeo & David Gegeo (2004), "Discourse is action with social consequences" (p. 244). Discourse can help to give us a structure for thinking about the subject, and the outcomes could be liberating or debilitating (as in maintaining a dominant culture). The dominant discourse is the material that fills traditional educational psychology textbooks. For example, when we consider physics or biology, we will encounter a particular language, a specialized set of concepts, particular research methods, etc., that are used for study or discussion. Educational psychology also has a discourse comprised of a particular academic language, a specialized set of concepts, research methods, etc. This discourse builds a structure which facilitates the way teachers have come to view the field of educational psychology: the study of learners and learning.

Teachers frequently rely on textbooks as compendiums of knowledge for the discourse of educational psychology. Because these books are often written by scholars of the discipline, the students studying educational psychology consider that these textbooks contain the sole truth of the subject. On one level, students are correct because textbooks do contain the "truth" of a subject, or at least what is taken as true. Take a look at a typical educational psychology textbook and you'll see many are over 600 pages. It would seem that these exhaustive textbooks could not possibly leave anything out of the discussion. However, this is not true. The discourse we find in textbooks is usually the dominant discourse of the discipline. It is what many educational psychologists think pre-service teachers should learn. It is often written by well-known names in education; it appears neutral, and such texts have been used for decades as a way to

introduce newcomers into the profession. As such it is powerful. However, these encyclopedias of the discipline, massive as they are, do not contain the whole truth of how learning and effective teaching happens. Wrapped in the guise of current information within glossy, recent editions, much of what is represented as the most current information is no longer seen as appropriate information in a diverse and multicultural world. For example, "research has seriously challenged the notion that the 'stages' of human development are universal in the Piagetian sense" (Watson-Gegeo & Gegeo, 2004, p. 244), yet the theory of Piaget is still considered an essential educational psychology topic. And it is often included in the Praxis exams.

Since the development of the foundational aspects of the discipline of educational psychology, there have been many new perspectives and ways of thinking about learners and learning. My perspective is that important new material has been left out completely or covered incompletely, and emphasis has been give to materials that are passé or material that does not serve all students' educational experience. Therefore, I think an important question is: Why we would still use materials that don't serve to enhance the educational experience of today's students? How can this field disregard the contributions of critical constructivism and feminist theory?

The discourse of the discipline of educational psychology has been in the process of being gathered formally for just about a century, and it has been collected by members of a particular community. These folks speak a language through which they communicate with each other and with those who will apply the tenants of the discipline. Members of the educational psychology community are led by well-known names in the discipline, and they tend to agree with the major concepts of the discipline. When I say "agree," I recognize that there are often disagreements and debates among members of this discursive community. Consequently, much of what this scholarly community says is the truth, or at least worthwhile, gets put into textbooks, pronounced at conferences, and is rewarded by professional organizations. Throughout the history of the discipline of educational psychology, there have been many controversies, disagreements, and arguments regarding what is said regarding the scientifically proven facts and how these scientific theories should be applied to teaching (Watson-Gegeo & Gegeo, 2004). This dimension of history of educational psychology is important, yet it is rarely mentioned to students aside from mentioning a few dissenting voices.

Modernist project

Much of what the educational psychology community agrees is the appropriate discourse of the field has evolved from a modernist worldview. Modernism is the term used to describe the period beginning with the Copernican revolution and extending until the end of World War II. The main theme of modernists is that the world can be described logically and through application of scientific thinking. The philosopher Rene Descartes (1596–1650) contributed, "I think; therefore, I am": the cornerstone value of modernist thinking. Members of the modernist community want to discover the scientific truth about students and teaching; they want to discover what makes students do what is desired so that our students can learn more effectively. Science, especially much of educational psychology's research efforts, is viewed as the gateway to this truth. It is viewed as being part of progress. Science holds the promise of progress as it is purported to give teachers control of the classroom and, thereby, make students' behavior predictable. Perhaps to understand the modern worldview it is helpful to consider a pre-modern worldview.

For a pre-modern worldview we can look at earlier times, before scientific technologies were developed and humans turned to their own reasoning for answers. In these times people came

to know the truth from folk stories, from God, or from the king; what was believable was mediated by their representatives. Very simply put, the truth was transmitted to the common folks through those in power, or those given the authority to speak. The discourse of those speaking with power at the time was rife with superstition, magic, and fantasy. Common folks were told about the world, how the world worked, and who they were through these representatives. In this world, the earth was the center of the universe.

In *Precious Bane*, Mary Webb tells the complex story of Prudence Sarn, who was born with a clef palate, sometimes referred to as a harelip. The story is set in the countryside of England early in nineteenth century, a time when multiple influences like folklore and superstition helped to shape life in the society in which Pru lived. Rather than the congenital influences that we understand today, folklore held that a harelip was the result of a curse resulting from a hare, or rabbit, running across the path of an expectant mother at a particular time in her baby's gestation. The result was the child's being born with a lip resembling that of a hare. This characteristic was thought to be the "mark of the devil," and often people, even children, born with the characteristic were feared and scorned. Pru's life was influenced by this mark of distinction as she responded to what others thought about her and how they treated her.

Today, this thinking seems ridiculous because it is based on superstition. In pre-modern times though, this was a powerful perspective. People's lives were certainly marked by such conditions. The work of modernity was to undo superstitions such as this. The power of "man's" rationality, through use of the scientific method, was thought to "replace pre-modern fantasy, faith, and superstition with scientific knowledge" (Gallagher, 2003, p. 39). As Usher and Edwards (1994) tell us, science now becomes the guarantor and route to truth, and when we have found the truth, we are free.

They write: "The emancipation of humanity thus requires that people are given access to scientific knowledge, since the condition of their emancipation is that they live subject to the 'laws' uncovered by science" (p. 172).

The research of education psychology is set firmly in the modern era's desire for truth, freedom, control, and progress. Pre-modern ways of thinking have been replaced by science. Now, science tells us about the world, how it works, and our place in the world. However, the discipline did not just appear, whole and complete, with smooth unfolding. As a discipline educational psychology developed over time as the number of children attending formal schools grew and teachers needed ways of organizing them for education.

As a discipline, educational psychology is just a bit younger than psychology. Although issues that we consider the concepts of educational psychology, e.g., learning and testing, can claim a long history dating back to the ancient philosophers, I would like to recognize the "father" of educational psychology, Edward L. Thorndike (1874–1949). The first formal attempt to gather the discourse was in 1910 with the first publication of the American Psychology Association journal *The Educational Psychologist* with Thorndike as the editor. Some, Levine (2004) for example, have paid him homage because of "Professor Thorndike's enormous contributions to the field of educational psychology" (p. 173). Educational psychology texts generally name him as a founding person of the field as well. It matters that Thorndike is regarded as the father of this discipline.

Thorndike matters because he set in motion a particular research agenda based on the question of how learning happens and how teachers can control and increase learning in their students. It's important that we understand Thorndike's perspective. His work was influential in making the field more scientific, which was very important to scholars at the beginning of the twentieth century. The

more a discipline looked scientific, the more it could be considered legitimate. To reinforce a more scientific authority, Thorndike retreated to a laboratory and chose cats as his favorite subjects. For example one of his questions was how a cat learns to escape from a box. From this experimentation grew laws of learning that directed teachers in exactly what they needed to do in order to get students to do what they wanted them to do. Direct instruction is the progeny of teaching and learning from this perspective.

Thorndike wasn't the only one interested in how learning happened. Thorndike's contemporaries William James (1842–1910) and John Dewey (1859–1952) were also interested in the phenomenon of learning. However, while Thorndike was more scientific in his approach, both James and Dewey expressed a fundamentally philosophical understanding of the teaching and learning process. I think it's important to mention that James was troubled by his former student Thorndike's approach. He feared that the discoveries that emanated from the lab were but small peppercorns of truth that in the end would result in a mountain of misrepresentation of the truth, not the certain formula acclaimed by Thorndike. In his famous text *Talks to Teachers,* William James counsels teachers:

> I say moreover that you make a great, a very great mistake, if you think that psychology, being the science of the mind's laws, is something from which you can deduce definite programmes (sic) and schemes and methods of instruction for immediate schoolroom use. Psychology is a science, and teaching is an art; and sciences never generate arts directly out of themselves. An intermediary inventive mind must make the application, by using its originality. (http://www.des.emory.edu/mfp/tt1.html)

Despite the tensions raised by these two very different perspectives, the scientific approach to learning grew and was further developed by B. F. Skinner. In Skinner's perspective, **behavioral psychology,** all learners, e.g., pigeons, dog, cats, or chil-

Behavioral psychology
A scientific paradigm that proves that behavior is controlled.

dren are responding organisms subjected to the same laws and able to be trained and/or controlled by the same set of conditions established by teachers in the educational environment. Learning could be mapped on grids and measured, with speed as a decisive factor. The technological culture of the 20th century found this perspective very appealing. This was a perfect example of applying modernist thinking to educating children: pure science.

This modernist perspective was also fueled by developments in Europe. For example, in 1904 in France Alfred Binet (1857–1911) had been asked by the ministry of education to devise a method whereby children could be sorted according to their ability to access education. France had mandated universal education so children formerly excluded from schools because of learning difficulties would now attend school. These children would be placed in separate classes according to their ability to learn. Binet, along with a colleague, Theodore Simon, devised a test for measuring **intelligence**, which they termed the intelligence quotient or IQ. Now, educators had the methods to improve learning as well as a way to measure it.

Intelligence

A construct that includes logical thinking, linguistic ability, etc.

The term *intelligence* is a good example of the project of modernity. We educators use it so frequently; yet, we may be thinking of very different aspects of a person's mind. Further confusing this notion of intelligence, the term *cognitive ability* is often substituted for intelligence. Textbooks often report research educational psychologists have done related to these concepts: intelligence and cognition. For example, Howard Gardner's work on multiple intelligences is usually mentioned. Robert Sternberg's triatic theory of intelligence and Vygotsky's socio-historical perspective, among others, are also commonly discussed. However, the traditional educational psychology text's discourse turns quickly to ways of measuring intelligence and intelligence tests, and the thorny issues of what these mental processes have to do with emotion or other less rational mental dynamics (Watson-

Gegeo & Gegeo, 2004). Defining intelligence is the controversial piece of the discussion.

Santrock (2008) has said that intelligence is an "abstract, broad concept, that it is not surprising that there are so many different ways to define it" (p. 115). This well-known author explains that, "unlike height, weight, and age, intelligence cannot be directly measured. You can't peer into a student's head and observe the intelligence going on inside" (p. 115). However, in the typical educational psychology text, the conversation always gets around to a discussion of IQ tests. The assumption is clear that intelligence is a solid construct; yet the scientific community has always been conflicted about just what intelligence is: fluid, crystallized, or multifarious. It strikes me as strange that intelligence, a concept that is difficult to define, has so many sure ways to be measured.

Measuring this elusive thing called intelligence is problematic. What is rarely mentioned in traditional texts is that these IQ tests aren't measuring intelligence in the same way metric scales measure height and weight. They are measuring in an ordinal way. Ordinal numbers put things in order or rank from first to last. Those who respond to the most number of tasks or questions correctly get the highest ranking; their scores are placed in order, just ahead of those who respond to fewer test items correctly, on the so-called normal curve. We've all seen this pictorial description of a general population. It is often referred to as a bell curve because of its resemblance to the shape of a bell with most scores congregating around the middle.

Unfortunately, what results from these tests is an image that more closely represents the socioeconomic background of the students more than any so-called intelligence. In other words, what these tests tell us is something most educators (and the public) already know, i.e., those with the most resources, who are able to access schools with up-to-date textbooks and technological materials, where teachers enjoy high status, generally do very well on intelligence tests. Yet, despite this obvious bias toward white, middle-class students, schools in the U.S. continue to grow the testing business, although the rate of return regarding information reaped from tests is so low. Ironically, the only valid reason to administer tests is to use the results to improve the educational experience for students, yet this rarely happens.

An often unexamined result of test scores is the marks students receive, literally and figuratively. This is a kind of "marking" that can give teachers, and sometimes the students themselves, a very limited understanding of students and who they are as learners. This marking becomes significant if students receive a limited form of educational experience because of this mark. These are referred to as high stakes tests. We find this ridiculous in *Precious Bane,* yet the main consumers of these tests, our students and their parents, hardly notice or discuss the negative, unintended consequences of these tests in our current educational situation.

For example, schools often use scores from tests to track students, the result of which can cause different educational experiences. Tracking is a controversial issue, which is often presented in the most neutral of tones. Santrock (2008) explains that, "Between-class ability grouping (tracking) consists of grouping students based on their ability or achievement. . . . [and] has long been used in schools as a way to organize students, especially at the secondary level" (p. 129). He cites critics who argue that this practice "stigmatizes students who are consigned to low-track classes" (p. 129). Further, Santrock explains that critics assert that "tracking is used to segregate students according to ethnicity and socioeconomic status because higher tracks have fewer students from ethnic minority and impoverished backgrounds . . . In this way tracking can actually replay segregation within schools" (p. 129–130).

The textbook seems to leave the judgment to the reader to draw their own conclusion. To learn more

about the student's perspective, I've had debates about tracking in my classroom. We read texts that contest the use of tracking. Pre-service teachers understand that tracking doesn't work, is unjust, and undemocratic. I can say that many students are outraged by this kind of treatment of children in U.S. schools. However, I question whether this issue, and many others of social justice, are taken up in traditional educational psychology classes. It has been over 20 years since Jeannie Oakes exposed the deleterious effects of tracking in her classic work *Keeping Track: How Schools Structure Inequality* (1985). This text was selected by the *American School Board Journal* and celebrated as a "Must Read" book when it was first published. Sadly, it is infrequently read or even mentioned in today's educational psychology courses.

Why is the use of test scores a viable factor in the tracking of students? This scientific technology helps to advance the feeling of *meritocracy;* a quality that most Americans like to believe is operative in our schools. It has the veneer or mask of an objective and fair way to measure something that can't be measured, i.e., intelligence. This notion of intelligence then morphs into ability and eventually achievement.

Technical Rationality

From a modernist, and purely logical worldview, problems that are encountered in schooling, e.g., organizing students, have a technical solution. Therefore, these solutions can often have a scientific loading, like the one standardized testing gives to tracking. Tracking seems to work, and teachers find it appealing because it appears to make their very difficult job just a little easier. However, this is a vulgar pragmatism (Cherryholms, 1988), in other words—it works. Tracking has an efficiency that appeals to educators who see the school as a factory. We can organize students as in an industrial model; but, an unintended consequence is exposed. The unintended consequence is that the low track is devalued by the school, and their educational opportunities become severely limited. I question: what should educational psychologists do in the face of these poor schooling practices?

Progress

Traditional educational psychology has been more concerned, I believe, with passing on the discipline rather than helping pre-service teachers explore more appropriate and socially just ways to assist students in their learning. We have made some improvements in the last 100 years, and these advancements need greater recognition within the field. At the end of the twentieth century educational psychologists espoused a shift in thinking regarding the field. For example Salomon (1995) asserted that educational psychologists now accept that learning is social. This is a dramatic shift in understanding as, for most of the twentieth century, the focus was the changes of behavior in the individual learner and what was going on in the person's mind. Salomon also explains the error in what he calls the "plague of reductionism," which occurs when a complex process, like learning, is broken down in to multiple, seemingly simpler, parts. These are the peppercorns that concerned William James. Although this call from Salomon and others came as the twentieth century ended, this perspective has not yet made its way into educational psychology textbooks used in today's courses.

Anderson, Blumenfeld, Pintrich, Clark, Marx, and Peterson (1995) express the shift in perspective well when they said: "Currently the heart of a contemporary psychological perspective is an image of learners as active constructors of meaning, and an image of learning as an act of construction through social interacting in many contexts" (p. 145). This is also a paradigm shift from concentration on the isolated individual.

Why Does the Discourse Need to Be Challenged?

The traditional text of educational psychology needs to be challenged for many reasons, but most importantly because it is a powerful discourse in the way it describes, excludes, includes, and constructs our students. Educational psychology can be a powerful force in schooling today. Pre-service teachers need to see the contributions of educational psychology as critical to the successful implementation of their classroom practices.

Challenging the Dominant Discourse

There are several helpful and effective ways in which we can challenge the dominant discourse of educational psychology that can assist students in looking at the way learning is enhanced. Key components of successful post-modern classrooms include the following.

Be Critical

Critics are held in esteem by the public: a literary critic, a music critic, a film critic. At other times critics can be thought to be people who make a habit of fault finding, who just carp on issues. I espouse a critical literacy; a literacy whereby we can read the word in the sense of decoding letters and symbols and arriving at meaning, yet we apply an added dimension to our reading. With critical literacy we read the word and the world as Freire (1992) insists. We are active in that we engage a text rather than just consume it. Sometimes we need to take an oppositional stance toward a text, and talk back to a text (hooks, 1989). We can only accomplish this critical reading if we are aware of subtexts and pretexts. From whose viewpoint is this text written? What are the political, cultural, economic underpinnings and values that support the text?

This kind of critique is a postmodern critique. Just as modernity leveled a critique against pre-modern ways of thinking, postmodernism levels a critique against modernism. The dominant discourse of educational psychology is what Usher and Edwards (1994) are talking about in the following quote: "The grand narratives of science, truth, and progress are discourses—'realities' we have created by and for ourselves. Stories we tell ourselves about the real, or more likely, stories told by more powerful others on our behalf" (p. 28).

Intertextual Reading

Intertextual reading is reading texts against each other. Texts are never neutral although some strive to take on a neutral voice. There are texts that contest and resist what the dominant discourse lays before students. There are texts that strive to present another voice, or a corrective to much of what is often taken for granted. An example would include the texts I've mentioned on tracking.

Ask Questions

We need to ask better questions as educators and students. For example, we need to inquire how well a program is working for this child instead of continuing of our continued obsession with how our students did test. In our current NCLB milieu we are so mired in paperwork, reporting, and test preparation that we hardly give credence to the fact that students are struggling in our schools as we use "scientifically approved" methods.

A question I always need to ask is *cui bono*? It is an ancient question coming from the Roman philosopher Cicero. By asking *cui bono*, I mean "who benefits?" from a particular way of thinking and acting. What we learn and then implement has a definite effect on our students' lives. For example, the tracking issue does more than simplify the instructional problem of teaching to multiple levels of student achievement. Tracking keeps the poor and slow students separated from the middle class and aspiring ones. Therefore, we must ask *cui bono* in all circumstances of school life. Who benefits from our grading systems, our assessment practices,

our methods of communication with parents and the community?

Many of our educational practices need to be challenged. You may have experienced some of these ill-conceived policies. Perhaps some of our readers have been told that they are not good students; that they shouldn't go to college, or, conversely, that they are better than other students. My mantra has become "says who?" Educational policies carrying negative consequences for our students need to be questioned and challenged.

Although I single out educational psychology in this chapter, I believe that all discourses need to be challenged, even this one. Now, that could keep a person pretty busy; however, the unexamined life is not for educated people. It is human nature to simply accept stories about the world, how it works, our place in the world, and ourselves. I believe that it is the educator's responsibility to teach students to question the status quo and to push for applications of social justice and equal opportunities for all students.

In this text, the authors have asked you to consider important issues of educational psychology and to apply critical thinking and query within your teaching skills, knowledge, and disposition. The authors of this text are united in their unfaltering belief in the possibility for the positive development of the soul and minds of all of our students. For you, the pre-service teacher, we hope to ignite the same fire and passion for the profession. Educational psychology is an art when we apply our attention to the whole student and respectfully deal with them within the social milieu they inhabit.

References

Anderson, L. M., Blumenfeld, P., Pintrich, P. R., Clark, C. M., Marx, R. W., & Peterson, P. (1995). Educational psychology for teachers: Reforming our courses, rethinking our roles. *Educational Psychology, 30*(3), 143–157.

Cherryholms, C. H. (1988). *Power and criticism: Post-structural investigations in education.* New York: Teachers College Press.

Damasio, A. (1994). *Descartes' error: Emotion, reason, and the human brain*. New York: Grosset/Putnam.

Freire, P. (1992). *Pedagogy of the oppressed*. New York: Seabury Press. (Original work published in 1972).

Gallagher, S. (2003). *Educational psychology: Disrupting the dominant discourse*. New York: Peter Lang Publishing, Inc.

hooks, B. (1989). *Talking back*. Boston: South End Press.

James, W. (n.d.). Talks to teachers. Retrieved on May 5 from http://www.des.emory.edu/mfp/tt1.html

Miller, J.B. (2003). Telling the truth about power. In *Research and Action Report 25* (1 Fall/Winter). Wellesley, MA: Wellesley College for Women.

Oakes, Jeannie (1985). *Keeping Track: How Schools Structure Inequality*. Birmingham, N.Y.: Vail-Ballou Press.

Salomon, G. (Ed.) (1995). Reflections on the field of educational psychology by the out-going journal editor. *Educational Psychology, 30*(3), 143–157.

Santrock, J. W. (2008). *Educational psychology* (3rd Edition). Boston: McGraw Hill.

Usher, R., & Edwards, R (1994). *Postmodernism and education*. New York: Routledge.

Watson-Gegeo, K. & Gegeo, D. (2004). Deep culture: Pushing the epistemological boundaries. In G. Goodman & K. Carey (Eds.), *Critical Multicultural Conversations*. Cresskill, NJ: Hampton Press.

A Glossary of Educational Psychology Terms

Acquisition: Literally meaning receiving, the acquisition of a new language is complex. Acquisition of a new language ranges from rudimentary vocabulary to mastery of the second language.

Affect: Feelings or emotions that are expressed by the students. This word is used as both a noun and a verb (affects or affected) describing feelings. For example, the music affected us deeply.

Affective domain: The entire world of feelings that the student expresses or is exposed to within his or her intrapersonal and interpersonal world. How a student feels is directly related to his or her ability to attend, concentrate, and learn.

Agency: The individual's ability to control her own destiny or life decisions. The agentic process fights for free will or personal power against forces of control or domination.

Assessment: This is a broad term that includes both formative and summative evaluations of student work. Assessment may be conducted using various forms: quizzes, tests, observations, authentic forms (art portfolios, etc.), standardized achievement tests, or personal reflection.

Aversive punishment: A strong, negative form of reprimand or agent of punishment; for example, scolding, yelling, spanking, or any other harsh form of negative consequence.

Backward design: This is a process of educational curriculum planning where the end result is considered first. After determining what teachers want their students to know, they then design instructional projects and assessments to measure the acquisition of learning along the way.

Baggage: This term is a metaphor describing things you carry with you from the past. For example, I wouldn't learn from that teacher because she reminded me of someone I didn't like.

Bias: A tendency to be opinionated or to favor one side over another. Examples include bias toward your school, race, religious preference, sexual orientation or other. Bias can be subtle or overt as in discrimination.

Binaries: Either/or juxtapositions. Conceiving a problem or solution in black or white: right or wrong. This thinking is considered reductive and is typically, though not exclusively, adolescent. For example: a song is either "awesome," or "it stinks."

Canon: A comprehensive collection of information, typically books of literature, representing a field or discipline. For example: the canon of American literature includes Gary Soto, Phil Levine, Emily Dickinson, Charles Simac, and Mary Oliver as representative poets.

Classroom management: The traditional term used to describe the controlling of classroom behavior. These authors prefer the process of developing a positive classroom culture of learning.

Cognitive: The acts of perceiving, thinking, and or remembering. These are mental processes. For example, reasoning is a cognitive process.

Cognitive apprenticeship: Using the analogy to traditional apprentice relationships (learning trades from an accomplished artisan; i.e., a carpenter, plumber, or electrician), the students apprentice under the teacher by modeling the intellectual and social behaviors exemplified by the teacher. Coaching is also an example of cognitive apprenticeship.

Communication context: The context is affected by the atmosphere or timing of the communication. Taking someone's words out of context would be a way to imbue false meaning to a communication. For example, if the president of the university said, "It is important to also have fun during your four years of rigorous study as you attend the college," the message is not "It is important to . . . have fun."

Concrete operations stage of development: Piaget described this stage from approximately 7 years of age through approximately 12 years of age as the time of the development of adult-like logical thinking skills.

Constructivism: The pedagogical perspective on learning that suggests that we create our own reality and the knowledge to support it. We make sense of the world through building upon prior knowledge. For example, Piaget stated that we assimilate new knowledge into existing schemes to support our current ideation.

Cooperative learning: This instructional strategy makes use of Vygotsky's socially motivated learning to increase student participation and engagement. For example, using small groups of students (2–5 per group) students have the opportunity to use oral language and to share opinions with one another.

Critical constructivism: Expanding upon constructivists' belief that individuals create their own reality, critical constructivists argue that the struggle to end the oppression of poor people, to stop the subjugation of women and under-represented groups, and to abolish the perpetuation of racism must be a significant part of one's life purpose. Learning is both a knowledge building and an emancipation tool for the liberation of both students and teachers. Critical constructivists support the growth of the individual and changes in the situation or context in which they are living. For example, critical constructivists elicit active expressions of social justice and social change to provide true democracy and egalitarianism within society.

Critical educators: Individuals who *are conscious of the social and political implications of teaching, and strive to* teach for social justice. Often these teachers ascribe to the teaching of a mentor, Paulo Freire. Friere's liberatory pedagogy has been the inspiration for thousands of educators world-wide.

Critical pedagogy: This is the emancipatory educational philosophy of educational and social practice introduced by Paulo Freire (1921–1997). Freire was a Brazilian educator who worked for the improvement of people's literacy to free them from the shackles of ignorance and poverty. Ending oppression through education was Freire's life hope and work.

Cultural collision: The experience of clashing cultures often represented by white, middle-class educators teaching in inner-city schools. For example, this experience as portrayed by actress Hilary Swank in the film, *Freedom Writers.*

Cultural pluralism: This is the combination of diverse cultural groups and represents a multicultural mix of identities. A metaphor for the mixing of multiple cultures is a salad, i.e., a unity with all parts maintaining their unique identities as they mix together.

Direct instruction: The processes of lecturing, explaining, and structured teaching where the teacher follows a specific script throughout the.instructional process. Sometimes considered the opposite of constructivism, this process can be an effective tool for teaching students needing clear and concise explanations for basic comprehension or fact learning.

Discovery learning: Often attributed to Jerome Bruner, this process involves student investigations into specific subject learning through experiential, first-hand connections. Rather than simply instructing students in the process of reading, Bruner suggested that we learn to read as we study a topic of interest.

Discursive practices: The act of rationally arguing to support or critique a topic. For example, discursive practice includes the use of reasoning to defend an argument. Discourse is a formal discussion of a topic.

Dissonance: This describes cacophony or harsh sounds. Dissonance also relates to a state of unrest or disharmony.

Ebonics: African-Americans vernacular English. The roots (Ebony = black and Phonics = pertaining to speech / sounds) are combined in this 1980's neologism.

Emancipatory pedagogy: This is a philosophy of education that espouses the belief that all people are entitled to receive a free and appropriate public education and that the aims of this education are to further one's ability to pursue a life characterized by liberty in life-style, vocation, and the selection of personal family values.

Feminism: This is a term used to describe a philosophic approach based upon the belief that women have social, economic, and political rights equal to men. Jean Miller's work considers the concept of *mutual enhancement* as a core component of feminist theory. For example, in education, mutual enhancement would refer to both the teacher and the students as being learners

Formal operations stage of development: Piaget described this stage as the last of the developmental sequence. From

approximately age 14, adolescents begin to comprehend abstract thought and concepts such as philosophy and other abstract phenomena (i.e., money is a medium of exchange).

Formative assessment: This is an evaluation of student learning that is used to evaluate on-going instruction and to plan for future teaching or re-teaching. Formative assessment is used by the teacher during varying time periods to review student progress and to consider future instructional decisions.

Hegemony: The process of the domination of one person, state, or entity over another. Often hegemony is an insidious process that requires the consent of the governed. For example, individuals either volunteer or are forced to relinquish personal agency to another. The connotation is negative, e.g., students placed in a low-track high school class feel they are not as worthy of a good education as those in an honors track.

High-stakes testing: The use of assessments, generally single standardized tests, to determine significant outcomes for students. For example, in California, the High School Exit Exam can be the sole determinant of high school graduation.

Hip-Hop: Popular youth culture identified with particular styles of music (rap, gangsta rap), clothing, language and accoutrements associated with (generally, not exclusively) urban, African-American and Latino identities.

Homework: This is a traditional form of assignment for the reinforcement of classroom work; however, the research on homework's value is mixed. In the primary grades, homework is more often a measure of cultural capital: if the student has a supportive home/family situation where homework can be accomplished. Parent educational levels can also be a covariant in homework success.

Idiomatic expressions: These are expressions used in speech that are peculiar to a region or a group. For example, to say someone died, the idiomatic expression is, "They kicked the bucket." A second language learner's literal interpretation of this would be confusing.

Institutionalized racism: This is a process of discrimination of one group over another through the mis-application of rules and authority. For example, racial profiling by police (white police disproportionally arresting black citizens) or schools with disproportionate numbers of disciplinary actions toward one group over another.

Intelligence: This is a hotly debated construct. Traditional definitions of intelligence focused on logical thinking, long-term memory, and other exclusively mental processes, which are thought to be measured on intelligence tests. More recent work by Gardner and others propose broader conceptualizations of intelligence such as body, feeling, interpersonal, intrapersonal, and other intelligences.

Interpersonal communication: This refers to all interaction, verbal and non-verbal, between people. Interpersonal communication is both an art and a science of interaction, and it can occur within multiple media.

Intrapersonal communication: This refers to personal reflection and the self-talk that a person creates to further understanding of thoughts and action. Intrapersonal communication could include journaling, internal dialogue, or other forms of rumination.

Involuntary immigrants: Individuals or groups who were coerced to come to a country. John Ogbu coined this term to refer to African Americans brought to America as slaves. Ogbu claimed that as an involuntary immigrant, one may be less willing to assimilate to the values of the new culture.

Learning-centered: This is a term used interchangeably with student-centered instruction. The focus is upon process and environment as well as the content of learning situations. Teachers understand that students are active in the meaning-making process and provide multiple opportunities for student engagement and responsibility.

Lesson plans: This is a tool to use as a part of the teacher's instructional strategies. Lesson plans direct the teacher as a recipe guides the cook. Creative deviations from a lesson plan are like spices, but the basic plan gives the teacher clear goals and objectives to pursue.

Liberatory pedagogy: This is a philosophy of education that works to free people from the oppression of poverty and social injustice. Liberatory pedagogy is the work of social justice educators. Examples of this pedagogy include community organizing to stop violence, promotion of equal treatment of all students, and the hiring of staff representative of the student body and community.

Long-term memory: This is the final stop in the memory process. Information is stored in this register for later retrieval. As is suggested by the name, information can remain in this part of the brain indefinitely. Most items in long-term memory are 'over-learned'; for example, George Washington was the first president of the United States.

Media: This is the plural of medium. Media are methods of communication such as face-to-face, radio, television, Internet, or other means.

Meritocracy: This is a term referring to the cultural myth that if people work hard enough they will achieve status and capital commensurate with their efforts. This is exemplified by the Horatio Alger story. The roots of the causal concept of work directly equating with success date back to the Puritan ethics of the seventeenth century.

Message interference: This term describes the effect of distortion upon message effects. Distortion changes the intent of the message. Examples of distortion include intentional distortion (lying), propaganda, gossip, or physical distortions such as crowd noise.

Metacognition: This is often referred to as 'thinking about thinking.' Metacognition allows a student the opportunity to reflect on his own learning. This is a valuable tool for reinforcing long-term memory and self-regulating learning.

Meta-analysis: The deconstruction of an argument that goes beyond the obvious. Meta implies taking something beyond the simple or rudimentary. For example, looking at the root causes of suspension/expulsion policies may disclose issues of institutionalized racism.

Misogynistic: Misogynists are individuals who hate women. The roots (gyn = woman and miso = disdain/hatred) are combined to reflect this most aversive attitude toward women. Examples in Hip-Hop culture include identifying women generally as "ho's" (prostitutes/whores) and "bitches."

Moral development: This relates to the development of beliefs that are considered right or wrong. Kohlberg is credited for early work on this subject and the development of a sequence of understanding right and wrong as pre-conventional, conventional, and post-conventional. Moral or character education has had a strong following in the post-Columbine and post-Enron years.

Mutual enhancement: This is a feminist term borrowed from Jean Miller. In a mutually enhancing situation, both participants receive benefit. For example, in the classroom, both teachers and students can be learners and growth occurs for both participants.

Normal or norms: This is a technical term from psychometrics and statistics used to describe a 'normal' population. From this perspective statisticians can generate conceptions of average; i.e., mean, median, and mode. Norm-referenced testing is a process of distributing a population in a way that it conforms to the laws of distribution. Norm-referenced tests unfairly represent the knowledge of the test takers.

Objective: Being objective implies that the observer is only seeing the facts of the situation. There is an emotional detachment in objectivity, and the situation is alleged to be viewed fairly from this perspective. For example: teachers need to be emotionally objective in dealing with their student's behavior.

Pedagogy: The practice of teaching, including methods and content. A pedagogy is based on a particular philosophy of education, which included the set of beliefs that form the basis upon which the teacher makes instructional decisions. In the case of this book, the example is critical constructivism.

Praxis: The practice of critical pedagogy or teaching for liberation. Freire insists that our work as teachers always includes reflection and action.

Preoperational Stage of Development: Piaget considered the time from age two through age six as a time of language development, and children can imagine reality outside their immediate senses. Sometimes referred to as the magic years, children in this stage often believe in Santa, the tooth fairy, and other imaginary people.

Reflective practice: This is the process of thinking about your experience. The teacher is immersed in hundreds of interactions and the performance of thousands of actions every day. Some of these actions and interactions are either mistakes or not appropriate to the situation. By reflecting on the work of the day, it is possible to learn to correct faulty decisions or actions.

Reinforcer: A term from behavioral psychology meaning any action that has the effect of continuing or maintaining a behavior. For example, if students are praised for completing their daily work and following the praise they continue to show good work effort, the praise may have been a positive reinforcer.

Resiliency: Literally, this term means the ability to bounce back. In psychology it means to recover from trauma, and it is dependent upon psycho-social strength from strong, supportive families, friends, or others. Resiliency helps a child recover from traumatic events such as a loss of a close family member, divorce, etc.

Scaffolding: Providing academic or psychosocial support for student learning. A scaffold is a structure to help raise the student's participation. Examples may include auditory assis-

tance (reading the material to the student), psychomotor support (providing word processing systems for help with written language), or visual support (displaying or providing alternative information sources such as printed notes).

Self-efficacy: A concept developed by Albert Bandura and used to describe a person's combined thoughts and feelings concerning their ability (personal agency) to function within particular contexts. For example, teachers' self-efficacy is built upon their sense of their ability to control difficult students, large classes, special needs children, and other requirements of their professional identity.

Self-esteem: A construct used to describe how individuals feel and think about themselves. A high or low self-esteem may be appropriate to the individual or it may be over- or underestimated. The self-esteem may be specific to any one area such as body image, intellectual ability, social skills, or family.

Semiotics: The study of signs and symbols. These investigations allow the student the ability to understand the meaning of communicative behavior; for example, media.

Sensori-motor stage of development: Piaget identified the first stage of development as the time of learning through the senses: sight, sound, touch and taste. From birth through approximately the first two years of life, children come to understand their world through sensory perception.

Sensory register: This is the first stop for information in the memory. Information comes in to consciousness for a second or two and is either processed into short-term memory or is instantly forgotten.

Social justice: The consideration of equality and freedom of opportunity within common educational, employment, or political practices affecting an individual's daily living. Equal opportunity to be given a free and appropriate public education (F.A.P.E.) is an example.

Social justice pedagogy: A philosophy of education that places issues of emancipation and liberation at the forefront of why one teaches. The practice of the teacher is directed at addressing issues of violence toward and oppression of children and their families.

Standardized assessment: Any form of testing that requires specific, timed and controlled assessment practices. Standardized assessments are generally commercially produced and rely on a combination of norm-referenced and criterion-referenced validity.

Standards: The specific criterion describing the content required for instruction. Standards-based instruction has been a topic of debate since the passing of NCLB. The questions surround who decides which curriculum is of value and what should be taught?

Stereotypes: Stereotypes are over-generalizations about groups or individuals representing specific groups. Examples include, "All Jewish people. . . ."; "Everyone from Harvard. . . ."; or "All Republicans. . . ." Stereotypes involve prejudging of individuals based on misrepresentations.

Subjective: Being subjective implies an emotional attachment to the event or situation. For example, parents view their children's behavior subjectively. It is extremely difficult to be distanced or detached when considering one's own child.

Summative assessment: This is a concluding assessment. Summative assessments may be standardized tests given at the end of the year. These assessments may also include final exams or other global evaluations.

Tao: Literally meaning "The Way," Tao is a concept of simplicity taken from the Chinese philosophy of Taoism. Acceptance of the natural order of the universe is an underlying precept. For example, "Accept is the way (Tao) of Zen."

Teacher centered: Similar to subject centered in focus, in teacher-centered instruction, the teacher maintains control and direction of the classroom and its inhabitants. For example, in a lecturing mode, the attention is focused on the teacher's instruction.

Technical rationality: This term is based on the understanding that the world, or the world of the classroom, can be predicted and controlled because certain rules are in play. For example, if a teacher want to control learning there are particular practices that will work toward this end; if learning doesn't occur it is because the practices have been implemented incorrectly.

Third world: This is a term used to describe the least developed nations of the world. Most generally, these are countries consumed by poverty and severe inequalities regarding health care, education, and economic opportunities. Examples include Zimbabwe and Bangladesh. The erroneous assumption implied by the ranking 'third' is the implication that these countries are less prestigious than first (highly industrialized) or second world (Communist) countries.

Transformative discourse: Conversations that are life changing. The term indicates deep levels of communication that go beyond simple and elementary chit-chat.

Wait time: This is the period of time a teacher should pause between asking a question and expecting students to answer. Because of differing processing times, some students may still be processing the question while another responds, and consequently, they might miss the answer. A suggested wait time is three to five seconds.

Contributors

Floyd D. Beachum is an Assistant Professor in the Department of Administrative Leadership at the University of Wisconsin – Milwaukee (UWM). He teaches the following courses: Organizational Change and Team Leadership, Leadership in Educational Organizations, Leadership in Multicultural Organizations, and Urban Educational Issues. His research interests include: leadership in urban education, moral and ethical leadership, and social justice issues K-12 schools. He is co-editor of the book, *Urban Education for the 21st Century: Research, Issues, and Perspectives*.

Karen T. Carey is currently serving as the Interim Dean of the College of Science and Mathematics at California State University, Fresno. Dr. Carey received her Ph. D. in school psychology from the University of Cincinnati and was a school psychologist working with P-12 students for over 25 years. Her most recent books include *Critical Multicultural Conversations* (Hampton Press) and *Ubiquitous Assessment* (Peter Lang Publishing).

Jeffrey M. R. Duncan-Andrade holds a joint appointment as the Assistant Professor of Raza Studies and Education and Co-director of the Educational Equity Initiative, Cesar Chavez Institute, San Francisco State University (415-522-5020; jandrade©sfsu.edu) and he teaches Sociology of Education at East Oakland Community High School.

Suzanne Gallagher is an associate professor in the School of Education at Gwynedd-Mercy College in Gwynedd Valley, Pennsylvania. Prior to coming to post-secondary education she worked in elementary education as a classroom teacher and administrator. Lang published her first book *Educational Psychology: Disrupting the Dominant Discourse* in 2003.

Greg S. Goodman is an assistant professor in the School of Education and Human Services at Clarion University of Pennsylvania. His career has included working as a school psychologist, school counselor, alternative education teacher, and outdoor education instructor. His most recent book is *The Outdoor Classroom*.

Tamar Jacobson, Ph.D., is Assistant Professor and coordinator of the early childhood section in the Teacher Education Department at Rider University, New Jersey. Currently, Jacobson serves on the Advocacy Committee of the National Association of Early Childhood Teacher Educators (NAECTE), was selected to participate on the Consulting Editors Panel for the NAEYC, and is a Fellow in the Child Trauma Academy. Her first book: *Confronting Our Discomfort: Clearing the Way For Anti-Bias*, was published by Heinemann in 2003.

Binbin Jiang is an Associate Professor in the Department of Educational Leadership of the Bagwell college of Education at Kenensaw State University. She has over 20 years of experience in teaching and educational administration in China and United States. Her research and publications are in the areas of Teaching English as a second and foreign language, multicultural education, international education, and professional development in cross-cultural contexts.

Patricia Liotta Kolencik is an associate professor in the Education Department at Clarion University of Pennsylvania, Clarion, Pa. She received her Doctorate in Education from the University of Pittsburgh, Pittsburgh, Pa. Prior to coming to Clarion University, Kolencik taught at the high school level for 27 years. In addition to the publication of her dissertation, *"Building Collaborative Partnerships in the Learning Community."* she has authored a professional handbook for elementary teachers entitled, *Teaching with Books that Heal.*

Dr. Carlos R. McCray is an Assistant Professor at Georgia State University in the Department of Educational Policy Studies. His research interests deal with building level leadership, multicultural education, and organizational diversity. He has published in international and regional research journals, and he has presented research at international, national, and regional conferences and consulted with school districts in the states of Ohio, Alabama, and Wisconsin. He is a member of numerous professional organizations including the American Educational Research Association and University Council for Education Administration.

Joanne A. Washington, Ph.D., is an associate professor in the Department of Mass Media Arts, Journalism and Communication Studies at Clarion University of Pennsylvania (jwashington@clarion. edu). She has traversed a varied career path including stops as a jazz musician, television producer, account executive and college residence advisor. Her research focus is on the impact of media and popular culture on the learning achievements of black and brown youth.

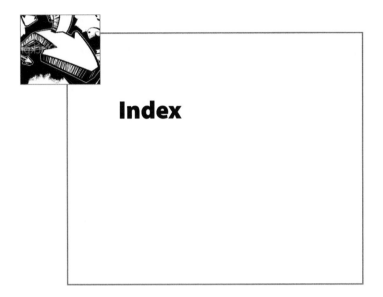

Index

Studies in the Postmodern Theory of Education

General Editors
Joe L. Kincheloe & Shirley R. Steinberg

Counterpoints publishes the most compelling and imaginative books being written in education today. Grounded on the theoretical advances in criticalism, feminism, and postmodernism in the last two decades of the twentieth century, Counterpoints engages the meaning of these innovations in various forms of educational expression. Committed to the proposition that theoretical literature should be accessible to a variety of audiences, the series insists that its authors avoid esoteric and jargonistic languages that transform educational scholarship into an elite discourse for the initiated. Scholarly work matters only to the degree it affects consciousness and practice at multiple sites. Counterpoints' editorial policy is based on these principles and the ability of scholars to break new ground, to open new conversations, to go where educators have never gone before.

For additional information about this series or for the submission of manuscripts, please contact:

Joe L. Kincheloe & Shirley R. Steinberg
c/o Peter Lang Publishing, Inc.
29 Broadway, 18th floor
New York, New York 10006

To order other books in this series, please contact our Customer Service Department:

(800) 770-LANG (within the U.S.)
(212) 647-7706 (outside the U.S.)
(212) 647-7707 FAX

Or browse online by series:
www.peterlang.com